Lecture Notes in Computer Science 2901

Edited by G. Goos, J. Hartmanis, and J. van Leeuwen

T0224693

Springer

Berlin
Heidelberg
New York
Hong Kong
London
Milan
Paris
Tokyo

François Bry   Nicola Henze
Jan Małuszyński   (Eds.)

Principles and Practice of Semantic Web Reasoning

International Workshop, PPSWR 2003
Mumbai, India, December 8, 2003
Proceedings

Springer

Series Editors

Gerhard Goos, Karlsruhe University, Germany
Juris Hartmanis, Cornell University, NY, USA
Jan van Leeuwen, Utrecht University, The Netherlands

Volume Editors

François Bry
Ludwig-Maximilians-Universität München, Institut für Informatik
Oettingerstr. 67, 80538 München, Germany
E-mail: Francois.Bry@informatik.uni-muenchen.de

Nicola Henze
Universität Hannover, Institut für Informationssysteme
Appelstr. 4, 30167 Hannover, Germany
E-mail: henze@kbs.uni-hannover.de

Jan Ma luszyński
Linköping University, Deptartment of Computer and Information Science
58183 Linköping, Sweden
E-mail: janma@ida.liu.se

Cataloging-in-Publication Data applied for

A catalog record for this book is available from the Library of Congress.

Bibliographic information published by Die Deutsche Bibliothek
Die Deutsche Bibliothek lists this publication in the Deutsche Nationalbibliografie;
detailed bibliographic data is available in the Internet at <http://dnb.ddb.de>.

CR Subject Classification (1998): H.4, H.3, I.2, F.4.1, D.2

ISSN 0302-9743
ISBN 3-540-20582-9 Springer-Verlag Berlin Heidelberg New York

Springer-Verlag is a part of Springer Science+Business Media

springeronline.com

© Springer-Verlag Berlin Heidelberg 2003
Printed in Germany

Typesetting: Camera-ready by author, data conversion by Olgun Computergrafik
Printed on acid-free paper   SPIN: 10971512   06/3142   5 4 3 2 1 0

Preface

The *Semantic Web* is a major endeavor aimed at enriching the existing Web with metadata and processing methods so as to provide Web-based systems with advanced (so-called intelligent) capabilities, in particular with *context-awareness* and *decision support*.

The advanced capabilities striven for in most Semantic Web application scenarios primarily call for *reasoning*. Reasoning capabilities are offered by existing Semantic Web languages, such as BPEL4WS, BPML, ConsVISor, DAML-S, JTP, TRIPLE, and others. These languages, however, were developed mostly from functionality-centered (e.g., ontology reasoning or access validation) or application-centered (e.g., Web service retrieval and composition) perspectives. A perspective centered on the reasoning techniques (e.g., forward or backward chaining, tableau-like methods, constraint reasoning, etc.) complementing the above-mentioned activities appears desirable for Semantic Web systems and applications. The workshop on "Principles and Practice of Semantic Web Reasoning," which took place on December 8, 2003, in Mumbai, India, was the first of a series of scientific meetings devoted to such a perspective.

Just as the current Web is inherently heterogeneous in data formats and data semantics, the Semantic Web will be inherently heterogeneous in its reasoning forms. Indeed, any single form of reasoning turns out to be irreal in the Semantic Web. For example, ontology reasoning in general relies on monotonic negation (for the metadata often can be fully specified), while databases, Web databases, and Web-based information systems call for non-monotonic reasoning (for one would not specify non-existing trains in a railway timetable); constraint reasoning is needed when dealing with time (for time intervals have to be dealt with), while (forward and/or backward) chaining is the reasoning of choice when coping with database-like views (for views, i.e., virtual data, can be derived from actual data using operations such as join and projections).

This book contains articles presented at the first workshop on "Principles and Practice of Semantic Web Reasoning" (PPSWR 2003). The workshop addressed both reasoning methods for the Semantic Web and Semantic Web applications relying upon various forms of reasoning.

The workshop organizers invited three papers on *Foundations of Semantic Web Reasoning*: A methodology for a framework and component technology for Semantic Web applications, based on layered frameworks and the semantic separation principle of architecture systems, is proposed in "Composing Frameworks and Components for Families of Semantic Web Applications." "Semantic Web Logic Programming Tools" discusses recent contributions from logic programming to Semantic Web research and proposes well-founded semantics for the WWW. In "Web Rules Need Two Kinds of Negation" it is argued that the Semantic Web will benefit from distinguishing between open and closed predicates using both strong negation and negation-as-failure.

Accepted papers for the workshop discuss Reasoning in Practice, Query and Rule-languages, and Semantics & Knowledge Representation: *Reasoning in Practice* is demonstrated via the embedding of personalization techniques in a distributed reasoning architecture, suitable for the Semantic Web, as proposed in "Towards the Adaptive Semantic Web." "On Reasoning on Time and Location on the Web" shows the integration of temporal and locational reasoning into XML query and transformation operations. An approach to interpret Semantic Web and Web services in a framework of multi-agent interoperation systems is proposed in "Reasoning about Communicating Agents in the Semantic Web."

Query and Rule Languages are developed. A visual query language for XML, based on a positional approach, is proposed in "A Visual Language for Web Querying and Reasoning." A web query language for data retrieval for adaptation, and formalisms for expressing adaptation functionality are shown in "XML Document Adaptation Queries (XDAQ): an Approach to Adaptation Reasoning Using Web Query Languages." "On Types for XML Query Language Xcerpt" discusses type systems for rule languages and algorithms for automatically checking the correctness of rule-language programs. A conceptual logic programming language for reasoning about ontologies in a rule-based manner is proposed in "Integrating Description Logics and Answer Set Programming."

Finally, the issues of *Semantics and Knowledge Representation* are investigated. "Extracting Mathematical Semantics from LaTeX Documents" allows the mapping from mathematical information in LaTeX documents to MathML. Automatic reasoning in the knowledge representation language Attempto Controlled English is the aim of "Reasoning in Attempto Controlled English." "Systematics and Architecture for a Resource Representing Knowledge About Named Entities" introduces special resources for formalizing and encoding types of information for named entities.

The first workshop on "Principles and Practice of Semantic Web Reasoning" took place as a satellite event of the 19th International Conference on Logic Programming (ICLP 2003), thus bringing closer together such scientific communities as the Logic Programming, Adaptive Web, and Web communities, each concerned with reasoning on the conventional Web and the Semantic Web. Because of the very positive resonance this first workshop on "Principles and Practice of Semantic Web Reasoning" caused in the international research community, the organizers intend to continue this new workshop series.

Mumbai, December 8, 2003   François Bry, University of Munich
                                            Nicola Henze, University of Hannover
                                            Jan Małuszyński, University of Linköping

Organization

Executive Committee

Workshop Coordinator François Bry, University of Munich
Program Committee Chair Nicola Henze, University of Hannover
Proceedings Chair   Jan Małuszyński, University of Linköping

Program Committee

François Bry, University of Munich, Germany
Georg Gottlob, University of Vienna, Austria
Nicola Henze, University of Hannover, Germany
Lalana Kagal, University of Maryland, Baltimore County, USA
Luis Moniz Pereira, Universidade Nova de Lisboa, Portugal
Jan Małuszyński, University of Linköping, Sweden
Massimo Marchiori, W3C and University of Venice, Italy
Wolfgang Nejdl, University of Hannover, Germany

Table of Contents

Composing Frameworks and Components for Families of Semantic Web Applications

Uwe Aßmann*

Research Center for Integrational Software Engineering (RISE)
Linköping University, Sweden
uwe.assmann@ida.liu.se

Abstract. This paper outlines a first methodology for a framework and component technology for Semantic Web applications, *layered constraint frameworks*. Due to the heterogeneity of the Semantic Web, different ontology languages will coexist. Applications must be able to work with several of them, and for good reuse, they should be parameterized by them. As a solution, we combine layered frameworks with architecture systems and explicit constraint specifications. Layered constraint frameworks can be partially instantiated on 6 levels, allowing for extensive reuse of components and variability of applications. Not only that applications can be instantiated for a certain product or web service family, also architectural styles, component models, and ontology languages can be reused or varied in applications. And hence, for the first time, this proposes a reuse technology for ontology-based applications on the heterogeneous Semantic Web.

Programmers are lazy. They do not want to develop their programs over and over again, but want to reuse already existing parts in new applications. They want to be more productive and quicker than the competitor. (In short, they want to earn more money than their competitors.) Also the success of the Semantic Web depends on that applications can be produced very quickly and with a short time-to-market. Parts of ontology-based applications must be reused in other ontology-based applications. To this end, an appropriate reuse technology should be developed that treats many different ontologies, and, since these will be written in different languages, also different ontology languages. In particular, this problem is important for web services, since we would like to engineer *service families* instead of single services. So, how can we build product and service families for ontology-based applications?

For standard software, software engineering has developed several well-known reuse concepts, one of them being *frameworks* [14]. A framework captures the *commonalities* of an application domain in a code skeleton. This skeleton can be

---

* Work partially supported by European Community under the IST programme - Future and Emerging Technologies, contract IST-1999-14191-EASYCOMP [6,7]. The authors are solely responsible for the content of this paper. It does not represent the opinion of the European Community, and the European Community is not responsible for any use that might be made of data appearing herein.

F. Bry et al. (Eds.): PPSWR 2003, LNCS 2901, pp. 1–15, 2003.
© Springer-Verlag Berlin Heidelberg 2003

reused in several applications by parameterizing it with application specific code (*variabilities*). This permits a company building product families [13]. For the technical realization of frameworks, the concept of *components* plays an important role. Frameworks are built of components, software blocks with *variation points (hot spots)* that can be instiantiated to blocks without variation points. Essentially, frameworks are larger components, i.e., collections of precomposed components, which can be instantiated to products of a product family. Fig. 1 contains a little example. On top, a framework is drawn, consisting of several components with several hot spots (white circles) and several *frozen* spots (grey circles), bound to inner components. To instantiate the framework towards an application, all hot spots of the framework have to be bound to components, such that an application is complete (on the bottom). Hence, a framework is *composed* out of components and is composed with other components to applications.

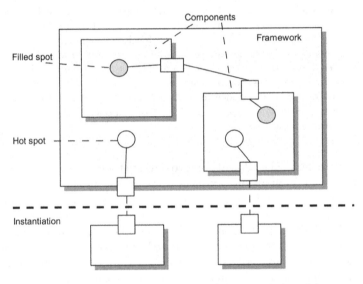

Fig. 1. A sketch of a framework with hot spots (white circles) and frozen spots (grey circles). It can be instantiated to an application (below).

Unfortunately, the usual framework technology cannot directly applied to the Semantic Web, since the Web had been planned and designed as a distributed, loosely coupled, and heterogeneous medium. Hence, on the Semantic Web, there will be always different approaches for ontologies and ontology languages. Applications will have to use components written in different ontology languages. However, usually, a framework is very much tied to its underlying language and cannot deal with components written in different languages. Hence, for the Semantic Web, there is a need for a generic framework technology that supports a family of ontology languages.

As a simple example, consider to construct a web service family for travel arrangements. The service family should offer services, such as information about single travels, information on best price or shortest travel time, selection between different competitors, and finally, booking and payment. However, travel booking systems live in a heterogeneous environment. They must interoperate with many other systems that have very different background and technology. For instance, hotel information, flight booking, rental car information, public transport systems, are all provided by different organisations that cannot integrate these systems easily. Hence, a web-based travel booking system will have to contact many different systems, which will in the future rely on many ontologies and ontology languages. So, if a family of travel booking web services should be developed, components that had been developed with an ontology language have to be varied with components written in other languages. Usual framework technology does not permit this.

Beyond frameworks, there is a second reuse technology in software engineering that is interesting in this respect. *Architecture systems* split off the architecture of an application from the application-specific components [8]. The architecture is specified with an *architectural language*, while the components are written in a standard language. Since architectural languages provide a specific language for the architectural level, it can be argued that they are more expressive and adequate for architectures than frameworks. For our problem, an architectural language offers a decisive advantage: its semantics is specified independently of the semantics of the component language and poses only minimal requirements on some selected language constructs. On the other hand, the component language is independent of the architectural language. Hence, an architectural language can easily work with several component languages at the same time, allowing for heterogeneous applications. In the following, we call this principle *semantic separation*[1].

From architectural languages, we can learn how to arrive at truly generic frameworks for the Semantic Web. In this paper, we combine semantic separation with standard framework technology, resulting in a new generic framework technology, *layered constraint frameworks*. This technology goes far beyond standard framework technology and is particularly suited for Semantic Web applications. Firstly, layered constraint frameworks are based on *layered frameworks* [4]. Layered frameworks are application frameworks that are applied for product families of a certain application domain, e.g., in the banking domain, in which applications can be divided into abstraction layers that contribute a certain concern to the application. (A *concern* captures partial knowledge about the application, abstracted from a certain viewpoint). A major advantage of a layered framework is that all concerns, i.e., all layers, can be exchanged independently of each other [4].

---

[1] In particular, the semantic separation principle holds for the *static semantics*, i.e., the part of the semantics that can be evaluated statically, for instance, to compile the languages to binary form. The static semantics can be specified with constraint specifications, such as type constraints.

Secondly, a layered constraint framework inherits the benefits of semantic separation for all concerns of an application, not only the architecture. Essentially, this means that every layer carries a separate set of semantic constraints for a certain concern. This set of constraints can be used to check the layer's implementation on consistency. Together with their layer, the constraints can be exchanged independently of the constraints of other layers.

Thirdly, layered constraint frameworks are interesting for the Semantic Web because the semantic constraints can be specified in an ontology language, so that we use ontology languages to describe frameworks for applications based on ontology languages. This reuses Semantic Web technology for a framework technology on the Semantic Web, *bootstrapping* the technology.

Lastly, layered constraint frameworks do not only explicitly capture application or architectural concerns, but also capture the semantics of component languages and component models. A layered constraint framework can be used for application domains with several ontology languages, which is essential for Semantic Web applications. Hence, layered constraints frameworks also generalize current framework technology considerably.

The structure of the paper is as follows. First, we present the ideas of layered frameworks in more detail. Then, we explain the major concerns of a web-based application in a product family or service family (Sec. 2). We argue that the concerns can be ordered into layers, so that the layered framework technology can be applied (Sec. 3). We show that, on every layer, semantic constraints play a major role to check the consistency of a layer's implementation and that these constraints are also partially ordered. This leads to the definition of layered constraint frameworks. Then, we show several examples how a layered constraint framework can be instantiated to diverse Semantic Web applications (Sec. 4). Finally, we conclude with an agenda for further research.

1   Layered Frameworks

Layered Frameworks have been invented for product lines of banking applications [4]. In this application domain, a framework has to be instantiated in pretty diverse contexts. For instance, not only the product must be varied, but also the bank and its customer rules. Also, the organizational structure of the bank plays an important role since it poses requirements on the rights for accesses and actions. Investigating these scenarios, it was discovered that the concerns and the products form a kind of matrix. Fig. 2 shows the main concerns in a layered diagram. On top, the concern of the applications is shown, in the middle layers the concern of the bank's organizational structure, and on the bottom the core concepts of the banking domain. Usually, an entity of an application, such as the account, is not restricted to the banking domain, but crosscuts all layers. In the figure, three product entities are shown, a telephone banking account, a ATM account, and a telephone banking loan. Thus, an application entity usually has many concerns, or *roles*, which it has to play, with respect to a layer of the application. On the other hand, the layers of the framework build on top of

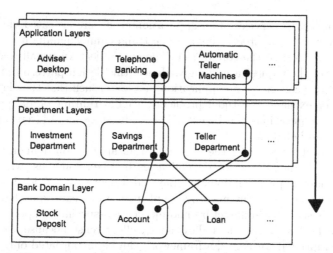

Fig. 2. The concerns of a banking application and some of the products.

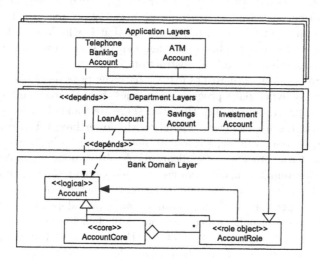

Fig. 3. The ROLEOBJECT pattern realizes the concerns of a banking application with a core object and layer-specific role objects.

each other, i.e., are hierarchically ordered. Hence, the application layers need the concepts of a bank's departments, and these in turn require the core business concepts of a bank.

The layering of the framework leads to an implementation that splits the application entities into layer-specific *role* objects that are linked by a *core* object. This pattern has been recorded as the ROLEOBJECT pattern [5]. The structure of this pattern ensures that, although upper layers require lower layers, every layer can be exchanged independently of each other (Fig. 3). Since a role object does not refer directly to its neighbor role objects in other layers, it only knows its core object (see the relations between core and role objects in the lower layer of Fig. 3). Hence, all services of an application entity are executed via the core object: whenever a role object gets a request and cannot handle it by itself, it forwards the request to the core object. The core object knows all role objects and distributes the request accordingly. Hence, this design pattern hides all information of one concern of an application in a layer, such that they layer's role objects can be exchanged without problems, even at runtime of an application. Furthermore, applications can be extended easily, since more layers with more role objects can be added.

Layered frameworks order the concerns of an application domain in dependent layers, i.e., they allow for dependencies between concerns, which is important for many application domains. Layered frameworks provide information hiding for their layers, such that layer implementations can be exchanged easily. The layers separate architecture and application-specific components. Most importantly, layered frameworks allow for excellent reuse because they can be partially instantiated. In Fig. 2, a framework can be instantiated only with the core business concepts, leaving hot spots in both layers above. Alternatively, it can be instantiated with the two lower layers, which leaves the hot spots of the application layers open. Hence, reuse actually occurs on n levels: every layer provides an additional level of reuse. And that is why layered frameworks are successful in business applications: they can be scaled over many different instantiations on different levels of abstraction.

Layered frameworks with ROLEOBJECT patterns bear resemblance to technologies, such as hyperspace programming (view-based programming [15]) or aspect-oriented programming [11]. However, there are some differences. In a layered framework, the upper layers depend on the lower layers, i.e., cannot exist without them. In our example, without business domain role objects and business department role objects, an application role object does not make sense. In view-based programming, usually, views are independent of each other. Then, in our example, all layers should be independent, which is not the case. On the other hand, in aspect-oriented programming, an aspect depends on the core of the system. However, usually, aspects are partners of each other and not stacked (although this is not impossible to achieve). Hence, layered frameworks play a somewhat different role: on the one hand, every layer clearly expresses a concern of the application and can be exchanged independently of the others; on the other hand, upper layers cannot live without lower layers and must be stacked on top of them. And this is the reason why we evolve them to frameworks for the Semantic Web: their layers model *dependent concerns* (Sec. 3). But before, we have to discuss, which concerns can be identified in a Semantic Web application, and that these depend on each other acyclically.

2   The Concerns of a Framework for Semantic Web Applications

In this section, we present a refined set of concerns for framework-based applications of a product line. It is refined, because we split the concerns of [4] into finer

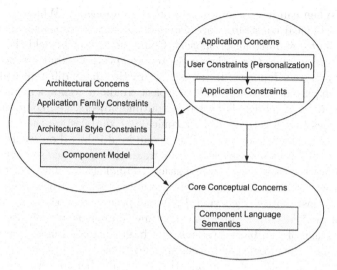

Fig. 4. Major concerns of an application, also of those based on Semantic Web technology.

concerns, and add some new ones. And this refined set of concerns enables us to treat applications for the Semantic Web, applications that use different ontology languages. In general, we assume that a concern consists of a specification or implementation, controlled by a set of semantic constraints that can check the consistency of the specification or implementation. In some concerns, the focus is on the specifications, in others on the constraints.

Fig. 4 gives an overview. Firstly, we distinguish a group of *application concerns*, divided into the user-specific concern and the application-specific concern. The personalization concern contains personalization constraints, such as *I want to use a Mozilla-style windowing theme*, while the application-specific concern contains specifications, such as *The system provides for Mozilla- or Opera-style windowing themes, but not IE-style*. Application constraints are conditions on these specifications, such as *In case of an inflamed foot, a diabetes patient needs a diabetes specialist and a dermatologist*. While for a new product, at least the user and application constraints have to be instantiated, all others might be reused from the framework. Clearly, the user concern depends on the application concern, but not vice versa. Also, the application concern depends on the architectural and the core conceptual concerns, but not vice versa.

The second group of concerns are the *architectural concerns*. On the software architecture level, we can distinguish between the *application-family constraints*, the *architectural style* of the application, and the *component model*. All concerns together form the architecture of an application. The central concern of this group, on which all others build, is the concern of the component model. A component model defines the syntax and semantics of the components of a framework. How does a component look? Which kinds of interfaces does it provide? When can it be composed to other components? Which are the operations [2]? Typical constraints are *Components can be composed at runtime* or *A component may have an event port*. Component models yield the base for single composition operations, the small-step compositions that are needed for framework-based development. In industrial practice many different component models are employed, however, only two basic kinds of component models exist. The first kind of models is based on runtime objects, i.e., components are runtime entities that are composed dynamically. Examples are the COM+ [12] or the EJB component models [10]. The second kind is based on composition of programs, i.e., components are sets of code fragments. *Invasive software composition* is such a fragment-based composition technology for Java [2], but there are many others, such as hyperspace programming [15], or aspect-oriented programming, at least in its static form [11]. We suppose that for the Semantic Web, both kind of models will be important: runtime component models are required for the dynamism of web-based systems, and fragment-based models are needed for composition of ontologies and other specifications.

The architectural style of an application forms another concern. Historically, architectural languages allowed only for specification of the application of an architecture. Later on, they were extended to express architectural styles, such as pipe-and-filter style, distributed-process style, or other general types of architectures. In this way, constraints for very general classes of architectures can be reused [1]. Typically a constraint in an architectural style prescribes the connections that are allowed between components, such a *Between two components, there should be a pipe (connection constraints)*.

A last concern in this group is the *application-family concern*. Often, companies would like to define not only constraints on an architectural style, but also describe a *reference architecture* that developers have to conform to. Application-family constraints prescribe how a framework can be instantiated with certain types of components (*instantiation constraints*), or which connections should be used on which level of the architecture. For instance, for a pipe-and-filter architecture an application-family constraint could be that *Only POSIX-defined filter components should be employed* or *On the outer level of the architecture, all pipes have to be encrypted*. Also core concepts of the application domain belong to this group. (Since [4] work in the banking domain, they call these *core business concepts*). In essence, application-family constraints play a large role within frameworks, because they adapt a very general architectural style to the needs of an application family. Obviously, application-family constraints depend on the architectural style, but not vice versa.

All concerns of this group form together the application's architecture. If the concerns are realized in a layered framework, several layers for every concern may be developed. For instance, both the business department layer of Fig. 2 and the core concept layer belong to the application-family concern.

The final group of concerns are the *core conceptual concerns*. At the moment, we consider in this group on the language of the components, but this will be refined in Sec. 3.

Ontologies play a role in several concerns. An ontology comprises the core concepts of an application domain, standardized for a large number of people. Hence, ontologies provide application and application-family constraints for a set of applications. Also, architectural styles, or even component models, can be specified with ontologies. In particular, if ontologies are based on inferencing (rule-based ontologies), there is hope that complex constraints and semantics can be expressed rather easily.

We do not claim that this list of concerns in framework-based applications is complete. Other concerns might be discovered that are worthwhile to be distinguished. However, already with the identified ones, we can achieve a better information hiding in framework-based applications. The next section will show how to order the concerns into a layered framework. This is possible, because the concerns depend are partially ordered (Fig. 4). Hence, we can encapsulate knowledge of a concern into one or several layers of a layered framework. Furthermore, we will show how to treat Semantic Web applications with their requirements on multiple ontology languages.

3   Layered Constraint Frameworks for Framework-Based Semantic Web Applications

This section proposes a framework technology for applications on the Semantic Web, guided by semantic constraints and ontologies. The main idea is to model the concerns of Sec. 2 as a layered framework. Every layer encapsulates a concern of a application. The layers differ in what they know about the component language, the component model, or the application style, so that they can be exchanged for variants easily. Additionally, on every layer, constraints (or ontologies) can be specified that specify a static semantics for the layer (*layered constraint framework*).

For better reuse, we propose to split and rearrange some of the concerns of Sec. 2. In particular, we split the concern of the component model in three different layers, the layer of the *generic component model*, the layer of *composition time*, and the layer of the *concrete component model*. The generic component model layer encapsulates all knowledge about components in general, such that it can be reused on upper layers. The composition time layer deals with the two basic kinds of component models. Finally, the layer of the concrete component model contains all specific constraints of a component model. It remains in the architectural layer group.

Fig. 5 illustrates the layers of the framework. On the bottom, the generic component model layer is found. This layer is introduced mainly for reuse of component knowledge for different component languages. It knows about abstract components with variation points (hot and frozen spots), as well as composition operations. Typically, this can be expressed in constraints, such as *A component consists of subcomponents*, *A component has hot and frozen spots*, or *A composition operation has some arguments*. Using this layer, an architecture can be expressed very abstractly in form of a composition of abstract compo-

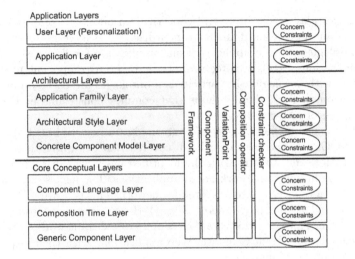

Fig. 5. The layers of a layered constraint framework. Application and central framework entities, such as component, variation point, or composition operator, crosscut all layers.

nents. However, the layer does not know which concrete component model, which component languages, nor which application it will be instantiated to.

The second layer provides information about the *time* of composition and the basic kind of component model, fragment-based models for compile-time, or runtime models for runtime. Also this layer does not know about the component language, so that its knowledge can be reused for different component languages.

The third layer is rather rich because it adds the knowledge about the semantics of the component language, which is in Semantic Web applications the ontology language. So, this layer knows about constraints such as *The product works with a component model for OWL, Datalog, or Prolog*. The layer does not yet know about constraints of the concrete component model.

The second and third layer group is structured in the way as Sec. 2 indicated. The second layer group realizes architectural specifications and constraints. The remaining constraints for a concrete component model are added by the fourth layer, the component model layer. It contains constraints, such as *The product works with EJB components and is based on transactions*. On top of this layer, constraints for the architectural styles are encapsulated. Above that, the application-family constraints get a layer.

Finally, the third group provides layers for application and user constraints.

We have indicated that the resulting layers depend on each other acyclically. Hence, they can be ordered into a layered framework. The dependencies of the semantic constraints are also acyclic. Hence, also the consistency checking can be distributed over the layers.

For a layered framework, we have to determine the application entities that crosscut all layers and can be realized with a ROLEOBJECT pattern. It is easy to see that all layers contain different abstractions of the notions framework, component, variation points, the composition operations and the constraint checker. Hence, at least the entities `Framework`, `Component`, `VariationPoint`, `CompositionOperation`, and `ConstraintChecker` should be implemented in all layers with role objects (Fig. 5).

Layered Specification of the Constraints. On every level of a layered constraint framework, constraints should be specified. To this end, all languages for semantic specifications can be used, however, in the context of the Semantic Web, it is appealing to employ ontology languages themselves. In the following, we give a short list of the involved specifications. Since ontology languages can be used, the specifications may be standardized to *concern ontologies* or *role ontologies*.

User and application layer constraints will be specified with public models for personalization and application constraints. In particular, personalization constraints should be standardized, to achieve a better interoperation for the customers in mobile applications.

On the architectural level, the constraints of the application family and the architectural style might form *composition ontologies*, ontologies that constrain the way how applications are plugged together. It is makes a lot of sense to define an ontology for architectural styles, since they are found in many applications throughout all areas. This standardization process is future work for the software architecture and framework communities. However, application-family constraints will probably hold only for single companies, since they define reference architectures for a certain product line.

On the level of the component model, also ontologies can be defined. A component model is even more general than an architectural style, and hence, appears in a lot more applications. Hence, it can be assumed that the most important component models will be defined by a standardized ontology.

Checking in a layered constraint framework should be implemented with the ROLEOBJECT pattern. The checker entity crosscuts all layers, has a core checker object and layer-specific role checker objects. Whenever a role checker object cannot answer a request, it delegates it to the core object, which in turn delegates it to the next layer-specific role checker. In this way, requests can always be answered, but the checker of one layer can be exchanged without changing other checkers. Hence, role objects that live in upper layers depend only on the core object and role objects in lower layers. This is guaranteed, if the constraint specifications also depend acyclically on each other. As we have explained above, this is the case.

In summary, if an application area has several concerns and the semantic constraints of the application framework acyclically depend on each other, it is possible to order the concerns in layers, and the ROLEOBJECT pattern can be used to implement the framework, also the checking of the semantic constraints.

4 Semantic Web Applications

Layered frameworks can be partially instantiated on every layer. For a rule-based language family, such as the RuleML family containing binary Datalog, Datalog,

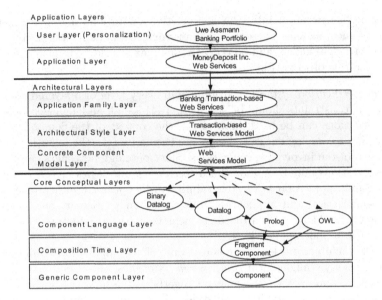

Fig. 6. Possible component models in the framework. All paths can be used to define a component model. Only the corresponding role objects in the component model layer have to be exchanged for new models.

Prolog, and DAML [9], this implies that many different applications, application frameworks, and component models can be instantiated.

Application to Different Ontology Languages. Fig. 6 shows a bunch of instantiations of the framework for these 4 rule-based ontology languages. The instantiations share several layers of the framework, but differ in the component language layer, i.e., the ontology languages. Hence, the layered constraint framework can instantiate 4 different web service models, each of them using a different ontology language. The layer principle guarantees that the languages can be exchanged for each other without modifying other layers.

In this scenario, all work that has been done for the abstract component model layer and the composition time layer can be reused for all ontology languages. Only on the component language layer, work cannot be shared. If the ontology languages are real subsets of each other, such as binary Datalog and Datalog, sharing is possible even in this layer.

Fig. 6 also illustrates why layered constraint frameworks are suited for the Semantic Web, in contrast to standard layered frameworks. Since a new group of core conceptual concerns is added, not only core application concepts and department structure can be varied, but also the language of the components and the component model in question. As explained in the introduction, this is required for Semantic Web applications.

Application to Different Architectural Styles. Fig. 7 shows variability in the architectural style. Two framework instantiations provide two different architec-

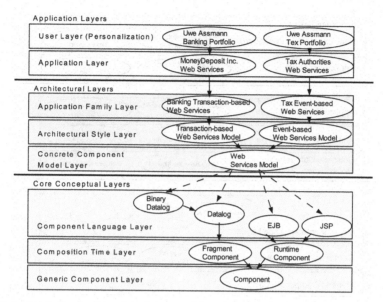

Fig. 7. Instantiations of a web service model with static and dynamic components for different application families.

tural styles for the same web service model. This is possible, if the underlying web service model contains enough functionality for both. Then, very different applications can be built on top of these two styles.

In this scenario, the variation appears in the architectural style layer. All work that has been done for the abstract component model layer, composition time layer, language layer, and concrete component models can be reused for all architectural styles.

Application to Component Models of Rule-based Languages. If the layered framework is instantiated up to the concrete component model layer, it provides a means for realizing component models of ontology languages. Fig. 8 shows how two web service component models can be instantiated and employed by two application families. Even if an ontology language does not support components well, it is easy to define a component model for it. This is possible due to the semantic separation principle and relies on fragment-based composition. The details go beyond this paper [2].

In this scenario, all work in the two lowest layers can be reused. The richer composition time and generic component layer are, the easier it is to instantiate a concrete component model for a new component language.

5   Conclusion

This paper has outlined a first methodology for a framework and component technology for Semantic Web applications. Due to the heterogenity of the Se-

14   U. Aßmann

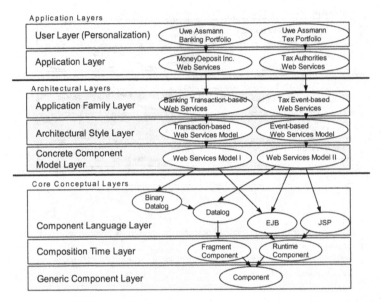

Fig. 8. Two instantiations of web service component models, both with static and dynamic components for different application families.

mantic Web, different ontology languages have to be treated, so that applications must be parameterized with them. As a solution, we combine the layered frameworks of [4] with the semantic separation principle of architecture systems, and enrich the resulting frameworks with layered constraint specifications. The results are manifold. We could identify 7 concerns of Semantic Web applications: user, application, application-family, architectural style, concrete component model, component (ontology) language, composition time, and generic component model concern. The layered frameworks can be partially instantiated on 6 levels, proving excellent potential for reuse. Not only that applications can be instantiated for a certain product or web service family, also architectural styles, component models, and ontology languages can be varied. And hence, for the first time, this proposes a reuse technology for ontology-based applications on the Semantic Web.

A Research Agenda. Much work remains to be done. For a concrete framework, the interfaces of each layer have to be precisely specified. What may an upper layer assume about lower layers? A standardization with ontologies of the Semantic Web would be desirable for every layer. As we have seen above, this might be possible for some layers, but is less probably for others. How far can standardization go? Since ontology languages do not support components and composition very well, we should use the framework to define concrete component models for them. How simple is this process? Finally, does the proposed framework technology scale for large applications?

Building an actual implementation of the proposed framework will take some time, however, the concepts are well-founded because they are derived from solid framework technology for large applications. Currently, our group refactors our software composition framework for Java towards the presented architecture [16]. The goal is to provide a layered constraint framework for the Semantic Web community in the near future.

References

1. Gregory D. Abowd, Robert Allen, and David Garlan. Formalizing style to understand descriptions of software architecture. *ACM Transactions on Software Engineering and Methodology*, 4(4):319–364, October 1995.
2. Uwe Aßmann. *Invasive Software Composition*. Springer-Verlag, February 2003.
3. Francois Bry and alia. Rules in a Semantic Web Environment (REWERSE). 6th Framework Network of Excellence, European Commission, Accepted NoE, August 2003. Leading European network on Semantic Web. Prof. Aßmann is leader of the Working Group I3 on Composition and Typing.
4. Dirk Bäumer, Guido Gryczan, Rolf Knoll, Carola Lilienthal, Dirk Riehle, and Heinz Züllighoven. Framework development for large systems. *Communications of the ACM*, 40(10):52–59, oct 1997.
5. W. Silberski M. Wulf Bäumer, D. Riehle. Role object. In *Conf. On Pattern Languages of Programming (PLOP)*, 1997.
6. The EASYCOMP Consortium. EASYCOMP: Easy Composition in Future Generation Component systems, Project-Nr. IST-1999-14191, February 2000. Aßmann, Uwe (ed.).
7. The EASYCOMP Consortium. EASYCOMP home page. http://www.easycomp.org, August 2000.
8. David Garlan and Mary Shaw. An introduction to software architecture. In V. Ambriola and G. Tortora, editors, *Advances in Software Engineering and Knowledge Engineering*, volume 1, pages 1–40, Singapore, 1994. World Scientific.
9. RuleML Initiative. RuleML initiative for xml-based rule-based languages (home page). http://www.ruleml.org.
10. JavaSoft. *Enterprise Java Beans (TM)*, April 2000. Version 2.0.
11. Gregor Kiczales, John Lamping, Anurag Mendhekar, Chris Maeda, Cristina Lopes, Jean-Marc Loingtier, and John Irwin. Aspect-oriented programming. In *Proceedings of the European Conference on Object-Oriented Programming (ECOOP 97)*, volume 1241 of *Lecture Notes in Computer Science*, pages 220–242. Springer, Heidelberg, 1997.
12. Juval Löwy. *COM and .NET*. O'Reilly, Sebastopol, CA, 2001.
13. Michael Mattsson, Jan Bosch, and Mohamed E. Fayad. Framework integration problems, causes, solutions. *Communications of the ACM*, 42(10):80–87, October 1999.
14. Heinz-Willi Schmidt. Systematic framework design by generalization. *Communications of the ACM*, 40(10):48–51, October 1997.
15. Peri Tarr, Harold Ossher, William Harrison, and Stanley M., Jr. Sutton. N degrees of separation: Multi-dimensional separation of concerns. In *Proceedings of ICSE'99*, pages 107–119, Los Angeles CA, USA, 1999.
16. The COMPOST Consortium (Linköping University and Karlsruhe University). COMPOST home page. http://www.the-compost-system.org, April 2003.

Semantic Web Logic Programming Tools

Jóse Júlio Alferes, Carlos Viegas Damásio, and Luís Moniz Pereira

Centro de Inteligência Artificial - CENTRIA
Departamento de Informática, Faculdade de Ciências e Tecnologia
Universidade Nova de Lisboa, 2829-516 Caparica, Portugal
{jja,cd,lmp}@di.fct.unl.pt

Abstract. The last two decades of research in Logic Programming, both at the theoretical and practical levels, have addressed several topics highly relevant for the Semantic Web effort, providing very concrete answers to some open questions.
This paper describes succinctly the contributions from the Logic Programming group of Centro de Inteligência Artificial (CENTRIA) of Universidade Nova de Lisboa, as a prelude to a description of our recent efforts to develop integrated standard tools for disseminating this research throughout the interested Web communities. The paper does not intended to be a survey of logic programming techniques applicable to the Semantic Web, and so the interested reader should try to obtain the missing information in the logic programming journals and conferences.

1 Introduction

The eXtensible Markup Language provides a way of organizing data and documents in a structured and universally accepted format. However, the tags used have no predefined meaning. The W3C has proposed the Resource Description Framework (RDF) for exposing the meaning of a document to the Web community of people, machines, and intelligent agents [26].

Conveying the content of documents is just a first step for achieving the full potential of the Semantic Web. Additionally, it is mandatory to be able to reason with and about information spread across the World Wide Web. The applications range from electronic commerce applications, data integration and sharing, information gathering, security access and control, law, diagnosis, B2B, and of course, to modelling of business rules and processes.

Rules provide the natural and wide-accepted mechanism to perform automated reasoning, with mature and available theory and technology. This has been identified as a Design Issue for the Semantic Web, as clearly stated by Tim Berners-Lee et al in [10]:

> *"For the semantic web to function, computers must have access to structured collections of information and sets of inference rules that they can use to conduct automated reasoning."*

> *"The challenge of the Semantic Web, therefore, is to provide a language that expresses both data and rules for reasoning about the data and that allows rules from any existing knowledge-representation system to be exported onto the Web."*

F. Bry et al. (Eds.): PPSWR 2003, LNCS 2901, pp. 16–32, 2003.

"Adding logic to the Web – the means to use rules to make inferences, choose courses of action and answer questions – is the task before the Semantic Web community at the moment."

Logic Programming is about expressing knowledge in the form of rules and making inferences with these rules. A major advantage of Logic Programming is that it provides an operational reading of rules and a declarative reading with well-understood semantics. In this paper we defend the use of Generalized Extended Logic Programs [29], i.e. logic programs with both (monotonic) explicit negation and (non-monotonic) default negation, as an appropriate expressive formalism for knowledge representation in the Web.

An important feature of Logic Programming is that it is able to deal with negative knowledge, and to express closed world assumptions. Expressing and reasoning with negative knowledge is fundamental for advanced applications but these capabilities are currently lacking in the existing and proposed Web standards. This is clearly identified as a limitation/feature of RDF, in the latest W3C Working Draft of RDF Semantics [24]:

"RDF is an assertional logic, in which each triple expresses a simple proposition. This imposes a fairly strict monotonic discipline on the language, so that it cannot express closed-world assumptions, local default preferences, and several other commonly used non-monotonic constructs."

The introduction of (non-monotonic) default negation brought new theoretical problems to Logic Programming, which were addressed differently by the two major semantics: Well-founded Semantics [21] (WFS) and Stable Model Semantics [22] (SM).

We start this paper by defending the use of Well-founded based semantics as an appropriate semantics for Semantic Web rule engines, and by illustrating its usage. We then proceed, in section 4 to describe our W4 project – Well-Founded Semantics for the WWW – which aims at developing Standard Prolog inter-operable tools for supporting distributed, secure, and integrated reasoning activities in the Semantic Web, and describe the implementations already developed within the project.

The Semantic Web is a "living organism", which combines autonomously evolving data sources/knowledge repositories. This dynamic character of the Semantic Web requires (declarative) languages and mechanisms for specifying its maintenance and evolution. It is our stance that also in this respect Logic Programming is a good choice as a representational language with attending inference and maintenance mechanisms and, in section 5, we briefly describe our recent research efforts for defining and implementing logic programming systems capable of dealing with updates and knowledge-base evolution.

2   The Case for Well-Founded Based Semantics

As mentioned above, in this paper we propound the use of Generalized Extended Logic Programs [29] as an appropriate expressive formalism for knowledge representation in the Web. A Generalized Extended Logic Program is a set of rules of the form:

$$L_0 \leftarrow L_1, \ldots, L_n$$

where literals $L_0, L_1, \ldots, L_n$ are objective literals, say A or $\neg A$, or default negated objective literals, say $not\, A$ or $not\, \neg A$, with A an atom of a given first-order language. Without loss of generality, a non-ground rule stands for all its ground instances. Notice that two forms of negation are available, namely default (or weak) negation not and explicit (or strong) negation $\neg$, and can occur both in the head (L_0) and body ($L_1, \ldots, L_n$) of the rule.

Default negation is non-monotonic and captures what is believed or assumed false (closed-world assumption), whilst explicit negation is monotonic and expresses what is known to be false (open-world assumption). The rationale of the two forms of negation is better grasped with the following example attributed to McCarthy:

Example 1. Suppose a driver intends to cross a railway and must make a decision whether he should proceed or stop. The two major possibilities he has to encode the knowledge in a logic programming language are captured by the rules:

$$1)\ cross \leftarrow \neg train \qquad 2)\ cross \leftarrow not\, train$$

Rule 1) represents the usual behaviour of a safe driver by stating that he can cross the rail tracks only when he has explicit evidence that a train is not approaching. The second rule represents the situation of a careless driver that advances whenever there is no evidence that a train is approaching (i.e. believes/assumes the train is not approaching).

The introduction of default negation brought new theoretical problems, which were addressed differently by the two major semantics for logic programs: Well-Founded Semantics [21] (WFS) and Stable Model Semantics [22] (SM). We suggest the use of Well-Founded based Semantics as an appropriate semantics for Semantic Web rule engines, by the following reasons:

– The adopted semantics for definite, acyclic and (locally) stratified logic programs, coinciding with Stable Model Semantics.
– Defined for every normal logic program, i.e. with default negation in the bodies, no explicit negation and atomic heads.
– Polynomial data complexity with efficient existing implementations, namely the SLG-WAM engine implemented in XSB [30].
– Good structural properties.
– It has an undefined truth-value.
– Many extensions exist over WFS, capturing paraconsistent, incomplete, and uncertain reasoning.
– Permits update semantics via Dynamic Logic Programs and EVOLP.
– It can be readily "combined" with DBMSs, Prolog, and Stable Models engines.

The minimal Herbrand model semantics for definite logic programs [20] (programs without default and explicit negation) is well-understood and widely accepted. Both Well-Founded Semantics and Stable Model Semantics coincide with the minimal Herbrand model semantics for definite logic programs.

A major advantage of WFS is that it is possible to assign a unique model to every normal logic program, in constrast to SM semantics. The same applies to the several extensions of WFS treating explicit negation, supporting paraconsistent reasoning forms [16], which we shall discuss in the following section.

The existence of an undefined logical value is fundamental for Semantic Web aware inference engines. On the one hand, in a distributed Web environment with communication failures and non-ignorable response times, a "remote" logic inference can be assumed undefined, while the computation proceeds locally. If the remote computation terminates and returns an answer, then the undefined truth-value can be logically updated to true or false. On the other hand, rule bases in the Web will naturally introduce cycles through default negation. Well-Founded Semantics deals with these cycles through default negation by assigning the truth-value undefined to the literals involved. In this particular situation, Stable Models may not exist or may explode.

The computation of the Well-Founded Model is tractable, contrary to Stable Models, and efficient implementations exist, notably the XSB Prolog engine [30]. XSB resorts to tabling techniques, ensuring better termination properties and polynomial data complexity. Tabling is also a good way to address distributed query evaluation of definite and normal logic programs. The XSB Prolog supports a full first-order syntax, which is not fully available in the state-of-the art Stable Model engines [9,31]. Moreover, the latests XSB Prolog 2.6 distribution is integrated with the SModels system, and thus applications can better exploit both Well-Founded and Stable Model semantics.

In summary, Well-Founded Semantics can be seen as the light-inference basic mechanism for deploying **today** complex Semantic Web rule-based applications, and Stable Model Semantics a complementary semantics for addressing other complex reasoning forms.

3   Knowledge Representation with Explicit Negation

In this section we illustrate the use of explicit and default negation for representing ontological knowledge, which may be contradictory and/or incomplete. The ability to deal and pinpoint contradictory information is a desirable feature of Semantic Web rule system, since it is very natural to obtain conflicting information from different sources. Classical logic assigns no model to an inconsistent theory, and therefore it is not fully appropriate as a general knowledge representation formalism for the Semantic Web. This limitation is inherited by the classical logic based formalisms like RDF(S) [26,24,12], DAML+OIL [13], and OWL [17].

An interesting example is the case of taxonomies. The example is a natural one since our common sense knowledge of the animal world is rather limited, and new species are discovered frequently. We present some examples showing the capabilities of our own Generalized Paraconsistent Well-founded Semantics with Explicit Negation, $WFSX_P$ for short. For a full account and all the formal details, the reader is referred to [3,14,16].

Example 2. Consider the following common-sense rules for identifying birds and mammals:

- Oviparous warm-blooded animals with a bill are birds;
- Hairy warm-blooded animals are mammals;
- Birds are not mammals and vice-versa;
- Birds fly;
- Mammals nurse their offspring.

This chunk of knowledge can be represented by the following extended logic program rules:

$$bird(X) \leftarrow bill(X), warm\_blood(X), oviparous(X).$$
$$\neg bird(X) \leftarrow mammal(X).$$
$$flies(X) \leftarrow bird(X).$$

$$mammal(X) \leftarrow hair(X), warm\_blood(X).$$
$$\neg mammal(X) \leftarrow bird(X).$$
$$nurses(X) \leftarrow mammal(X).$$

If the information regarding dogs and ducks is correctly filled in one gets the expected results. We just add to the program the set of facts:

$hair(dog).\ warm\_blood(dog).\quad bill(duck).\ warm\_blood(duck).\ oviparous(duck).$

The model of the above program under $WFSX_P$ entails the following expected conclusions:

$$\left\{ \begin{array}{l} mammal(dog), nurses(dog), \neg bird(dog), not\ bird(dog), not\ flies(dog), \\ bird(duck), flies(duck), \neg mammal(duck), not\ mammal(duck), \\ not\ nurses(duck) \end{array} \right\}$$

Now on a trip to Australia the user discovers there are some creatures named platypus which lay eggs, have warm blood, sport a bill, and are hairy! A nice contradiction is obtained from the program containing the facts:

$hair(platypus).\ warm\_blood(platypus).\ bill(platypus).\ oviparous(platypus).$

The model entails the following new conclusions:

$$\left\{ \begin{array}{l} mammal(platypus), \neg mammal(platypus), \\ not\ mammal(platypus), not\ \neg mammal(platypus), \\ nurses(platypus), not\ nurses(platypus), not\ \neg nurses(platypus), \\ bird(platypus), \neg bird(platypus), not\ bird(platypus), not\ \neg bird(platypus), \\ flies(platypus), not\ flies(platypus), not\ \neg flies(platypus) \end{array} \right\}$$

The remarkable points about this example are manifold. First, contradictory information can coexist with safe one without interfering with each other; in particular, we must not relinquish the information about dogs and ducks. Second, we can detect a contradiction both about the *mammal* and the *bird* predicates (both *mammal* and ¬*mammal* hold, as well as *bird* and ¬*bird*), its consequences are propagated, and we are aware that the knowledge about platypuses regarding nursing and flying capabilities depends on contradiction. This is recognized by noticing that *nurses(platypus)* and *not nurses(platypus)* hold, while ¬*nurses(platypus)* is absent from the model [15]. Third, the right solution is covered by the program's model: platypus are mammals, do not fly, and nurse their progeny. Finally, it is unsound to have a heuristic rule saying to drop all objective (or default) knowledge. For platypus we want to retain that they nurse their descendants but discard the *fly(platypus)* conclusion.

The rationale of *WFSX_P* is to non-trivially extract the maximum number of conclusions from contradictory information. This provides the user with the information necessary to decide what to do, since all possible scenarios are taken into account. The user is warned about some potential problems, and is up to him to take the right decision. This is possible due to the adoption of the Coherence Principle, which relates both forms of negation: *"If something is known to be false then it should be believed false: if ¬A holds then not A should hold; if A holds then not ¬A should hold".*

If A and ¬A hold, then by coherence, one should have *not* ¬A and *not* A. This produces a localized explosion of consequences which are propagated by the semantics only to the dependant literals, and not to the whole model. The same semantics can be exploited to represent taxonomies with exceptions, expressing general absolute (i.e. non-defeasible) rules, defeasible rules, exceptions to defeasible rules and to other exceptions, explicitly making preferences among defeasible rules. We assume that in the presence of contradictory defeasible rules we prefer the one with most specific information.

Example 3. Consider the following statements, corresponding to the hierarchy depicted in Figure 1:

(1) Mammals are animals.
(2) Bats are animals.
(3) Birds are animals.
(4) Penguins are birds.
(5) Dead animals are animals.

(6) Normally animals don't fly.
(7) Normally bats fly
(8) Normally birds fly
(9) Normally penguins don't fly
(10) Normally dead animals don't fly

the following individuals

(11) Pluto is a mammal.
(12) Tweety is a bird.
(13) Joe is a penguin.

(14) Dracula is a bat.
(15) Dracula is a dead animal.

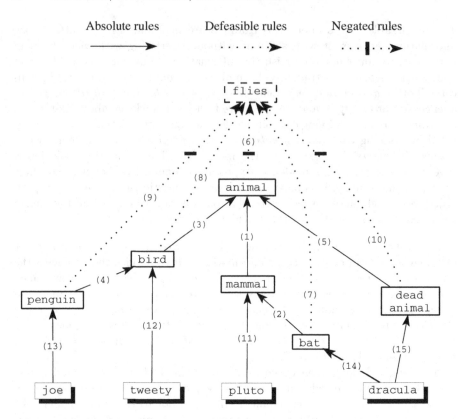

Fig. 1. A non-monotonic hierarchical taxonomy

and the preferences

(16) Dead bats do not fly though bats do.
(17) Dead birds do not fly though birds do.
(18) Dracula is an exception to the above preferences.

The above hierarchy can be represented by the program:

(1) $animal(X) \leftarrow mammal(X)$ (4) $bird(X) \leftarrow penguin(X)$
(2) $mammal(X) \leftarrow bat(X)$ (5) $animal(X) \leftarrow dead\_animal(X)$
(3) $animal(X) \leftarrow bird(X)$

(6) $\neg flies(X) \leftarrow animal(X), \neg flying\_animal(X), not\,flies(X)$
     $\neg flying\_animal(X) \leftarrow not\,flying\_animal(X)$
(7) $flies(X) \leftarrow bat(X), flying\_bat(X), not\,\neg flies(X)$
     $flying\_bat(X) \leftarrow not\,\neg flying\_bat(X)$
(8) $flies(X) \leftarrow bird(X), flying\_bird(X), not\,\neg flies(X)$
     $flying\_bird(X) \leftarrow not\,\neg flying\_bird(X)$

(9) $\neg flies(X) \leftarrow penguin(X), \neg flying\_penguin(X), not\ flies(X)$
        $\neg flying_penguin(X) \leftarrow not\ flying\_penguin(X)$

(10) $\neg flies(X) \leftarrow dead\_animal(X), \neg flying\_dead(X), not\ flies(X)$
        $\neg flying\_dead(X) \leftarrow not\ flying\_dead(X)$

(11) $mammal(pluto) \leftarrow$ (14) $bat(dracula) \leftarrow$
(12) $bird(tweety) \leftarrow$ (15) $dead\_animal(dracula) \leftarrow$
(13) $penguin(joe)$

with the implicit hierarchical preference rules (prefer most specific information):

$$flying\_animal(X) \leftarrow bat(X), flying\_bat(X)$$
$$flying\_animal(X) \leftarrow bird(X), flying\_bird(X)$$
$$\neg flying\_bird(X) \leftarrow penguin(X), \neg flying\_penguin(X)$$
$$flying\_dead(X) \leftarrow bat(X), flying\_dead\_bat(X).$$

and the explicit problem statement preferences:

(16) $\neg flying\_bat(X) \leftarrow dead\_animal(X), bat(X), \neg flying\_dead\_bat(X)$
        $\neg flying\_dead\_bat(X) \leftarrow not\ flying\_dead\_bat(X)$

(17) $\neg flying\_bird(X) \leftarrow dead\_animal(X), bird(X), \neg flying\_dead\_bird(X)$
        $\neg flying\_dead\_bird(X) \leftarrow not\ flying\_dead\_bird(X)$

(18) $flying\_dead\_bat(dracula) \leftarrow$

The model of this programs is non-contradictory, and we get the expected results, namely that Pluto and Joe don't fly, and that Dracula and Tweety do fly.

The above rules can be automatically generated from the description of the hierarchies, as shown elsewhere [6]. As for WFS, the advantage of $WFSX_P$ is that the computation of the well-founded model is tractable, is defined for every Generalized Extended Logic Program in particular for contradictory programs. Furthermore, we are able to detect dependencies on contradiction just by looking at the model. Generalized Answer Set Semantics based [23,29] is an extension of Stable Model Semantics for Generalized Extended Logic Programs, and is very appropriate for the declarative representation of complex problems, but inherits the same problems of Stable Model Semantics; moreover it explodes when faced with contradiction.

4   The W4 Project: Well-Founded Semantics for the WWW

The W4 project aims at developing Standard Prolog inter-operable tools for supporting distributed, secure, and integrated reasoning activities in the Semantic Web. The results of the W4 project are expected to contribute to the recently approved REWERSE European Network of Excellence. The long-term objectives are:

- Development of Prolog technology for XML, RDF, and RuleML.
- Development of a General Semantic framework for RuleML, including default and explicit negation, supporting uncertain, incomplete, and paraconsistent reasoning.
- Development of distributed query evaluation procedures for RuleML, based on tabulation, according to the previous semantics.
- Development of Dynamic Semantics for evolution/update of Rule ML knowledge bases.
- Integration of different semantics in RuleML (namely, Well-Founded Semantics, Answer Sets, Fuzzy Logic Programming, Annotated Logic Programming, and Probabilistic Logic Programming).

We have started the implementation efforts from the previously described theoretical work and implementations, and the RuleML [25] language proposal. A full RuleML compiler is already available for an extension of the hornlog frament of RuleML (see [32]). The W4 RuleML compiler supports default and explicit negation both in the heads and in the bodies of rules, as well as assert statements of EVOLP programs (see section 5). The semantics implemented is Paraconsistent Well-founded Semantics with Explicit Negation. We now shortly illustrate the use of the W4 RuleML with an example session:

Example 4. Consider the taxonomy of Example 3 encoded in RuleML format. E.g., one of the rules used for capturing the sentence "Normally, bats fly" is:

$$flies(X) \leftarrow bat(X), flying\_bat(X), not \neg flies(X).$$

with the following corresponding RuleML encoding:

```
<imp>
 <_head>
   <atom> <_opr><rel>flies</rel></_opr> <var>X</var> </atom>
 </_head>
 <_body>
   <and>
     <atom> <_opr><rel>bat</rel></_opr> <var>X</var> </atom>
     <atom> <_opr><rel>flying bat</rel></_opr> <var>X</var> </atom>
     <not><neg>
         <atom> <_opr><rel>flies</rel></_opr> <var>X</var> </atom>
     </neg></not>
   </and>
 </_body>
</imp>
```

The whole rule base is loaded as follows:

```
| ?- loadRules( ruleML( 'taxonomy.ruleml' ) ).
yes
```

The same predicate is capable of reading ordinary Prolog and NTriple files. After loading its rule bases, the user can start querying them, a tuple-at-a-time, with the **demo/2** predicate. The first argument is the name of a loaded

rule base and the second the query in the usual Prolog syntax, extended with
the unary operators **not** and **neg** for representing default and explicit negation,
respectively:

```
| ?- demo( animals, flies(X) ).
X = Dracula; X = Tweety;
no
| ?- demo( animals, neg flies(X) ).
X = Joe; X = Pluto;
no
| ?- demo( animals, ( animal(X), not flies(X) ) ).
X = Pluto; X = Joe;
no
```

The **demo/2** predicate invokes a meta-interpreter that implements $WFSX_P$
semantics via a program transformation into normal logic programming under WFS, making use of the tabling primitives of XSB-Prolog. The predicate
queryRules/3 allows the user to collect all the answers to a query in a list, or
write them in XML format to an output stream. The first argument is the rule
based being queried, the second is a list of terms of the form **query(Goal,
Label, ListofVars)** with the several queries to issue, and finally the last argument is either a variable or an output stream.

```
| ?- queryRules(animals, [query( flies(X), q1, [animal=X] )], Ans).
Ans = [[answer(q1,[animal = Dracula]),answer(q1,[animal = Tweety])]]

| ?- queryRules(animals, [query( flies(X), q1, [animal=X] ),
                         query( neg flies(X), q2, [non=X])], Ans).
Ans = [[answer(q1,[animal = Dracula]),answer(q1,[animal = Tweety])],
       [answer(q2,[non = Joe]),answer(q2,[non = Pluto])]]

| ?- queryRules(animals, [query( flies(X), q1, [animal=X] )],userout).
<answers>
 <_answer><_rlab><ind>q1</ind></_rlab>
         <_subst><var>animal</var><ind>Dracula</ind></_subst>
 </_answer>
 <_answer><_rlab><ind>q1</ind></_rlab>
         <_subst><var>animal</var><ind>Tweety</ind></_subst>
 </_answer>
</answers>

| ?- queryRules(animals, [query( flies(X), q1, [animal=X]),
                         query( neg flies(X) , q2, [non=X])], userout).
<answers>
 <_answer><_rlab><ind>q1</ind></_rlab>
         <_subst><var>animal</var><ind>Dracula</ind></_subst>
 </_answer>
 <_answer><_rlab><ind>q1</ind></_rlab>
         <_subst><var>animal</var><ind>Tweety</ind></_subst>
 </_answer>
 <_answer><_rlab><ind>q2</ind></_rlab><_subst>
```

```
              <var>non</var><ind>Joe</ind></_subst>
   </_answer>
   <_answer><_rlab><ind>q2</ind></_rlab><_subst>
              <var>non</var><ind>Pluto</ind></_subst>
   </_answer>
</answers>
```

Mark that the answer may be labelled with user-provided labels in order to identify the corresponding query, and variables can be given user-understandable names. The format of answers is not specified in the RuleML proposal.

The W4 RuleML compiler supports several rulebases, imported from RuleML files, Prolog files, or NTriples files. A converter from Prolog syntax to RuleML syntax and from RuleML syntax to Prolog syntax is included. An experimental RDF(S) engine is also provided, and makes extensive use of the tabling facilities of the XSB Prolog engine. By exploiting the NMR features of the new XSB Prolog 2.6, support will be provided for Stable Models and Answer Set Semantics. The package was originally developed for XSB Prolog 2.5, but porting to other Prolog systems is foreseen.

There are some open issues, namely the definition of remote Goal invocation method via the exchange of SOAP messages, and the selection of distributed query evaluation algorithms and corresponding protocols. A standard integration of RuleML with ontologies is still lacking. Further applications, testing, and evaluation is required for the construction of practical systems.

5   Updates and the Evolution of Rule Bases

One of the features for which we developed research work, and corresponding implementations is that of updates and evolution of rule-based knowledge bases. While logic programming can be seen as a good representation language for static knowledge, as we have just shown, if we are to move to a more open and dynamic environment typical of, for example, the agency paradigm, we must consider ways and means of representing and integrating knowledge updates from external sources, but also inner source knowledge updates (or self updates). In fact, an agent not only comprises knowledge about each state, but also knowledge about the transitions between states. The latter may represent the agent's knowledge about the environment's evolution, coupled to its own behaviour and evolution rules. Similar arguments apply to the Semantic Web. In it, knowledge is stored in various autonomous sources or repositories, which evolve with time, thus exhibiting a dynamic character. Declarative languages and mechanisms for specifying the Semantic Web's evolution and maintenance are in order, and we have recently worked towards this goal.

To address these concerns we first introduced *Dynamic Logic Programming (DLP)* [5] ([19] addressed similar concerns). According to DLP, knowledge is given by a linearly ordered sequence of generalized extended logic programs that represent distinct and dynamically changing states of the world. Each of the states may contain mutually contradictory and overlapping information. The semantics of DLP ensures that all previous rules remain valid (by inertia) so long as they are not contradicted by newer (prevailing) rules.

We have developed two implementations of DLP[1]:

- One of them implements exactly the semantics defined in [5] which is a stable models based semantics. This implementation is provided as a pre-processor of sequences of generalized programs into programs that run under the DLV system [9] for computing the stable models.
- The other implementation is based on a generalization of the well-founded semantics [21] for sequences of programs, which is sound though not complete with respect to the semantics in [5]. The advantages of using a well-founded based semantics rather than a stable models based one can be found in section 2. This implementation consists of a meta-interpreter of sequences of programs, and runs under XSB-Prolog [30]. With it, one can consult sequences of generalized programs, as well as update the running sequence with with set or another of generalized rules. Queries to literals can be posed to the current (latest) state, or to any other previous state. It is also possibly to ask in which of the states some literal holds.

Recently we have integrated a mechanism of preferences [7], which generalizes the preferences of [11] to sequences of programs. The implementation of updates with preferences is based on a pre-processor into DLV programs, according to a transformation defined in [4].

To cope with updates of knowledge coming from various sources, we extended DLP and developed *Multi-dimensional Dynamic Logic Programming - (MDLP)* [28]. DLP allows to encode a single update dimension, where this dimension can either be time, hierarchy strength of rules, priorities, etc. With MDLP more than one of these dimensions can be dealt within a single framework (allowing e.g. to model the evolution over time of hierarchically organized sets of rules). The MDLP implementation is enacted as a meta-interpreter running under XSB-Prolog. With it, Directed Acyclic Graphs (DAGs) of programs can be consulted (with a special syntax for representing the graph), and queries can be put to any of the programs in the DAG.

With these languages and implementations logic programs can describe well knowledge states and also sequences and DAGs of updating knowledge states. It's only fit that logic programs be utilized to describe the transitions between knowledge states as well. This can be achieved by associating with each state a set of transition rules to obtain the next state. However, till recently, *LP* had sometimes been considered less than adequate for modelling the dynamics of knowledge change over time, because typical update commands are defined by it. To overcome this limitation, we have introduced and implemented the language LUPS [8] (related languages are EPI [18] and KABUL [27]).

LUPS is a logic programming command language for specifying logic program updates. It can be viewed as a language that declaratively specifies how

---

[1] All implementations mentioned in this section can be found at:
http://centria.di.fct.unl.pt/~jja/

to construct a Dynamic Logic Program by means of successive update commands. A sentence U in LUPS is a set of simultaneous update commands that, given a pre-existing sequence of logic programs, whose semantics corresponds to our knowledge at a given state, produces a new DLP with one more program, corresponding to the knowledge that results from the previous sequence after performing all the simultaneous update commands. A program in LUPS is a sequence of such sentences. The most simple LUPS command is **assert** *Rule*, that simply asserts a rule in the next program of the running sequence. Other more elaborate commands of LUPS take care of retraction of rules, persistent assertion of rules, cancellation of persistent assertions, event assertion and persistent event assertion. For example, the command for persistent rule assertion is of the form **always** *Rule* **when** *Conds*, which from the moment it is given, till cancelled, whenever *Conds* are true *Rule* is asserted. As with DLP, two implementations have also been developed for LUPS, one stable models based, running as a pre-processor into DLV programs, and another running as a meta-interpreter in XSB-Prolog.

More recently, we have worked on a general language, christened EVOLP (after EVOlving Logic Programs) [1], that integrates in a simple way the concepts of both DLP and LUPS, through a language much closer to that of traditional logic programs than the one of LUPS. EVOLP generalizes logic programming to allow specification of a program's own evolution as well as evolution due to external events, in a single unified way, by permitting rules to indicate assertive conclusions in the form of program rules. EVOLP rules are simply generalized LP rules plus the special predicate assert/1, which can appear both in heads or bodies of rules. The argument of assert/1 can be a full-blown EVOLP rule, thus allowing for the nesting of rule assertions within assertions to make it possible for rule updates to be themselves updated down the evolution line. The meaning of a sequence of EVOLP rules is given by sequences of models. Each sequence determines a possible evolution of the knowledge base. Each model determines what is true after a number of evolution steps (i.e. a state) in the sequence: a first model in a sequence is built by "computing" the semantics of the first EVOLP program, where assert/1 is as any other predicate; if *assert(Rule)* is true at some state, then the program must be updated with *Rule* in the next state; this updating, and the "computation" of the next model in the sequence, is performed as in DLP.

The current implementation of EVOLP is a meta-interpreter that runs under XSB-Prolog. With it, it is possible to consult sequences of sets of EVOLP rules, as well as update the running sequence with a new set of rules. Queries to literals can be made in the current (later) state, or in any other previous state or interval of states. It is also possibly to ask in which of the states is some literal true. We are now in the process of integrating the EVOLP implementation (which, as mentioned above, encompasses both the features from DLP and LUPS) into the W4 RuleML compiler described in section 4, that already supports EVOLP's syntax . This work, which we expect to finish soon, will allow the usage of

EVOLP for taking care of the evolution and maintenance of RuleML rule bases in the Semantics Web.

We have applied these languages, and used the above mentioned implementations, in various domains, such as: actions, agents' architecture, specification of agents' behaviours, software specification, planning, legal reasoning, and active databases. References to this work, as well as the running examples, can be found in the URL above.

To illustrate the expressiveness of these languages, we briefly illustrate here how EVOLP can be employed to model an evolving personal assistant agent for email management able to: Perform basic actions of sending, receiving, deleting messages; Storing and moving messages between folders; Filtering spam messages; Sending automatic replies and forwarding; Notifying the user of special situations. All of this dependent on user specified criteria, and where the specification may change dynamically. More details on this application can be found in [2]. In this application messages are stored via the basic predicates $msg(Identifier, From, Subject, Body, TimeStamp)$ and $in(Identifier, Folder)$ for specifying in which folder the message is stored. New messages are simply events of the form $newmsg(msg(Identifier, From, Subject, Body)$. Basic actions can be easily modelled with EVOLP. For example, for dealing with incoming messages, all we have to specify is that any new message, arriving at time T, should be stored in the inbox folder, unless it is marked for deletion. If a message is marked to be deleted then it should not be stored in any folder. This can be modelled by the EVOLP rules:

$$assert(msg(M, F, S, B, T)) \leftarrow newmsg(M, F, S, B), time(T), not\ delete(M)$$
$$assert(in(M, inbox)) \leftarrow newmsg(M, F, S, B), not\ delete(M)$$
$$assert(not\ in(M, inbox)) \leftarrow delete(M), in(M, F)$$

Rules for filtering spam can then be added, as updates to the program, in a simple way. For example, if one wants to filter, and delete, messages containing the word "credit" in the subject, we simply have to update our program with:

$$delete(M) \leftarrow newmsg(M, F, S, B), spam(F, S, B)$$

$$spam(F, S, B) \leftarrow contains(S, credit)$$

Note that this definition of spam can later be updated, EVOLP ensuring that conflicts between older and newer rules are automatically resolved. For example, if later one wants to update the definition of spam, by stating that messages coming from one's accountant should not be considered as spam, all one has to do is to update the program with the rule:

$$not\ spam(F, S, B) \leftarrow contains(F, my\_accountant)$$

With this update, EVOLP ensures that messages from the accountant are not considered spam, even if they contain the word "credit" in the subject, and the user doesn't have to worry about guaranteeing, manually, the consistency of later rules with previous ones.

As an example of a more complex rule, consider that the user is now organizing a conference, and assigns papers to referees. Suppose further that he wants to automatically guarantee that, after receipt of a referee's acceptance, any message about an assigned paper is forwarded to the corresponding referee. In EVOLP terms, this means that if a message is received from the referee accepting to review a given paper, then a rule should be asserted stating that new messages about that paper are to be sent to that referee:

$$assert(send(R, S, B) \leftarrow newmsg(M, F, S, B), contains(S, PId),$$
$$assign(PId, R) \quad)$$
$$\leftarrow newmsg(M, R, PId, B), contains(B, \text{'accept'})$$

For an illustration of more elaborate rules, showing other features of EVOLP, such as the possibility of dynamically changing the policies of the agent triggered by internal or external conditions, for commands that span over various states, etc, the reader is referred to [2].

6   Conclusion

In our opinion, Well-Founded Semantics should be a major player in RuleML, properly integrated with Stable Models. A full-blown theory is available for important extensions of standard WFS/SMs, addressing many of the open issues of the Semantic Web. Most extensions resort to polynomial program transformations, namely those for evolution and update of knowledge bases. They can handle uncertainty, incompleteness, and paraconsistency. Efficient implementation technology exists, and important progress has been made in distributed query evaluation. An open, fully distributed, architecture is being elaborated and proposed.

Acknowledgments

The work summarized here has been developed by us in collaboration with João Alcântara, António Brogi, Pierangelo Dell'Acqua João Leite, Teodor Przymusinski, Halina Przymusinska, and Paulo Quaresma (cf. publications below). We would like to thank all of them for this joint work.

Part of the work on logic programming updates has been supported by projects FLUX "Flexible Logical Updates" (POSI/SRI/40958/2001) , funded by FEDER, and TARDE "Tabulation and Reasoning in a Distributed Prolog Environment" (EEI/12097/1998), funded by FCT/MCES.

References

1. J. J. Alferes, A. Brogi, J. A. Leite, and L. M. Pereira. Evolving logic programs. In S. Flesca, S. Greco, N. Leone, and G. Ianni, editors, *Proceedings of the 8th European Conference on Logics in Artificial Intelligence (JELIA'02)*, volume 2424 of *LNAI*, pages 50–61. Springer-Verlag, 2002.

2. J. J. Alferes, A. Brogi, J. A. Leite, and L. M. Pereira. Logic programming for evolving agents. In M. Klusch, A. Omicini, and S. Ossowski, editors, *Proceedings of the 7th International Cooperative Information Agents (CIA'03)*, LNAI. Springer-Verlag, 2003.

3. J. J. Alferes, C. V. Damásio, and L. M. Pereira. A logic programming system for non-monotonic reasoning. *Special Issue of the Journal of Automated Reasoning*, 14(1):93–147, 1995.

4. J. J. Alferes, P. Dell'Acqua, and L. M. Pereira. A compilation of updates plus preferences. In S. Flesca, S. Greco, N. Leone, and G. Ianni, editors, *Proceedings of the 8th European Conference on Logics in Artificial Intelligence (JELIA'02)*, volume 2424 of *LNAI*, pages 62–73. Springer-Verlag, 2002.

5. J. J. Alferes, J. A. Leite, L. M. Pereira, H. Przymusinska, and T. C. Przymusinski. Dynamic updates of non-monotonic knowledge bases. *The Journal of Logic Programming*, 45(1–3):43–70, September/October 2000. A short version appeared in A. Cohn and L. Schubert (eds.), *KR'98*, Morgan Kaufmann.

6. J. J. Alferes and L. M. Pereira. *Reasoning with logic programming*, volume 1111 of *Lecture Notes in Artificial Intelligence*. Springer-Verlag, 1996.

7. J. J. Alferes and L. M. Pereira. Updates plus preferences. In M. O. Aciego, I. P. de Guzman, G. Brewka, and L. M. Pereira, editors, *Proceedings of the 7th European Conference on Logics in Artificial Intelligence (JELIA'00)*, volume 1919 of *LNAI*, pages 345–360. Springer-Verlag, 2000.

8. J. J. Alferes, L. M. Pereira, H. Przymusinska, and T. Przymusinski. LUPS: A language for updating logic programs. *Artificial Intelligence*, 132(1 & 2), 2002. A short version appeared in M. Gelfond, N. Leone and G. Pfeifer (eds.), *LPNMR'99*, Springer LNAI 1730.

9. The DLV Project: A Disjunctive Datalog System (and more).
http://www.dbai.tuwien.ac.at/proj/dlv/, 2000.

10. Tim Berners-Lee, James Hendler, and Ora Lassila. The Semantic Web. *Scientific American*, May 2001.

11. G. Brewka and T. Eiter. Preferred answer sets for extended logic programs. *Artificial Intelligence*, 109, 1999. A short version appeared in A. Cohn and L. Schubert (eds.), *KR'98*, Morgan Kaufmann.

12. D. Brickley and R.V. Guha. RDF Vocabulary Description Language 1.0: RDF Schema, 23 January 2003 (work in progress).
http://www.w3.org/TR/2003/WD-rdf-schema-20030123/.

13. D. Connolly D., F. van Harmelen, I. Horrocks, D.L. McGuinness, P.F. Patel-Schneider, and L.A. Stein. DAML+OIL (March 2001) Reference Description.
http://www.w3.org/TR/daml+oil-reference.

14. Carlos Viegas Damásio and Luís Moniz Pereira. Default negated conclusions: why not ? In R. Dyckhoff, H. Herre, and P. Schroeder-Heister, editors, *Proc. of the 5th International Workshop on Extensions of Logic Programming (ELP'96)*, number 1050 in LNAI, pages 103–117, 1996.

15. Carlos Viegas Damásio and Luís Moniz Pereira. A paraconsistent semantics with contradiction support detection. In Jürgen Dix, Ulrich Furbach, and Anil Nerode, editors, *Proceedings of the 4th International Conference on Logic Programming and Nonmonotonic Reasoning (LPNMR'97)*, volume 1265 of *Lecture Notes in Artificial Intelligence*, pages 224–243, Castelo de Dagstuhl, Alemanha, July 1997. Springer.

16. Carlos Viegas Damásio and Luís Moniz Pereira. A survey of paraconsistent semantics for logic programas. In D. Gabbay and P. Smets, editors, *Handbook of Defeasible Reasoning and Uncertainty Management Systems*, volume 2, Reasoning with Actual and Potential Contradictions. Coordenado por P. Besnard e A. Hunter, pages 241–320. Kluwer Academic Publishers, 1998.

17. M. Dean, G. Schreiber, F. van Harmelen, J. Hendler, I. Horrocks, D.L. McGuinness, P.F. Patel-Schneider, and L.A. Stein. OWL Web Ontology Language Reference, 18 August 2003 (Candidate Recommendation).
    http://www.w3.org/TR/2003/CR-owl-ref-20030818/.

18. T. Eiter, M. Fink, G. Sabbatini, and H Tompits. A framework for declarative update specifications in logic programs. In *IJCAI'01*. Morgan-Kaufmann, 2001.

19. T. Eiter, M. Fink, G. Sabbatini, and H. Tompits. On properties of update sequences based on causal rejection. *Theory and Practice of Logic Programming*, 2(6), 2002.

20. M. Van Emden and R. Kowalski. The semantics of predicate logic as a programming language. *Journal of ACM*, 4(23):733–742, 1976.

21. A. Van Gelder, K. A. Ross, and J. S. Schlipf. The well-founded semantics for general logic programs. *Journal of the ACM*, 38(3):620–650, 1991.

22. M. Gelfond and V. Lifschitz. The stable model semantics for logic programming. In R. Kowalski and K. A. Bowen, editors, *5th International Conference on Logic Programming*, pages 1070–1080. MIT Press, 1988.

23. M. Gelfond and V. Lifschitz. Logic programs with classical negation. In Warren and Szeredi, editors, *7th International Conference on Logic Programming*, pages 579–597. MIT Press, 1990.

24. P. (Editor) Hayes. RDF semantics, 23 January 2003 (work in progress).
    http://www.w3.org/TR/2003/WD-rdf-mt-20030123/.

25. The Rule Markup Initiative. http://www.ruleml.org/.

26. O. Lassila and R. Swick. Resource description framework (RDF) model and syntax specification, 22 February 1999. http://www.w3.org/TR/REC-rdf-syntax/.

27. J. A. Leite. *Evolving Knowledge Bases*. IOS Press, 2003.

28. J. A. Leite, J. J. Alferes, and L. M. Pereira. Multi-dimensional dynamic knowledge representation. In T. Eiter, W. Faber, and M. Truszczynski, editors, *Proceedings of the 6th International Conference on Logics Programming and Non-Monotonic Reasoning (LPNMR'01)*, volume 2173 of *LNAI*, pages 365–378. Springer-Verlag, 2001.

29. V. Lifschitz and T. Woo. Answer sets in general non-monotonic reasoning (preliminary report). In B. Nebel, C. Rich, and W. Swartout, editors, *Proceedings of the 3th International Conference on Principles of Knowledge Representation and Reasoning (KR-92)*. Morgan-Kaufmann, 1992.

30. The XSB Logic Programming Systems. http://xsb.sourceforge.net, 2003.

31. The smodels system. http://www.tcs.hut.fi/Software/smodels/, 2000.

32. The W4 RuleML compiler. http://centria.fct.unl.pt/~cd/projectos/w4/.

Web Rules Need Two Kinds of Negation

Gerd Wagner

Eindhoven University of Technology, Faculty of Technology Management
G.Wagner@tm.tue.nl
http://tmitwww.tm.tue.nl/staff/gwagner

Abstract. In natural language, and in some knowledge representation systems, such as extended logic programs, there are two kinds of negation: a weak negation expressing non-truth, and a strong negation expressing explicit falsity. In this paper I argue that, like in several basic computational languages, such as OCL and SQL, two kinds of negation are also needed for a Web rule language.

1 Introduction

In [Wag91], I have argued that a database, as a knowledge representation system, needs two kinds of negation to be able to deal with partial information. The present paper is an attempt to make the same point for the Semantic Web.

Computational forms of negation are used in imperative programming languages (such as *Java*), in database query languages (such as *SQL*), in modeling languages (such as *UML/OCL*), in production rule systems (such as *CLIPS* and *Jess*) and in logic programming languages (such as *Prolog*). In imperative programming languages, negation may occur in the condition expression of a conditional branching statement. In database query languages, negation may occur in at least two forms: as a *not* operator in selection conditions, and in the form of the relational algebra *difference* operator (corresponding to the SQL *EXCEPT* operator). In modeling languages, negation occurs in constraint statements. E.g., in OCL, there are several forms of negation: in addition to the *not* operator in selection conditions also the *reject* and the *isEmpty* operators are used to express a negation. In production rule systems, and in logic programming languages, a negation operator *not* typically occurs only in the condition part of a rule with the operational semantics of *negation-as-failure* which can be understood as classical negation under the preferential semantics of stable models.

We show in section 2 that negation in all these computational systems is, from a logical point of view, not a clean concept, but combines classical (Boolean) negation with negation-as-failure and the strong negation of three-valued logic (also called *Kleene negation*). In any case, however, it seems to be essential for all major computational systems to provide different forms of negation. Consequently, we may conclude (by common sense induction) that the Semantic Web also needs these different forms of negation.

F. Bry et al. (Eds.): PPSWR 2003, LNCS 2901, pp. 33–50, 2003.

In natural language, there are (at least) two kinds of negation: a weak negation expressing non-truth (in the sense of "she doesn't like snow" or "he doesn't trust you"), and a strong negation expressing explicit falsity (in the sense of "she dislikes snow" or "he distrusts you"). Notice that the classical logic law of the excluded middle holds only for the weak negation (either "she likes snow" or "she doesn't like snow"), but not for the strong negation: it does not hold that "he trusts you" or "he distrusts you"; he may be neutral and neither trust nor distrust you.

A number of knowledge representation formalisms and systems, discussed in section 4, follow this distinction between weak and strong negation in natural language. However, many of them do not come with a model-theoretic semantics in the style of classical logic. Instead, an inference operation, that may be viewed as a kind of proof-theoretic semantics, is proposed.

Classical (two-valued) logic cannot account for two kinds of negation because two-valued (Boolean) truth functions do not allow to define more than one negation. The simplest generalization of classical logic that is able to account for two kinds of negation is *partial logic* giving up the classical bivalence principle and subsuming a number of 3-valued and 4-valued logics. For instance, in 3-valued logic with truth values $\{f, u, t\}$ standing for *false, undetermined* (also called *unknown* or *undefined*) and *true*, weak negation (denoted by $\sim$) and strong negation (denoted by $\neg$) have the following truth tables:

p	$\sim p$
t	f
u	t
f	t

p	$\neg p$
t	f
u	u
f	t

Notice the difference between weak and strong negation in 3-valued logic: if a sentence evaluates to u in a model, then its weak negation evaluates to t, while its strong negation evaluates to u in this model. Partial logics allow for *truth-value gaps* created by partial predicates to which the law of the excluded middle does not apply.

However, even in classical logic, where all predicates are total, we may distinguish between predicates that are completely represented in a database (or knowledge base) and those that are not. The classification if a predicate is completely represented or not is up to the owner of the database: the owner must know for which predicates she has complete information and for which she does not. Clearly, in the case of a completely represented predicate, negation-as-failure amounts to classical negation, and the underlying completeness assumption is also called *Closed-World Assumption*. In the case of an incompletely represented predicate, negation-as-failure only reflects non-provability, but does not allow to infer the classical negation. Unfortunately, neither CLIPS/Jess nor Prolog support this distinction between 'closed' and 'open' predicates.

Open (incompletely represented total) predicates must not be confused with partial predicates that have truth-value gaps. The law of the excluded middle, $p \vee \neg p$, applies to open predicates but not to partial predicates.

For being able to make all these distinctions and to understand their logical semantics, we have to choose partial logic as the underlying logical framework. Partial logic allows to formally distinguish between falsity and non-truth by means of strong and weak negation. In the case of a total predicate, such as being an odd number, both negations collapse:

$$\sim odd(x) \text{ iff } \neg odd(x),$$

or in other words, the non-truth of the atomic sentence $odd(x)$ amounts to its falsity. In the case of a partial predicate, such as *likes*, we only have the relationship that the strong negation implies the weak negation:

$$\sim likes(she,snow) \text{ if } \neg likes(she,snow),$$

but not conversely. Also, while the double negation form '$\neg \sim$' collapses (according to partial logic, see [Wag98]), the double negation form '$\sim \neg$' does not collapse: not disliking snow does not amount to liking snow. Classical logic can be viewed as the degenerate case of partial logic when all predicates are total.

2   Negative Information, Closed Predicates and Two Kinds of Negation in the Semantic Web

We claim that, like in the cases of UML/OCL, SQL and extended logic programs, also for Web rules one needs two kinds of negation. This applies in particular to RDF(S), OWL and RuleML. We first discuss this problem briefly for the case of RDF(S), N3 and RuleML. Then in Section 3 and 4, we discuss it both for the established languages/technologies of UML/OCL, SQL, Jess, and Prolog, and for knowledge representation formalism. Finally, in Section 5, present its logical foundation.

2.1   Expressing Negative Information in RDF

The *FIPA RDF Content Language Specification* (see www.fipa.org) that specifies how RDF can be used as a message content language in the communication acts of FIPA-compliant agents proposes a method how to express negated RDF facts to *'express belief or disbelief of a statement'*. For this purpose an RDF statement (expressed as a 'subject-predicate-object' triple corresponding to *objectID-attribute-value*) is annotated by a truth value *true* or *false* in a `<fipa:belief>` element as in the following example:

```
<fipa:Proposition>
  <rdf:subject>RDF Semantics</rdf:subject>
  <rdf:predicate rdf:resource="http://description.org/schema#author"/>
  <rdf:object>Ora Lassila</rdf:object/>
  <fipa:belief>false</fipa:belief>
</fipa:Proposition>
```

This example expresses the negated sentence

Ora Lassila is not the author of 'RDF Semantics'.

It shows that there is a need to extend the current syntax of RDF, so as to be able to express negative information.

2.2 Closed Predicates and Negation-as-Failure in RDF/S

As opposed to the predicate 'is the author of', there are also predicates for which there is no need to express negative information because the available positive information about them is complete and, consequently, the negative information is simply the complement of the positive information.

For instance, the W3C has complete information about all official W3C documents and their normative status (http://www.w3.org/TR/ is the official list of W3C publications); consequently, the predicate *is an official W3C document* should be declared as closed in the W3C knowledge base (making a 'local' completeness assumption)[1]. This consideration calls for a suitable extension of RDFS in order to allow making such declarations for specific predicates.

For sentences formed with closed predicates it is natural to use negation-as-failure for establishing their falsity (anything not listed on that page cannot be a W3C recommendation). So, a query language for RDF should include some form of negation-as-failure.

2.3 Default Rules in RuleML and N3

The RuleML standardization initiative has been started in August 2000 with the goal of establishing an open, vendor neutral XML-based rule language standard. The official website of the RuleML initiative is `www.ruleml.org`.

The current 'official' version of RuleML (in July 2003) has the version number 0.84. In [BTW01], the rationale behind RuleML 0.8 and some future extensions of it is discussed, while [Wag02] provides a general discussion of the issues of rule markup languages.

An example of a derivation rule involving strong negation (for making sure that something is definitely not the case) and negation-as-failure (for expressing a default condition) is the following:

A car is available for rental if it is not assigned to any rental order, does not require service and is not scheduled for a maintenance check.

This rule could be marked up in RuleML as shown below. Strong negation is expressed by `<neg>` while negation-as-failure is expressed by `<naf>`. Notice that it is important to apply `<neg>`, and not `<naf>`, to `requiresService` in order to make sure, by requiring explicit negative information, that the car in question does not require service (the car rental company may be liable for any consequences/damages caused by a failure of this check).

---

[1] This example is due to Sandro Hawke, see [DDM].

```
<imp>
  <_head>
    <atom>
      <_opr>isAvailable</_opr>
      <var>Car</var>
    </atom>
  </_head>
  <_body>
    <and>
      <atom>
        <_opr>RentalCar</_opr>
        <var>Car</var>
      </atom>
      <neg>
        <atom>
          <_opr>requiresService</_opr>
          <var>Car</var>
        </atom>
      </neg>
      <naf>
        <atom>
          <_opr>isSchedForMaint</_opr>
          <var>Car</var>
        </atom>
      </naf>
      <naf>
        <atom>
          <_opr>isAssToRentalOrder</_opr>
          <var>Car</var>
        </atom>
      </naf>
    </and>
  </_body>
</imp>
```

However, the last condition of the rule, expressed with `<naf>`, is a default condition requiring only that there is no information about any assignment of the car in question. In N3, one can test for what a formula does not say, with `log:notIncludes`. In the following example (taken from [BL]), we have a rule stating that if the specification for a car doesn't say what color it is, then it is black:

```
this log:forAll :car. { :car.auto:specification log:notIncludes
{:car auto:color []}}
=> {:car auto:color auto:black}.
```

In this rule, the `log:notIncludes` operator expresses a negation-as-failure in a similar way as the isEmpty operator of OCL and the IS NULL operator of SQL.

3   Negations in UML/OCL, SQL, CLIPS/Jess and Prolog

UML/OCL, SQL, CLIPS/Jess and Prolog may be viewed as the paradigm-setting languages for *modeling, databases, production rules* and (logical) *derivation rules*. We discuss each of them in some more detail.

3.1   Negation in UML/OCL

The Unified Modeling Language (UML) may be viewed as the paradigm-setting language for software and information systems modeling. In the UML, negation occurs in Object Constraint Language (OCL) statements. There are several forms of negation in OCL: in addition to the *not* operator in selection conditions also the *reject* and the *isEmpty* operators are used to express a negation. OCL allows partially defined expressions and is based on a 3-valued logic where the third truth value, denoted by $\bot$, is called *undefined*.

The above rule for rental cars defines the derived Boolean-valued attribute `isAvailable` of the class `RentalCar` by means of an association `isAssignedTo` between cars and rental orders and the stored Boolean-valued attributes `requiresService` and `isSchedForMaint`. All these concepts are shown in the UML class diagram in Figure 1.

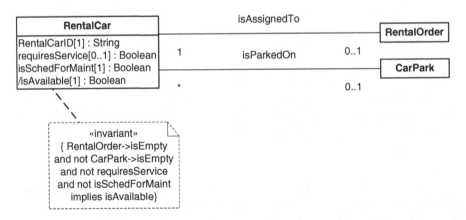

Fig. 1. This UML class diagram shows two classes, `RentalCar` and `RentalOrder`, and the functional association `isAssignedTo` between them. The Boolean-valued attribute `isAvailable` is a derived attribute whose definition is expressed by the attached OCL constraint.

Notice that `requiresService` is defined as an optional attribute (that need not always have a value). This reflects the fact that whenever a rental car is returned by a customer, it is not known if it requires service until its technical state is checked. Only then this attribute obtains a value true or false[2]. As opposed to `requiresService`, `isSchedForMaint` is defined as a mandatory attribute that must always have a value, reflecting the fact that the car rental company always knows if a car is or is not scheduled for a maintenance check.

Since the Object Constraint Language (OCL) of UML does not allow to define derivation rules, we have to express the definition of the derived attribute `isAvailable` by means of an OCL invariant statement:

```
context RentalCar inv:
  RentalOrder->isEmpty
    and not requiresService
    and not isSchedForMaint
  implies isAvailable
```

This integrity constraint states that for a specific rental car whenever there is no rental order associated with it, and it does not require service and is not scheduled for maintenance, then it has to be available for a new rental. It involves three forms of negation:

1. the first one, `RentalOrder->isEmpty`, expresses the negation-as-failure *there is no information that the car is assigned to any rental order*;
2. the second one, `not requiresService`, is strong negation; and
3. the third one, `not isSchedForMaint`, is classical negation.

We discuss each of them in more detail.

The *not* Operator. The negation in `not isSchedForMaint` is classical negation, since `isSchedForMaint` is defined as a mandatory Boolean-valued attribute. However, the negation in `not requiresService` is strong negation, since `requiresService` is defined as an optional Boolean-valued attribute such that the truth value of the corresponding statement is *unknown* whenever the value of this attribute is NULL. Thus, viewing Boolean-valued attributes as *predicates*, we may say that UML allows for both (closed) total and partial predicates, such that *not* denotes classical (Boolean) negation when applied to a total predicate and strong (Kleene) negation when applied to a partial predicate.

The *isEmpty* Operator. The negation that is implicitly expressed by `RentalOrder->isEmpty` is negation-as-failure, since it evaluates to true whenever there is no information about any associated rental order. Notice, however, that having no information about any associated rental order does logically not imply that there is no associated rental order. Only in conjunction with a completeness assumption (either for the entire database or at least for the predicate concerned) can we draw this conclusion.

In summary, we have three kinds of negation in OCL: classical negation, strong negation and negation-as-failure.

---

[2] Notice that optional, i.e. partial, attributes in the UML correspond to SQL table columns admitting null values.

3.2   Negation in SQL

In SQL, negation may occur in various forms: as a NOT operator or as an IS NULL operator in selection conditions, or in the form of the EXCEPT table operator (corresponding to the relational algebra *difference* operator). SQL may be viewed as the paradigm-setting language for databases. It supports null values and incomplete predicates (whose truth-value may be *unknown*), and is based on a 3-valued logic with the truth values *true, unknown* and *false*, where NOT corresponds to strong negation [MS02].

The following SQL table definition implements the class RentalCar from the UML class diagram of Figure 1.

```
CREATE TABLE  RentalCar(
CarID              CHAR(20) NOT NULL,
requiresService    BOOLEAN,
isSchedForMaint    BOOLEAN NOT NULL,
isAvailable        BOOLEAN,
isAssignedTo       INTEGER REFERENCES RentalOrder
)
```

Notice that isSchedForMaint is defined as a mandatory ('not null') Boolean-valued column, whereas requiresService is defined as an optional Boolean-valued column and isAssignedTo as an optional reference to a rental order. Table 1 contains a sample population of the RentalCar table.

Table 1. A sample population of the RentalCar table.

CarID	requiresService	isSchedForMaint	isAvailable	isAssignedTo
23010	false	false	false	1032779
23011	false	false	true	NULL
23785	NULL	false	NULL	NULL
30180	true	true	false	NULL

In SQL databases, a *view* defines a derived table by means of a query. For instance, the derived table of available cars is defined as the view

```
CREATE VIEW AvailableCar( CarID)
  SELECT CarID FROM RentalCar
  WHERE isAssignedTo IS NULL
    AND NOT requiresService
    AND NOT isSchedForMaint
```

The SELECT statement in this view contains three negations:

1. the first one, isAssignedTo IS NULL, expresses the negation-as-failure stating that *there is no information that the car is assigned to any rental order*;

2. the second one, NOT requiresService, is strong negation; and

3. the third one, NOT isSchedForMaint, is classical negation.

We discuss each of them in more detail.

The *not* Operator. When applied to a complete predicate, SQL's *not* expresses classical negation, but when applied to an incomplete predicate, it expresses strong negation because SQL evaluates logical expressions using 3-valued truth functions, including the truth table for $\neg$ presented in the introduction.

When we ask the query *'which cars do* not *require service?'* against the database state shown in Table 1, using the SQL statement

```
SELECT CarID FROM RentalCar
WHERE NOT requiresService
```

we actually use strong negation because requiresService is an incomplete predicate (admitting NULL values). Thus, the resulting answer set would be $\{23010, 23011\}$. That SQL's *not* behaves like strong negation when applied to an incomplete predicate can be demonstrated by asking the query *'which cars require service or do* not *require service?'*:

```
SELECT CarID FROM RentalCar
WHERE requiresService OR NOT requiresService
```

leading to the result set $\{23010, 23011, 30180\}$. If *not* would be classical negation in this query, then, according to the law of the excluded middle, the answer should be the set of all cars from table RentalCar, that is $\{23010, 23011, 23785, 30180\}$. However, SQL's answer set includes only those cars for which the requiresService attribute has the value *true* or *false*, but not those for which it is NULL.

The *IS NULL* Operator. When we ask, however, 'which cars are *not* assigned to any rental order?' using the SQL statement

```
SELECT CarID FROM RentalCar
WHERE isAssignedTo IS NULL
```

leading to the result set $\{23011, 23785, 30180\}$, we use negation-as-failure because without a completeness assumption, the isAssignedTo IS NULL condition does not imply that there is really no associated rental order, but only that there is no information about anyone.

The *EXCEPT* Operator. Also, SQL's EXCEPT operator corresponds to Prolog's negation-as-failure *not*: a Prolog query expression "give me all objects x such that 'p(x) and not q(x)'" corresponds to the SQL expression 'P EXCEPT Q' where P and Q denote the tables that represent the extensions of the predicates p and q.

3.3   Negation in CLIPS/Jess and Prolog

CLIPS/Jess and Prolog may be viewed as the paradigm-setting languages for *production rules* and (computational logic) *derivation rules*. Both languages have been quite successful in the Artificial Intelligence research community and have been used for many AI software projects. However, both languages also have difficulties to reach out into, and integrate with, mainstream computer science and live rather in a niche. Moreover, while Prolog has a strong theoretical foundation (in computational logic), CLIPS/Jess and the entire production rule paradigm lack any such foundation and do not have a formal semantics. This problem is partly due to the fact that in production rules, the semantic categories of events and conditions in the left-hand-side, and of actions and effects in the right-hand-side, of a rule are mixed up.

While derivation rules have an if-*Condition*-then-*Conclusion* format, production rules have an if-*Condition*-then-*Action* format. To determine which rules are applicable in a given system state, conditions are evaluated against a fact base that is typically maintained in main memory.

In Prolog, the rule for available cars is defined by means of the following two rules:

```
availableCar(X) :-
  rentalCar(X),
  not requiresService(X),
  not isSchedForMaint(X),
  not isAssignedToSomeRental(X).

isAssignedToSomeRental(X) :-
  isAssignedTo(X,Y).
```

The second of these rules is needed to define the auxiliary predicate `isAssigned-ToSomeRental` because Prolog does not provide an existential quantifier in rule conditions for expressing a formula like $\neg \exists y(p(x,y))$. Although they include the possibility of using the nonmonotonic negation-as-failure operator, Prolog rules and deductive database rules (including SQL views) have a purely declarative semantics in terms of their intended models (in the sense of classical logic model theory). For rules without negation, there is exactly one intended model: the unique *minimal* model. The intended models of a set of rules with negation(-as-failure) are its *stable* models.

Production rules do not explicitly refer to events, but events can be simulated by asserting corresponding objects into working memory. A derivation rule can be simulated by a production rule of the form if-*Condition*-then-assert-*Conclusion* using the special action *assert* that changes the state of a production rule system by adding a new fact to the set of available facts.

The production rule system *Jess*, developed by Ernest Friedman-Hill at Sandia National Laboratories, is a Java successor of the classical LISP-based production rule system *CLIPS*. Jess supports the development of rule-based systems which can be tightly coupled to code written in the Java programming language. As in LISP, all code in Jess (control structures, assignments, procedure calls) takes the form of a function call. Conditions are formed with conjunction, disjunction and negation-as-failure. Actions consist of function calls, including the assertion of new facts and the retraction of existing facts.

In Jess, the rule for available cars is defined as

```
(defrule availableCar
  (and (RentalCar ?x)
       (not (requiresService ?x))
       (not (isSchedForMaint ?x))
       (not (isAssignedToSomeRental ?x)))
  =>
  (assert (availableCar ?x))
```

Both Prolog and Jess allow negation to be used only in the body (or condition) of a rule, and not in its head (in Jess, the head of a rule represents an action, so negation wouldn't make sense here, anyway), nor in facts. So, unlike in SQL, where a Boolean-valued attribute can have the value *false* as distinct from NULL corresponding to *unknown*, there is no possibility to represent and process explicit negative information. For instance, the negative fact that *the car with CarID=23010 does not require service*, expressed by the attribute-value pair *23010.requiresService=false* in Table 1, cannot be represented in Jess and Prolog. In both languages, *not* expresses negation-as-failure implementing classical negation in the case of complete predicates subject to a completeness (or 'Closed-World') assumption.

This shortcoming has led to the extension of normal logic programs by adding a negation for expressing explicit negative information, as proposed independently in [GL90,GL91], and in [PW90,Wag91].

4   Two Kinds of Negation in Knowledge Representation

A number of knowledge representation formalisms and systems follow the distinction between weak and strong negation in natural language which is also implicit in SQL. We mention just two of them:

- Logic programs with two kinds of negation (called *extended logic programs* in [GL90]).
- The IBM business rule system CommonRules (described in [Gro97,GLC99]) that is based on the formalism of extended logic programs.

Using two kinds of negation in derivation rules has been proposed independently in [GL90] and [Wag91]. Unfortunately, and confusingly, several different names and several different semantics have been proposed by different authors for these two negations. Strong negation has been called 'classical negation' and 'explicit negation', while negation-as-failure has been renamed into 'implicit negation' and 'default negation'. In particular, the name 'classical negation' is confusing because (the real) classical negation satisfies the law of the excluded middle while the 'classical negation' in extended logic programs does not. Apparently, the reason for choosing the name 'classical negation' is of a psychological nature: one would like to have classical negation, or at least some approximation of it. But that's exactly what partial logic is able to offer: for complete predicates, both strong negation and weak negation collapse into classical negation.

Unlike for logical theories in standard logics, the semantics of knowledge bases in knowledge representation formalisms is not based on all models of a knowledge base but solely on the set of all intended models. E.g., for relational databases the intended models are the 'minimal' ones in the intuitive sense of minimal information content. However, a satisfactory definition of minimally informative models is not possible in classical logic, but only in partial logics. Among all partial models of a KB the minimal ones are those that make a minimal number of atomic sentences true or false. This definition does not work for classical models where a sentence is false iff it is not true. So, classical models allow only an asymmetric definition of minimality: one may define that among all classical models of a KB the minimal ones are those that make a minimal number of atomic sentences true. However, this definition does not adequately capture the intuitive notion of minimal information content, since both the truth and the falsity of a sentence should count as information.

For a KB consisting of derivation rules with negation-as-failure, minimal model semantics is not adequate, because it does not account for the directedness of such rules. This is easy to see. Consider the knowledge base $\{p \leftarrow \text{not } q\}$. This KB has two minimal models: $\{p\}$ and $\{q\}$, but only $\{p\}$ is an intended model.

The model-theoretic semantics of derivation rules with negation-as-failure (e.g. in normal and extended logic programs) is based on the concept of stable (generated) classical models (see [GL88,HW97]). Under the preferential semantics of stable (generated) models, classical negation corresponds to negation-as-failure, or, in other words, negation-as-failure implements classical negation under the preferential semantics of stable (generated) models.

There is a kind of proof-theoretic semantics for normal logic programs, called *wellfounded semantics*, originally proposed by [vG88]. It should be rather considered an inference operation (or a proof theory) which is sound but incomplete with respect to stable model semantics.

The model-theoretic semantics of derivation rules with negation-as-failure and strong negation (e.g. in extended logic programs) is based on the concept of stable generated partial models (see [HJW99]). Under the preferential semantics of stable generated partial models, weak negation corresponds to negation-as-failure, or, in other words, negation-as-failure implements weak negation when applied to an incomplete predicate, and it implements classical negation when applied to a complete predicate.

Another model-theoretic semantics for extended logic programs, which is elegant but more complicated (since based on possible worlds), is the *equilibrium* semantics of [Pea99]. Other proposed semantics, such as the *answer set semantics* of [GL90,GL91] or the WFSX semantics of [PA92], are not model-theoretic and less general (they do not allow for arbitrary formulas in the body and head of a rule).

In the next section, we present the logical formalism needed to explain two kinds of negation.

5   Partial Logics with Two Kinds of Negation and Two Kinds of Predicates

This section is based on [HJW99, Wag98].

A function-free[3] partial logic *signature* $\sigma = \langle Pred, TPred, Const \rangle$ consists of a set of predicate symbols *Pred*, the designation of a set of total predicate symbols $TPred \subseteq Pred$, and a set of constant symbols *Const*.

5.1   Partial Models

We restrict our considerations to Herbrand interpretations since they capture the *Unique Name Assumption* which is fundamental in the semantics of databases and logic programming.

Definition 1 (Interpretation)   *Let $\sigma = \langle Pred, TPred, Const \rangle$ be a signature. A partial Herbrand σ-interpretation $\mathcal{I}$ consists of:*

1. *A set $U_{\mathcal{I}}$, called* universe *or* domain *of $\mathcal{I}$, which is equal to the set of constant symbols, $U_{\mathcal{I}} = Const$;*
2. *an assignment $\mathcal{I}(c) = c$ to every constant symbol $c \in Const$;*
3. *an assignment of a pair of relations $\mathcal{I}_t(p), \mathcal{I}_f(p)$ to every predicate symbol $p \in Pred$ such that*

$$\mathcal{I}_t(p) \cup \mathcal{I}_f(p) \subseteq U_{\mathcal{I}}^{a(p)},$$

and in the special case of a total predicate $p \in TPred$,

$$\mathcal{I}_t(p) \cup \mathcal{I}_f(p) = U_{\mathcal{I}}^{a(p)},$$

where $a(p)$ denotes the arity of p.

In the sequel we also simply say 'interpretation' ('satisfaction', 'model', 'entailment') instead of 'partial Herbrand interpretation' ('partial Herbrand satisfaction', 'partial Herbrand model', 'partial Herbrand entailment').

The class of all σ-interpretations is denoted by $\boldsymbol{I}_4(\sigma)$. We define the classes of *coherent*, of *total*, and of total coherent (or *2-valued*) interpretations by

$$\boldsymbol{I}_c(\sigma) = \{ \mathcal{I} \in \boldsymbol{I}_4(\sigma) \mid \mathcal{I}_t(p) \cap \mathcal{I}_f(p) = \emptyset \text{ for all } p \in Pred \}$$
$$\boldsymbol{I}_t(\sigma) = \{ \mathcal{I} \in \boldsymbol{I}_4(\sigma) \mid \mathcal{I}_t(p) \cup \mathcal{I}_f(p) = U_{\mathcal{I}}^{a(p)} \text{ for all } p \in Pred \}$$
$$\boldsymbol{I}_2(\sigma) = \boldsymbol{I}_c(\sigma) \cap \boldsymbol{I}_t(\sigma)$$

---

[3]   For simplicity, we exclude function symbols from the languages under consideration, i.e. we do not consider functional terms but only variables and constants; signatures without function symbols lead to a finite Herbrand universe.

The model relation $\models$ between a Herbrand interpretation and a sentence is defined inductively as follows.

Definition 2 (Satisfaction)

$$\mathcal{I} \models p(c_1, \ldots, c_m) \iff \langle c_1, \ldots, c_m \rangle \in \mathcal{I}_t(p)$$
$$\mathcal{I} \models \neg p(c_1, \ldots, c_m) \iff \langle c_1, \ldots, c_m \rangle \in \mathcal{I}_f(p)$$
$$\mathcal{I} \models {\sim} F \iff \mathcal{I} \not\models F$$
$$\mathcal{I} \models F \wedge G \iff \mathcal{I} \models F \ \& \ \mathcal{I} \models G$$
$$\mathcal{I} \models F \vee G \iff \mathcal{I} \models F \ \text{or} \ \mathcal{I} \models G$$
$$\mathcal{I} \models \exists x F(x) \iff \mathcal{I} \models F(c) \text{ for some } c \in Const$$
$$\mathcal{I} \models \forall x F(x) \iff \mathcal{I} \models F(c) \text{ for all } c \in Const$$

All other cases of compound formulas are handled by the following DeMorgan and double negation rewrite rules:

$$\neg(F \wedge G) \longrightarrow \neg F \vee \neg G \qquad \neg(F \vee G) \longrightarrow \neg F \wedge \neg G$$
$$\neg \exists x F(x) \longrightarrow \forall x \neg F(x) \qquad \neg \forall x F(x) \longrightarrow \exists x \neg F(x)$$
$$\neg \neg F \longrightarrow F \qquad \neg {\sim} F \longrightarrow F$$

in the sense that for every rewrite rule $LHS \longrightarrow RHS$, we define

$$\mathcal{I} \models LHS \iff \mathcal{I} \models RHS$$

Mod_* denotes the model operator associated with the system $\langle L(\sigma), \mathbf{I}_*, \models \rangle$, and $\models_*$ denotes the corresponding entailment relation, for $* = 4, c, t, 2$, i.e.

$$X \models_* F \quad \text{iff} \quad Mod_*(X) \subseteq Mod_*(\{F\})$$

Observation 1   *If only two-valued models are admitted, weak and strong negation collapse:*

$$\neg F \equiv_2 {\sim} F$$

5.2   Classical Logic as a Special Case of Partial Logic

Obviously, the entailment relation $\models_2$ corresponds to entailment in classical logic. The most natural way to arrive at classical logic from proper partial logic is to assume that all predicates are total: $TPred = Pred$. Under this assumption, the two entailment relations $\models_c$ and $\models_2$ of partial logic collapse.

Claim.   If $TPred = Pred$, then $\models_c = \models_2$.

5.3   Total Predicates and the Closed-World Assumption

In general, three kinds of predicates can be distinguished. The first distinction, proposed in [Koe66], reflects the fact that many predicates (especially in empirical domains) have truth value gaps: neither $p(c)$ nor $\neg p(c)$ has to be the case for specific instances of such *partial* predicates, like, e.g., color attributes which can in some cases not be determined because of vagueness.

Other predicates, e.g. from legal or theoretical domains, are *total*, and we then have, for instance, $m(S) \lor \neg m(S)$ and

$$\text{prime}(2^{77} - 1) \lor \neg\text{prime}(2^{77} - 1)$$

stating that Sophia is either married or unmarried, and that $2^{77} - 1$ is either a prime or a non-prime number. Only total predicates can be completely represented in a knowledge base. Therefore, only total predicates can be subject to a completeness assumption. For simplicity, a predicate is called *closed* whenever it is completely represented, otherwise it is called *open*.

For distinguishing between closed, open total and partial predicates, the schema of a knowledge base has to specify a set $Pred = \{p_1, \ldots, p_n\}$ of predicates (or table schemas), a set $TPred \subseteq Pred$ of total predicates, and a set $CPred \subseteq TPred$ of closed predicates.

Definition 3 (Completeness Assumption)   *For a knowledge base Y over a schema specifying a set of closed predicates* CPred, *we obtain the following additional inference rule for drawing negative conclusions,*

$$Y \vdash \neg p(c) \quad \text{if} \quad p \in CPred \ \& \ Y \vdash \sim p(c)$$

The completeness assumption, in a less general form, was originally proposed in [Rei78], under the name *Closed-World Assumption (CWA)*. Our form of the CWA relates explicit with default-implicit falsity, i.e. strong with weak negation. It states that an atomic sentence formed with a closed predicate is false if it is false by default, or, in other words, its strong negation holds if its weak negation does. It can also be expressed by means of the *completion $Compl(Y)$* of a knowledge base Y with respect to the set of closed predicates *CPred*:

$$Compl(Y) = \mathsf{Upd}(Y, \{\neg p(c) \mid p \in CPred \ \& \ Y \vdash \sim p(c)\})$$

A sentence F is inferable from Y if it can be derived from the *tertium-non-datur-closure* of $Comp(Y)$:

$$Y \vdash F :\Longleftrightarrow \mathsf{Upd}(Compl(Y), \{p(c) \lor \neg p(c) \mid p \in TPred - CPred\}) \vdash F$$

Notice that in definite knowledge bases (not admitting disjunctions), it is not possible to declare total predicates that are open. Therefore, in definite knowledge systems, $TPred = CPred$.

Observation 2   *For a knowledge base Y, it holds that*

1. *for any total predicate $p \in TPred$, and any constant (tuple) c, the resp. instance of the* tertium non datur *holds: $Y \vdash p(c) \lor \neg p(c)$;*
2. *if $q \in CPred$, then Y does not contain any indefinite information about q, i.e. $Y \vdash q(c)$, or $Y \vdash \neg q(c)$.*

5.4   Reasoning with Three Kinds of Predicates

Only certain total predicates can be completely represented in a KB. These closed predicates are subject to the completeness assumption. For example, the KB of a city may know all residents of the city, i.e. the completeness assumption holds for *resident*, but it does not have complete information of every resident whether (s)he is married or not because (s)he might have married in another city and this information is not available. Consequently, the completeness assumption does not apply to *married* in this KB.

The completeness assumption helps to reduce disjunctive complexity which is exponential in the number of open total predicates: if n is the number of unknown ground atoms which can be formed by means of predicates declared as total but open, then the knowledge base contains 2^n possible state descriptions.

We illustrate these distinctions with an example. Let m, r, s, l denote the predicates *married, resident, smoker* and *is_looking_at*, and let M, P, A stand for the individuals *Mary, Peter* and *Ann*. Let

$$Y = \{\{m(M),\, r(M),\, s(M),\, \neg m(A),\, \neg s(A),\, l(M, P),\, l(P, A)\}\}$$

be a knowledge base over a schema declaring the predicates m and r to be total, and the predicate r to be closed. The interesting queries we can ask Y and the resp. answers are:

1. Does a married person look at an unmarried one? Yes, but Y does not know who, either Mary at Peter, or Peter at Ann. Formally, it holds that

$$Y \ \vdash\ \exists x \exists y (l(x, y) \wedge m(x) \wedge \neg m(y))$$

   but there is no definite answer to this query, only an indefinite answer may be obtained:

$$\mathsf{Ans}(Y,\, l(x, y) \wedge r(x) \wedge \neg r(y)) = \{\{\langle M, P\rangle,\, \langle P, A\rangle\}\})$$

2. Does a resident look at a non-resident ? Yes, Mary at Peter.

$$\mathsf{Ans}(Y,\, l(x, y) \wedge r(x) \wedge \neg r(y)) = \{\{\langle M, P\rangle\}\}$$

   since $Y \vdash \neg r(P)$ if $Y \vdash \sim r(P)$.

3. Does a smoker look at a nonsmoker? No. Y is completely ignorant about Peter being a smoker or not: neither is he a smoker, nor is he a nonsmoker, nor is he a smoker or nonsmoker (as a partial predicate, s may have a truth value gap for this instance):

$$\mathsf{Ans}(Y,\, l(x, y) \wedge s(x) \wedge \neg s(y)) = \emptyset$$

6   Conclusion

Like many other computational systems and formalisms, also the Semantic Web would benefit from distinguishing between open and closed predicates using both strong negation and negation-as-failure. We have shown that partial logic is the logic of these two kinds of negation. Consequently, it would be important to generalize RDF and OWL from their current classical logic version to a suitable partial logic version and to combine them with RuleML.

References

BL.   Tim Berners-Lee. Reaching out onto the web. web document.
          http://www.w3.org/2000/10/swap/doc/Reach.
BTW01.   Harold Boley, Said Tabet, and Gerd Wagner. Design Rationale of RuleML:
          A Markup Language for Semantic Web Rules. In *Proc. Semantic Web
          Working Symposium (SWWS'01)*. Stanford University, July/August 2001.
DDM.   Stefan Decker, Mike Dean, and Deborah McGuinness. Requirements and
          use cases for a semantic web rule language. web document.
          http://www.isi.edu/ stefan/rules/20030325/.
GL88.   M. Gelfond and V. Lifschitz. The stable model semantics for logic program-
          ming. In R. A. Kowalski and K. A. Bowen, editors, *Proc. of ICLP*, pages
          1070–1080. MIT Press, 1988.
GL90.   M. Gelfond and V. Lifschitz. Logic programs with classical negation. In
          Proc. of Int. Conf. on Logic Programming. MIT Press, 1990.
GL91.   M. Gelfond and V. Lifschitz. Classical negation in logic programs and dis-
          junctive databases. *New Generation Computing*, 9:365–385, 1991.
GLC99.   B.N. Grosof, Y. Labrou, and Hoi Y. Chan. A declarative approach to busi-
          ness rules in contracts: Courteous logic programs in XML. In *Proc. 1st
          ACM Conference on Electronic Commerce (EC99)*, Denver, Colorado, USA,
          November 1999.
Gro97.   B.N. Grosof. Prioritized conflict handling for logic programs. In Jan
          Maluszynski, editor, *Proc. of the Int. Symposium on Logic Programming
          (ILPS-97)*. MIT Press, 1997.
HJW99.   H. Herre, J. Jaspars, and G. Wagner. Partial logics with two kinds of
          negation as a foundation of knowledge-based reasoning. In D.M. Gabbay
          and H. Wansing, editors, *What Is Negation?* Oxford University Press, 1999.
HW97.   H. Herre and G. Wagner. Stable models are generated by a stable chain. *J.
          of Logic Programming*, 30(2):165–177, 1997.
Koe66.   S. Koerner. *Experience and Theory*. Kegan Paul, London, 1966.
MS02.   Jim Melton and Alan R. Simon. *SQL:1999*. Morgan Kaufmann, San Fran-
          cisco, CA, 2002.
PA92.   Luís Moniz Pereira and José Júlio Alferes. Well founded semantics for logic
          programs with explicit negation. In B. Neumann, editor, *Proceedings of
          the European Conference on Artificial Intelligence (ECAI)*, pages 102–106.
          Wiley, 1992.
Pea99.   D. Pearce. Stable inference as intuitionistic validity. *Journal of Logic Pro-
          gramming*, 38:79–91, 1999.
PW90.   D. Pearce and G. Wagner. Reasoning with negative information I – strong
          negation in logic programs. In M. Kusch L. Haaparanta and I. Niiniluoto,
          editors, *Language, Knowledge and Intentionality*. Acta Philosophica Fennica
          49, 1990.
Rei78.   R. Reiter. On closed-world databases. In J. Minker and H. Gallaire, editors,
          Logic and Databases. Plenum Press, 1978.

vG88.   A. van Gelder. Negation as failure using tight derivations for general logic programs. In *Foundations of Deductive Databases and Logic Programming*, pages 149–176. Morgan Kaufmann, San Mateo (CA), 1988.

Wag91.   G. Wagner. A database needs two kinds of negation. In B. Thalheim and H.-D. Gerhardt, editors, *Proc. of the 3rd. Symp. on Mathematical Fundamentals of Database and Knowledge Base Systems*, volume 495 of *Lecture Notes in Computer Science*, pages 357–371. Springer-Verlag, 1991.

Wag98.   G. Wagner. *Foundations of Knowledge Systems – with Applications to Databases and Agents*, volume 13 of *Advances in Database Systems*. Kluwer Academic Publishers, 1998.
         See http://www.inf.fu-berlin.de/~wagnerg/ks.html.

Wag02.   Gerd Wagner. How to design a general rule markup language? In *Proceedings of the First Workshop on XML Technologies for the Semantic Web (XSW2002)*, Lecture Notes in Informatics, Berlin, June 2002. Gesellschaft für Informatik. invited paper.

Towards the Adaptive Semantic Web

Peter Dolog[1], Nicola Henze[2], Wolfgang Nejdl[1,2], and Michael Sintek[3]

[1] Learning Lab Lower Saxony, University of Hannover,
Expo Plaza 1, D-30539 Hannover, Germany
dolog@learninglab.de
http://www.learninglab.de/~dolog
[2] ISI- Knowledge-Based Systems, University of Hannover,
Appelstr. 4, D-30167 Hannover, Germany
{henze,nejdl}@kbs.uni-hannover.de
http://www.kbs.uni-hannover.de/~{henze,nejdl}
[3] German Research Center for Artificial Intelligence (DFKI) GmbH,
Knowledge Management Group,
Postfach 2080, D-67608 Kaiserslautern, Germany
Michael.Sintek@dfki.de
http://www.dfki.uni-kl.de/~sintek

Abstract. In this paper we show how personalization techniques from the area of adaptive hypermedia can be achieved in the semantic web. Our approach is based on rule-based reasoning enabled by semantic web technologies. The personalization techniques are formalized as reasoning rules. The rules are able to reason over distributed information resources annotated with semantic web metadata formats. This leads towards the realization of an adaptive semantic web idea which provides personalized, adaptive access to information, services, or other, distributed resources.

Keywords: adaptive hypermedia, personalization, adaptive web, semantic web.

1 Introduction

Adaptive web, as envisioned in [10], should provide users with optimized access to distributed electronic information on the web according to particular needs of individual users or group of users. The main problem of current web systems their inability to support different needs of individual users. This problem is mainly due to their incapability to identify those needs, and insufficient mappings of those needs to available resources (information/document).

The *semantic web* [6] initiative reflects this problem by "giving information a well-defined meaning, better enabling computers and people to work in cooperation". This can be achieved by making metadata about different resources explicit using standardized descriptions.

Foundations for designing an *adaptive web* can be found in existing personalization and adaptive systems. For example, *recommender systems* (cf. [33,4]) explore the usage of information entities (or products, services, etc.) in order

F. Bry et al. (Eds.): PPSWR 2003, LNCS 2901, pp. 51–68, 2003.

to point out further interesting information, products, services to a user. Adaptive hypermedia systems (cf.provide individual guidance through the hyperspace by modeling and reasoning about explicit user models that contain preferences, goals, and further characteristics of individual users.

However, their closed architecture, own formats used for representing information about a user, documents and knowledge concepts does not allow to provide a personalization in wider distributed context. The exchange of the information and data between those applications and providing well formed adaptive functionality also to external parties cannot be achieved currently.

A step towards adaptive web can be made by employing standardized description formats for metadata. This will allow us to reason over facts described in standardized metadata formats. More important, reasoning can be performed in wider context over distributed data. In this paper we investigate how to provide reasoning on the semantic web with special focus on personalization techniques.

Based on our experience in developing adaptive hypermedia systems for e-learning, we propose separation of metadata about documents, information covered in the documents, users and observations. We propose a separation of adaptation rules from the metadata. These encapsulated reusable adaptive functionalities allow us to reason over distributed metadata in the web.

After a brief introduction to adaptive hypermedia systems (section 2), section 3 discusses how we can benefit from lessons learned from adaptive hypermedia systems in the adaptive web. Section 4 discusses a logic-based formalization of adaptive hypermedia. Section 6 describe how we can prototype an adaptive web utilizing the logical characterization of adaptive hypermedia. Related work is briefly reviewed in section 7. Finally we provide some remarks on further work in section 8.

2   Background: Adaptive Hypermedia Systems

Adaptive hypermedia is an alternative to the traditional "one-size-fits-all" static approach of hypermedia systems [9]. Adaptive hypermedia systems (AHS) enlarge the functionality of hypermedia systems to personalize the underlying hypermedia system to the individual user.

Adaptive hypermedia systems usually perform the adaptation based on several user features they maintain. The user features are used to determine appropriate information presentation and navigation sequences through the information. The systems are able to learn new user features from the user interaction with a system or from information he provided. Thus, each user has an individual view and individual navigational possibilities for working with the hypermedia system.

A hypermedia system can be described as a graph:

A set of nodes (of text) and a set of edges between these nodes (links) (cf. [31]). Thus personalization techniques in AHS can be grouped into techniques that adapt the nodes, which means to select/modify/rearrange the content of the documents (so called *content-level adaptation*) or the edges, which means to select appropriate hypertext links, delete links, or generate new, previously non existing links (so called *navigational-level adaptation*).

The content-level adaptation focuses mainly on improving a local navigation of a user and his orientation in currently presented page or fragment. For example, such adaptive systems can provide different text or different media variants, which serve information at different level of detail, to users with different level of knowledge or expertise in some field. They can switch between different media types according to different user preferences or his learning style. They are able to hide or appropriately annotate the parts of presented information which are not suited for current user based on values of his features the system maintains.

The navigational-level adaptation is trying to improve user global orientation in hyperspace. This includes for example a support for making exploration of required information easier such as enabling, disabling, showing, hiding, removing links when it is appropriate, or sorting links according to user goals or preferences. They can annotate links to indicate whether the links are appropriate or relevant. They are able to generate next appropriate information and thus to guide a user.

A specific research branch in the area of adaptive hypermedia, adaptive educational systems, improve learner guidance by showing e.g. the next reasonable learning step to take or by the individual creation of learning sequences. They have shown to improve orientation by annotating hypertext links with hints according to the students learning progress, by adapting the teaching or presentation style to the specific needs of the student, and by supporting learners to find their own optimal learning strategy. We are building on our experience in the area of educational systems in this paper as well.

3 From Adaptive Hypermedia to Adaptive Web

On the (semantic) web, we are confronted with a much more complex situation compared to the usually "closed" adaptive hypermedia settings: there is no central point of control and data storage, since on the web data and services are distributed and change rapidly and unpredictably. Furthermore, data and metadata is represented in a multitude of formats: while there are several upcoming standards, especially RDF/S [39,38] and its extensions like DAML+OIL and OWL [15,30], to define metadata schemas and (domain) ontologies, there are no commonly-agreed upon concrete schemas for metadata in specific domains like e-learning, nor are there domain ontologies shared by a whole community. Although first approaches to such generally useful metadata schemas and domain ontologies exist, like LOM [28] (building upon DC [20]) for the description of e-learning resources and classification systems like ACM [2] as a common domain ontology to characterize computer science content, it is not expected that they will be generally accepted as they cannot deal with the specific details of concrete (local) applications.

As a result, we need mechanisms on an adaptive web that allow resources, metadata, and ontology concepts to be mapped to each other and to the concepts found in user profiles. The technologies to accomplish this are currently being developed in the semantic web community. Promising approaches include those based on (logical) mapping rules and description logics [12,29].

In order to provide personalized access to information on the web, we can therefore assume that the required mapping and integration technologies, in the style of wrappers and mediators in a web services (or P2P) architecture, are provided as part of the general semantic web infrastructure. What is missing for an adaptive web are the acquisition, representation, and usage of information about the users, i.e., their general preferences, interests, etc., and their specific situation and information need.

Because of the formal nature of resource metadata and domain ontologies on the semantic web, we propose a logic-based approach, building on the same technologies already developed for the semantic web. In the following sections, we will therefore first describe a general logic-based definition of adaptive educational hypermedia systems and then a specific prototype using the semantic web language TRIPLE [35].

4   Logic-Based Definition of Adaptive Educational Hypermedia Systems

In order to develop design-proposals for the *adaptive web* based on AHS techniques we have to analyze architecture and, even more important, data resources and data flow in AHS. A functionality-oriented definition of adaptive hypermedia given by Brusilovsky is [9]: "By adaptive hypermedia systems we mean all hypertext and hypermedia systems which reflect some features of the user in the user model and apply this model to adapt various visible aspects of the system to the user."

A logic-based definition of adaptive educational hypermedia systems has been proposed in [25]. Components of an AHS are therefore the *hypermedia system* which includes information about documents and their relations, the *user model* which stores characteristics of a user and possibly reasoning rules to derive additional user characteristics, and the *adaptation component* which determines the adaptive treatment provided for the particular user. During runtime, the system monitors a user's interaction to update the user model, thus a component for *observations* is necessary, too. Basis data required by the AHS can be found in the components "hypermedia system" (e.g. metadata about documents) and "observations" (e.g. usage data during runtime). The "user model" component processes data from both "hypermedia system" and "observations" to describe and reason about a user's characteristics. The "adaptation component" finally decides about beneficial adaptive treatments for a user based on data of the other three components. The component "hypermedia system" has been generalized to *document space* due to the fact that a hypermedia system requires stronger assumptions about the modeling of documents than we can expect to have in the World Wide Web.

Definition 1 (Adaptive Educational Hypermedia System [25]). *An adaptive educational hypermedia system (AEHS) is a Quadruple*

$$(\ DOCS, \ UM, \ OBS, \ AC \ ) \tag{1}$$

with

DOCS: Document Space: *A finite set of first order logic (FOL) sentences with constant symbols for describing documents (and knowledge concepts), and predicates for defining relations between these (and other) constant symbols.*

UM: User Model: *A finite set of FOL sentences with constant symbols for describing individual users (user groups), and user characteristics, as well as predicates and formulas for expressing whether a characteristic applies to a user.*

OBS: Observations: *A finite set of FOL sentences with constant symbols for describing observations, and predicates for relating users, documents / concepts, and observations.*

AC: Adaptation Component: *A finite set of FOL sentences with formulas for describing adaptive functionality.*

5 Example: Logically Describing an AEHS

In this section we will provide an example setting for illustrating the approach proposed in this paper. We will define an adaptive system called *SIMPLE* which can annotate information resources in order to give orientation by pointing out where to start learning, and by indicating more advanced concepts. The adaptation techniques in SIMPLE are well known techniques in existing adaptive hypermedia techniques. Our aim is to translate some well-explored techniques to the semantic web. Doing this, we show how personalization can be brought to the semantic web. Of course, more advanced adaptation techniques can be implemented, or new techniques can be investigated. The important step which will be illustrated in our example is to bring personalization to the logic level of the semantic web tower [5]: This requires the encapsulation of adaptation techniques for reuse (for example by formalizing adaptation techniques as logical formulas as done in [25]) and enabling adaptation techniques to reason over various information resource.

The following sections will describe the AEHS SIMPLE and its functionality in FOL, according to definition 1.

5.1 SIMPLE: Document Space

SIMPLE needs information about available information resources - like documents, knowledge concepts, etc. For the logical description we therefor need a set of n constant symbols (n corresponds to the number of documents in the document space) which name the documents (the URI of the documents respectively) and a set of s atoms (s corresponds to the number of concepts in the knowledge space) which name the knowledge concepts:

D_1, D_2, ..., D_n, C_1, C_2, ..., C_s.

The predicate "depends" states learning dependencies between these concepts: Concept C is required to understand C':

depends(C, C') for certain concepts $C \neq C'$.

Furthermore, the documents can be annotated with a non-empty set of concepts. This can be expressed by the hasConcept-predicate between documents and concepts. This can be compared to assigning a set of keywords to each document.

$\forall D\ \exists C$ hasConcept(D, C).

We cannot ensure that this constraint is fulfilled in the open world. However, this rule says that a valid metadata – annotation for the AEHS Simple requires that each document is related to at least one concept.

Further predicates between concepts and/or documents are possible but not required by this example of an AEHS.

5.2 SIMPLE: User Model

The adaptive system SIMPLE needs data from the user model - in order to reflect the user's actual learning progress and learning state. Again, the user model of SIMPLE is very straightforward and models only the user's knowledge state - further user characteristics can be considered as well.

SIMPLE's user model contains a set of m constant symbols, one for each individual (registered) user:

U_1, U_2, ..., U_m.

A rule defines that a concept C is assumed to be learned whenever the corresponding document has been visited by the user. Therefor, SIMPLE uses the constant symbol

Learned.

The rule for processing the observation that a concept has been learned by a user is given by:

$\forall U\ \forall C$
($\exists D$ keyword(D, C) $\wedge$ obs(D, U, Visited)
$\Longrightarrow$ p_obs(C, U, Learned).

5.3 SIMPLE: Observations

SIMPLE interpretes from the observations about a user's action with the personalized systems only whether a user has visited some page. The time s/he spend on this resource, or further information like information about the order in which the user has accessed resources, or further interactions, are not required for SIMPLE. Thus, one constant symbol for the observation whether a document has been visited is enough:

Visited.

A predicate is relating this observation to a user U and a document D:

obs(D, U, Visited) for certain D, U.

5.4   SIMPLE: Adaptation Component

The example system SIMPLE has the following adaptive functionality: It can annotate hypertext-links to documents by using the traffic light metaphor[9]. The traffic light metaphor belongs to the group of navigational-level adaptation techniques and assigns colors of a traffic light to point out the educational state of a hypertext link (more precisely, the educational state of the resource to which this hypertext link points to). E.g. a green color is used to indicate that a link leads to a resource which is *Recommended* to a learner (because he has sufficient pre-knowledge, or because of other reasons), a red color is used to show that visiting the hypertext link is *Not_Recommended* (because e.g. the user actually lacks some knowledge for successfully learn the resource in question). In addition, SIMPLE shows which links lead to documents that *Will_become_understandable* (annotated by a dark orange icon; the user has started to learn some of the necessary prerequisite knowledge), and documents that *Might_be_understandable* (translated into a yellow icon; the user has learned nearly all required prereq-uisite knowledge). A white icon in front of a link indicates that a user has *Already_visited* the resource belonging to the link.

To express the adaptation formulas, SIMPLE uses five constant symbols for representing the *learning state* of a document:

Recommended, Not_Recommended, Might_be_understandable,
Will_become_understandable, Already_learned.

The following formulas then describe the educational state of a document. For-mula_1 states that a document is **Already_learned** whenever the user has read the document

$\forall U \ \forall D$
obs(D, U, Visited)
$\Longrightarrow$ learning_state(D, U, Already_visited).

Formula_2 states that a document is **Recommended** for learning if *all* prerequisites for the keywords of this document are learned

$\forall U \ \forall D$
$\forall C \ \Big(\text{keyword}(D, C) \Longrightarrow \big(\forall C' \text{ depends}(C, C') \Longrightarrow \text{p\_obs}(C', U, \text{Learned}) \big) \Big)$
$\wedge \neg$ learning_state(D, U, Already_visited)
$\Longrightarrow$ learning_state(D, U, Recommended).

Formula_3 states that a document **Might_be_understandable** if at least some of the prerequisites have already been learned by this user:

$\forall U \; \forall D$
$(\; \forall C \; \text{keyword}(D, C) \Longrightarrow$
$(\; \exists C' \; \text{depends}(C, C') \Longrightarrow \text{p\_obs}(C', U, \text{Learned}) \;) \;)$
$\wedge \; \neg \; \text{learning\_state}(D, U, \text{Recommended})$
$\Longrightarrow \text{learning\_state}(D, U, \text{Might\_be\_understandable}).$

Formula_4 derives that a document Will_become_understandable if the user has some prerequisite knowledge for at least one of the document's keywords:

$\forall U \; \forall D$
$\exists C \; \text{keyword}(D, C) \Longrightarrow$
$(\exists C' \; \text{depends}(C, C') \Longrightarrow \text{p\_obs}(C', U, \text{Learned}) \;)$
$\wedge \; \neg \; \text{learning\_state}(D, U, \text{Might\_be\_understandable})$
$\Longrightarrow \text{learning\_state}(D, U, \text{Will\_become\_understandable}).$

$\forall U \; \forall D$
$\neg \; \text{learning\_state}(D, U, \text{Will\_become\_understandable})$
$\Longrightarrow \text{learning\_state}(D, U, \text{Not\_Recommended}).$

The translation of the learning_state into document_annotations with green, red, orange, yellow or white icons is straightforward, for example to annotate a document with a green ball, is expressed by

$\forall U \; \forall D$
$\text{learning\_state}(D, U, \text{Recommended})$
$\Longrightarrow \text{document\_annotation}(D, U, \text{Green\_Icon})$

6   Prototyping the Adaptive Web

The logically described adaptive educational hypermedia system SIMPLE, proposed in section 5 will be implemented in TRIPLE. The formal description of adaptive systems in FOL [25] allows us to reuse the adaptation rules in different contexts, here we will use them to access learning resources from the Sun Java Tutorial [13,14]. There exists a freely available online version[1] from the Sun Java Tutorial. We annotated the resources of the Sun Java Tutorial according to our document ontology as can be seen in the next section.

6.1   TRIPLE Overview

TRIPLE [34] is a rule language for the Semantic Web which is based on Horn logic and borrows many basic features from F-Logic [27] but is especially designed for querying and transforming RDF models.

TRIPLE can be viewed as a successor of SiLRI (Simple Logic-based RDF Interpreter [16]). One of the most important differences to F-Logic and SiLRI

---

[1] http://java.sun.com/docs/books/tutorial/

is that TRIPLE does not have fixed semantics for object-oriented features like classes and inheritance. Its modular architecture allows such features to be easily defined for different object-oriented and other data models like UML, Topic Maps, or RDF Schema. Description logics extensions of RDF (Schema) like OIL, DAML+OIL, and OWL that cannot be fully handled by Horn logic are provided as modules that interact with a description logic classifier, e.g. FaCT [26], resulting in a hybrid rule language.

Namespaces and Resources. TRIPLE has special support for namespaces and resource identifiers. Namespaces are declared via clause-like constructs of the form *nsabbrev := namespace.*, e.g., rdf := *"http : //www.w3.org/1999/02/22 −rdf − syntax − ns#"*. Resources are written as *nsabbrev:name*, where *nsabbrev* is a namespace abbreviation and *name* is the local name of the resource.

Statements and Molecules. Inspired by F-Logic object syntax, an RDF statement (triple) is written as: *subject[predicate → object]*. Several statements with the same subject can be abbreviated as "molecules":

$$\text{stefan[hasAge} \to 33; \text{isMarried} \to \text{yes}; \ldots]$$

Models. RDF models, i.e., sets of statements, are made explicit in TRIPLE ("first class citizens")[2]. Statements, molecules, and also Horn atoms that are true in a specific model are written as *atom@model* (similar to Flora-2 module syntax), where *atom* is a statement, molecule, or Horn atom and *model* is a model specification (i.e., a resource denoting a model), e.g.:

$$\text{michael[hasAge} \to 35]\text{@factsAboutDFKI}$$

TRIPLE also allows Skolem functions as model specifications. Skolem functions can be used to transform one model (or several models) into a new one when used in rules (e.g., for ontology mapping/integration):

$$O[P \to Q]@\text{sf}(m1, X, Y) \longleftarrow \ldots$$

Logical Formulae. TRIPLE uses the usual set of connectives and quantifiers for building formulae from statements/molecules and Horn atoms, i.e., $\land$, $\lor$, $\neg$, $\forall$, $\exists$, etc[3]. All variables must be introduced via quantifiers, therefore marking them is not necessary.

Clauses and Blocks. A TRIPLE clause is either a fact or a rule. Rule heads may only contain conjunctions of molecules and Horn atoms and must not contain (explicitly or implicitly) any disjunctive or negated expressions. To assert that a set of clauses is true in a specific model, a model block is used: *@model {clauses}*, or, in case the model specification is parameterized:

$$\forall \ Mdl \ @model(Mdl) \ \{clauses\}$$

---

[2] Note that the notion of *model* in RDF does not coincide with its use in (mathematical) logics.

[3] For TRIPLE programs in plain ASCII syntax, the symbols AND, OR, NOT, FORALL, EXISTS, <-, ->, etc. are used.

Semantics, Implementation. TRIPLE has been implemented via a translation to Horn Logic plus enactment by XSB [36], i.e., a Prolog with tabled resolution, giving it the well-founded semantics [37]. Details on the model-theoretic semantics of TRIPLE can be found in [17].

6.2   Facts about a Document

A simple structure for document meta data and relationships to other structures is depicted in fig. 1. The class `Document` is used to annotate a resource which is a document. Documents describe some concepts. The concepts are the main information entities from domain knowledge communicated by the documents (cf. [32]). Concept and Documents are related through `dc:subject` property. Documents can have its prerequisites. This is annotated by `dcterms:requires` property.

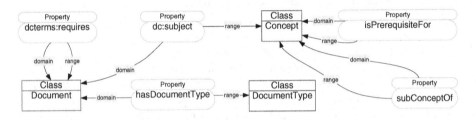

Fig. 1. Ontology for documents

An example of such resource can be a page describing object oriented class concept (URI of the resource is `sun_java:java/concepts/class.html`. Following example shows how such page can be annotated based on the document metadata structure.

```
sun_java:java/concepts/class.html[
rdf:type->doc:Document;
dc:subject->java:OO_Class;
...].

java:OO_Class[
rdf:type->doc:Concept;
doc:isPrerequisiteFor->doc:OO_Method;
...
].
```

The page is annotated with type `Document`. It describes information about classes (annotation `dc:subject -> OO_Class`). The `OO_Class` is of type Concept and is subconcept of `Classes_and_objects`. The `OO_Class` is prerequisite for the `OO_Method` concept.

The structure of the document metadata can be more complex. It can contain for example a slot for annotating a role of document, its type, level of covering particular concept in the document, roles of concept in particular document, position of particular document in document structure described by whole/part relationships and so on.

All of these relationships can enhance adaptation possibilities for example for construction of learning sequences based on user profile, annotating position of a user in the document structure, helping to identify main outcomes of a document based on roles and level of concept coverage, and so on.

6.3 Facts about a Domain

The dc:subject entries used in examples in previous section can be seen as facts about a domain. Facts about domain can form complex structures. For space limitation we show just a fragment of domain knowledge base about concepts for java programming. For the same reason we show just isa (subConceptOf) relationship between these concepts. Figure 2 depicts Programming_Strategies concept with its subconcepts: Object_Oriented, Imperative, Logical, and Functional. The OO_Class, OO_Method, OO_Object, OO_Inheritance, and OO_Interface are depicted as subconcepts of Object_Oriented.

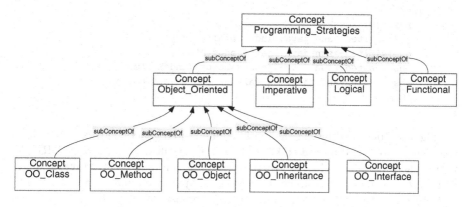

Fig. 2. Concept ontology for Java e-lecture

The facts about a domain and different relationships between the facts can be used for adaptation purposes quite successfully. The mentioned subConceptOf relationship can be for example utilized to recommend either more general documents introducing a concept of programming strategies in general, or to recommend more specific documents (resources) about object oriented programming strategy based on requirements, level of knowledge, or interest of a user.

Sequencing relationship is another relationship which can be used to recommend documents. A document (resource) which describes a concept (the concept appears in dc:subject slot in meta data about the document) from the beginning of the sequence will be recommended sooner than a document which describes a concept from the end of such a sequence.

A dependency relationship referring to whether a concept depends on another concept can be used as well. It can be used to recommend documents which describe dependent concepts together with a document describing a concept which was recommended by another rule.

6.4 Facts about the User Profile

We need to have explicit facts about a user to be able to recommend documents (resources) which are relevant to user interests. This facts can enclose information about user performance from courses within a domain, his goals and interests, preferences, and so on. Following simple example contains just some facts about resources visited by a user (for more complex user models see, e.g., [19]).

```
@simple:data{
...
kbs:henze[
        rdf:type->User;
        obs:visited->sun_java:'index.html'].

13s:dolog[
        rdf:type->User;
        obs:visited->sun_java:'index.html';
        obs:visited->sun_java:'java/index.html';
        obs:visited->sun_java:'java/concepts/index.html';
        obs:visited->sun_java:'java/concepts/object.html'].

}
```

The user identified by kbs:henze URI has visited general sun java introduction page represented by index.html. The user identified by 13s:dolog URI has visited the general introduction, the java introduction (sun_java:'java/index.html'), java concepts introduction (sun_java:'java/concepts/index.html'), and objects introduction (sun_java:'java/concepts/object.html').

Other facts and relationships between the facts can help to derive additional information which can improve recommendation results. For example a time spent on resource can be used to infer a level of knowledge gained from the resource.

6.5 Reasoning Rules for Adaptation

The adaptive system SIMPLE which we have implemented (see section 5) requires only view information about the user's characteristics. Thus, for our example we employed a very simple user model: This user model traces the users path in the learning environment and registers whenever the user has visited some learning resource.

The TRIPLE rules for adaptive functionality will be described in the following.

Following rule asserts that all triples from @simple:data view are also triples in the @simple:adaptation.

```
FORALL O,P,V O[P->V] <- O[P->V]@simple:data.
```

Following rules derive all documents, concepts, and users from metadata based on types taken from ontologies.

```
FORALL D document(D) <- D[rdf:type->Document].
FORALL C concept(C) <- C[rdf:type->Concept].
FORALL U user(U) <- U[rdf:type->User].
```

We need to derive observations about a user from metadata from user profile (see an example in section 6.4). The observations states whether particular user learned concept based on visiting a document describing the concept. The following rule derive all learned concepts.

```
FORALL C, U  p_obs(C, U, Learned) <- user(U) AND concept(C) AND
    EXISTS D (D[dc:subject->C] AND U[obs:visited->D]).
```

To derive appropriate recommendation annotation for particular user, prerequisite concepts of documents have to be learned by a user. Following rule derive concepts which are prerequisite concepts for a document being analyzed for recommendation. The prerequisite concepts are derived according to the doc:isPrerequisiteFor relationship.

```
FORALL D, C, Ck prerequisite_concepts(D, Ck) <-
    document(D) AND concept(Ck) AND
    D[dc:subject->C] AND Ck[doc:isPrerequisiteFor->C].
```

All previously mentioned rules are used in recommendation rules. We have five rules for recommendation annotations. The first one annotates a document which was visited.

```
FORALL D, U learning_state(D, U, Already_visited) <-
    user(U) AND document(D) AND U[obs:visited->D].
```

The second rule determines documents which are **Recommended**. The recommendation rule is performed according to a FOL sentence from section 5 that document is recommended if *all* prerequisite concepts for all of its concepts are learned.

```
FORALL D, U learning_state(D, U, Recommended) <-
    document(D) AND user(U) AND NOT learning_state(D, U, Already_visited)
    AND FORALL Ck (prerequisite_concepts(D, Ck) ->
        p_obs(Ck, U, Learned)).
```

The third rule derives less strong recommendation. It asserts that document Might_be_understandable if at least one prerequisite concept of for all of its concepts was learned.

```
FORALL D, U learning_state(D, U, Might_be_understandable) <-
    document(D) AND user(U)
AND NOT learning_state(D, U, Recommended)
AND NOT learning_state(D, U, Already_visited) AND
FORALL C (D[dc:subject->C] ->
    (EXISTS Ck (Ck[doc:isPrerequisiteFor->C]
    AND p_obs(Ck, U, Learned)))).
```

A document is annotated as Will_become_understandable if at least one prerequisite concept among its concepts was learned.

```
FORALL D, U learning_state(D, U, Will_become_understandable) <-
    document(D) AND user(U)
AND NOT learning_state(D, U, Recommended)
AND NOT learning_state(D, U, Might_be_understandable)
AND NOT learning_state(D, U, Already_visited)
AND EXISTS Ck (prerequisite_concepts(D, Ck) AND p_obs(Ck, U,
Learned)).
```

For all other cases a document is annotated as Not_recommended.

```
FORALL D, U learning_state(D, U, Not_recommended) <-
    document(D) AND user(U)
AND NOT learning_state(D, U, Recommended)
AND NOT learning_state(D, U, Might_be_understandable)
AND NOT learning_state(D, U, Already_visited)
AND NOT learning_state(D, U, Will_become_understandable).
```

A query which queries for documents and particular annotations about recommendation for particular user can look as follows.

```
FORALL U, D, L <- learning_state(D, U, L)@simple:adaptation.
```

A subset of results derived from our knowledge-base is:

```
U=doc:kbs:henze, D=sun_java:'index.html', L='Already_visited'
U=doc:13s:dolog, D=sun_java:'index.html', L='Already_visited'
U=doc:kbs:henze, D=sun_java:'java/concepts/message.html',
       L='Not_recommended'
U=doc:13s:dolog, D=sun_java:'java/concepts/message.html', L='Recommended'
...
```

The results show that the index.html document has learning state Already_visited for both users. Then the results say that the document message.html is Not_recommended to user identified by kbs:henze URI, and it is Recommended for the user identified by 13s:dolog.

The complete example of the rules used in this paper can be found in triple-file at http://www.learninglab.de/~dolog/seminar/seminar03files/ppswr03_triple_example.triple.

7   Related Work

Adaptive hypermedia has been studied normally in closed worlds, i.e. the underlying document space / the hypermedia system has been known to the authors of the adaptive hypermedia system at design time of the system. As a consequence, changes to this document space can hardly be considered: A change to the document space normally requires the reorganization of the document space (or at least some of the documents in the document space). To open up this setting for dynamic document or information spaces, approaches for so called *open corpus adaptive hypermedia systems* have been discussed [9,23]. Our approach to bring adaptive hypermedia techniques to the web will therefore contribute to the open corpus problem in AH.

Contributions to open corpus adaptive hypermedia can be found in the area of so called *open hypermedia systems*, too. Open hypermedia is an approach to relationship management and information organization for hypertext-like structure servers. Key features are the separation of relationships and content, the integration of third party applications, and advanced hypermedia data models allowing, e.g., the modeling of complex relationships. Approaches to open hypermedia have been discussed, e.g., in [1]. [3] aims to describe adaptive hypermedia techniques for open hypermedia by relating basic fundamental open hypermedia model concepts with adaptive hypermedia techniques. The work presented in this paper settles on more general descriptions of the data objects used in open hypermedia: Instead of using specific kinds of data objects [3], we use resources that are annotated by general RDF metadata. Because we provide a more expressive language for specifying contexts — Triple based queries and constraints — we can have more complex rules for specifying accessibility and usage in general. Behavior like update of user profiles can also be associated within the RDF annotation of the resource and as Triple programs. RDF annotations provide several possibilities for specifying relationships and association, as defined by the RDF schema, and domain ontologies are defined as RDF data again in the form of domain ontologies. Our work is also related to [23,24], and extends it by investigating the different standards relevant for adaptive functionalities in an open environment and how to use queries to implement that functionality. This work also extends our work published in [18] where we made first steps towards adaptive hypermedia based on logical characterization. We showed and implemented more complex rules in comparison to the work and we employed more powerful rule-based language for expressing adaptive functionality. The core differences are availability of models (views) in TRIPLE and direct support for namespaces and URIs.

If we compare our work with standard models for adaptive hypermedia systems such as the one used in AHA! [8] for example, we observe that they define several model like conceptual, navigational, adaptation, teacher and user models. Compared to our approach, these models either correspond to ontologies / taxonomies, to different schemas describing teacher and user profile, and to schemas describing the navigational structure of a course. We express adaptation functionalities as encapsulated and reusable Triple rules, while the adaptation model in AHA uses a rule based language encoded into XML. At the level of

concept or information items AHA! provides functionalities to describe requirements [7] for the resource, which state what is required from a user to visit that
information.

In our approach, we used the RDF-querying and transformation language
TRIPLE. Related approaches in the area of querying languages for the semantic
web can be found, e.g., in [11]. Here, a rule-based querying and transformation
language for XML is proposed. A web language for rules is currently under development of the Rule Markup-Language (RuleML) Initiative [4]. A discussion of
the interoperability between RuleML Logic programs and ontologies (coded in
OWL[5] (web ontology language) or DAML+OIL[6] (Darpa Agent Markup Language + Ontology Inference Layer) can be found in [21].

Reasoning in open worlds like the semantic web is not fully explored yet,
sharing and reusing of resources with high quality is still an open problem. In
this paper, we discussed first ideas on the application of rules and rule-based
querying and transformation language for the domain of adaptation.

8   Conclusions and Further Work

In this paper, we described an approach to personalization on the semantic
web based on reasoning. We have shown how known techniques from adaptive
hypermedia (which normally work in closed worlds) can be realized in an open
world setting like the semantic web. The logical characterization of adaptive
hypermedia enables the formalization of personalization techniques in a common
language (FOL). The rule-based language TRIPLE allowed us to implement
this functionality and reason over distributed metadata. The ontology based
metadata descriptions and thorough use of the ontologies in the descriptions
allowed us to employ monotonic reasoning.

However, the semantic web is characterized with non-complete information.
We would like to continue with experiments with the environment where we will
not have always complete information to derive conclusions. Thus additional
experiments either with non-monotonic reasoning, with additional heuristics to
derive conclusions from not complete information, or experiments with local
closed worlds [22] are needed.

On the other hand, we would like to investigate also more complex concept ontologies. In this paper we use just two types of relationships for relating
concepts, namely *isPrerequisiteFor* and *subConceptOf*. This includes for example decomposition of sequences into smaller parts or content packaging with
additional relationships in concept model (ontology), e.g., partOf, belongsTo,
and alternatives. In addition, we can consider explicit ontologies for educational
models which can provide us with complementary facts for improving conclusions
from personalization reasoning rules. This enables to add additional rules to enhance adaptive functionalities based on the facts modeled in knowledge-base by
utilizing additional relationships.

---

[4] http://www.dfki.uni-kl.de/ruleml/
[5] http://www.w3.org/2001/sw/WebOnt/
[6] http://www.w3.org/TR/daml+oil-reference

At the application level we also would like to experiment with different visualization strategies for displaying results of reasoning.

References

1. K. Anderson, R. Taylor, and E. Whitehead. Chimera: Hypermedia for heterogeneous software development environments. *ACM Transactions on Information Systems*, 18(3):211–245, 2000.
2. Association of Computing Machinery: The ACM computer classification system. http://www.acm.org/class/1998/, 2002.
3. C. Bailey, W. Hall, D. Millard, and M. Weal. Towards open adaptive hypermedia. In *Proccedings of the 2nd International Conference on Adaptive Hypermedia and Adaptive Web-Based Systems (AH 2002)*, Malaga, Spain, May 2002.
4. C. Basu, H. Hirsh, and W. W. Cohen. Recommendation as classification: Using social and content-based information in recommendation. In *Fifteenth National Conference on Artificial Intelligence*, pages 714–720, Madison, USA, 1998.
5. T. Berners-Lee. The semantic web - mit/lcs seminar. http://www.w3c.org/2002/Talks/09-lcs-sweb-tbl/.
6. T. Berners-Lee, J. Hendler, and O. Lassila. The semantic web. *Scientific American*, May 2001.
7. P. D. Bra, A. Aerts, D. Smits, and N. Stash. AHA! version 2.0. In *Proceedings of the AACE ELearn'2002 conference*, pages 240–246, Oct. 2002.
8. P. D. Bra, G.-J. Houben, and H. Wu. AHAM: A dexter-based reference model for adaptive hypermedia. In K. Tochtermann, J. Westbomke, U. Wiil, and J. Leggett, editors, *Proc. of ACM Conference on Hypertext and Hypermedia*, pages 147–156, Darmstadt, Germany, Feb. 1999.
9. P. Brusilovsky. Adaptive hypermedia. *User Modeling and User-Adapted Interaction*, 11(1-2):87–100, 2001.
10. P. Brusilovsky and M. Maybury. *The Adaptive Web*. Communications of the ACM, 2002.
11. F. Bry and S. Schaffert. A gentle introduction into xcerpt, a rule-based query and transformation language for xml. In *International Workshop on Rule Markup Languages for Buisiness Rules on the Semantic Web*, Sardinia, Italy, June 2002.
12. D. Calvanese, G. D. Giacomo, and M. Lenzerini. Ontology of integration and integration of ontologies. In *Proceedings of the 2001 Description Logic Workshop (DL 2001)*, 2001.
13. M. Campione and K. Walrath. The java tutorial. http://java.sun.com/docs/books/tutorial/.
14. M. Campione and K. Walrath. *The Java(TM) Tutorial: A Short Course on the Basics (3rd Edition)*. Addison-Wesley, 2000.
15. DAML+OIL, 2001. http://www.daml.org/2001/03/daml+oil-index.html.
16. S. Decker, D. Brickley, J. Saarela, and J. Angele. A query and inference service for RDF. In *QL'98 — The Query Languages Workshop*, Boston, USA, 1998. WorldWideWeb Consortium (W3C).
17. S. Decker, M. Sintek, and W. Nejdl. The model-theoretic semantics of triple.
18. P. Dolog, R. Gavriloaie, W. Nejdl, and J. Brase. Integrating adaptive hypermedia techniques and open rdf-based environments. In *Proc. of 12th International World Wide Web Conference*, Budapest, Hungary, May 2003.

19. P. Dolog and W. Nejdl. Benefits and challenges of the semantic web for user modelling. In *International Workshop on Adaptive Hypermedia and Adaptive Web-based Systems (AH 2003)*, Budapest, Hungary, 2003.
20. The Dublin Core Metadata Initiative. http://dublincore.org/.
21. B. N. Grosof, I. Horrocks, R. Volz, and S. Decker. Description logic programs: Combining logic programs with description logic. In *Twelfth International World Wide Web Conference*, Budapest, Hungary, May 2003.
22. J. Heflin and H. Munoz-Avila. Lcw-based agent planning for the semantic web. In *Ontologies and the Semantic Web. Papers from the 2002 AAAI Workshop WS-02-11*, pages 63–70, Menlo Park, CA, Nov. 2002.
23. N. Henze and W. Nejdl. Adaptation in open corpus hypermedia. *IJAIED Special Issue on Adaptive and Intelligent Web-Based Systems*, 12, 2001.
24. N. Henze and W. Nejdl. Knowledge modeling for open adaptive hypermedia. In *Proccedings of the 2nd International Conference on Adaptive Hypermedia and Adaptive Web-Based Systems (AH 2002)*, Malaga, Spain, 2002.
25. N. Henze and W. Nejdl. Logically characterizing adaptive educational hypermedia systems. In *International Workshop on Adaptive Hypermedia and Adaptive Web-based Systems (AH 2003)*, Budapest, Hungary, 2003.
26. I. Horrocks. The FaCT System, 2001.
    URL: http://www.cs.man.ac.uk/~horrocks/FaCT/.
27. M. Kifer, G. Lausen, and J. Wu. Logical foundations of object-oriented and frame-based languages. *Journal of the ACM*, 42:741–843, July 1995.
28. LOM: Draft Standard for Learning Object Metadata.
    http://ltsc.ieee.org/wg12/doc.html.
29. Z. Miklós, G. Neumann, U. Zdun, and M. Sintek. Querying semantic web resources using TRIPLE views. In *Proceedings of the 2nd International Semantic Web Conference (ISWC2003)*, Sanibel Island, Florida, USA, Oct. 2003.
30. OWL, 2003. http://www.w3.org/2001/sw/WebOnt/.
31. R. Rada. *Interactive Media*. Springer, 1995.
32. Reference model for an open archival information system (oais), 2002.
    http://ssdoo.gsfc.nasa.gov/nost/isoas/.
33. U. Shardanand and P. Maes. Social information filtering: Algorithms for automating "word of mouth". In *Proceedings of CHI'95 – Human Factors in Computing Systems*, pages 210–217, 1995.
34. M. Sintek and S. Decker. TRIPLE—A query, inference, and transformation language for the semantic web. In *1st International Semantic Web Conference (ISWC2002)*, June 2002.
35. M. Sintek and S. Decker. Triple - an rdf query, inference, and transformation language. In I. Horrocks and J. Hendler, editors, *International Semantic Web Conference (ISWC)*, pages 364–378, Sardinia, Italy, 2002. LNCS 2342.
36. SUNY. The XSB programming system. Dept. of Computer Science, SUNY at Stony Brook, 2000.
    URL: http://www.cs.sunysb.edu/~sbprolog/xsb-page.html.
37. A. van Gelder, K. Ross, and J. S. Schlipf. The well-founded semantics for general logic programs. *Journal of the ACM*, 38(3):620–650, 1991.
38. W3C. Resource Description Framework (RDF) Schema Specification 1.0, 2001.
    URL: http://www.w3.org/TR/2000/CR-rdf-schema-20000327/.
39. W3C. Semantic Web Activity: Resource Description Framework (RDF), 2001.
    URL: http://www.w3.org/RDF/.

On Reasoning on Time and Location on the Web

François Bry, Bernhard Lorenz, Hans Jürgen Ohlbach, and Stephanie Spranger

University of Munich, Germany
http://www.pms.informatik.uni-muenchen.de

Abstract. Reasoning on time and location is receiving increasing attention on the Web due to emerging fields like Web adaptation, mobile computing, and the Semantic Web. Web applications in these fields often refer to rather complex temporal, calendric, and location information. Unfortunately, today's Web languages and formalisms have merely primitive temporal and location data types and temporal and location reasoning capabilities – if any. This article reports on work in progress aiming at integrating temporal and locational reasoning into XML query and transformation operations. We analyze the problem and propose a concrete architecture. A prototype of the temporal reasoner, the WEB-CAL system has already been realized.

1 Introduction

The next generation of the World-Wide-Web must have *machine readable* and *machine understandable* Web content, and no longer just html pages – this is the now widely agreed vision of the 'Semantic Web' initiative [5]. The basic tool for the first step, to make Web content machine readable, is undisputedly XML. The second step, however, to make Web content machine understandable, seems to become a never ending story. Almost anything, human beings can think of, can become Web content. Making all this machine understandable, means formalizing the whole knowledge of mankind in a way that computers can work with; and this is the old vision of Artificial Intelligence. One can attack this problem in at least two ways. The first approach is to develop XML compatible knowledge representation and reasoning tools, and to leave the concrete formalization of knowledge with these tools to the application developers. RDF and OWL are systems of this kind. The second approach is to develop formal theories and mechanisms of particular concepts occurring in Web content, and to integrate these theories into the other XML mechanisms, in particular into XML query and transformation languages. Both approaches are complementary to each other in the same way as general purpose inference systems in logic are complementary to special theory reasoning.

In this paper we propose the development of special theories and XML mechanisms for the concepts time and location, and the integration into XML query and transformation languages. Our proposal goes far beyond the temporal data types of the W3C standard XML Schema [1,2,3], which has in fact no reasoning mechanisms and no location data types and operations.

F. Bry et al. (Eds.): PPSWR 2003, LNCS 2901, pp. 69–83, 2003.
© Springer-Verlag Berlin Heidelberg 2003

The time theory for XML we propose works with the WEBCAL system, a server for advanced calendrical calculations. The WEBCAL system is based on ideas first published in [13,14,15]. WEBCAL has an international dimension: it provides most of the calendar systems world-wide in use, with timezones, daylight savings time regulations, leap years, leap seconds etc. It also has an historical dimension: it models historical sequences of calendrical regulations, for example sequences of calendar systems, sequences of daylight savings time regulations, timezones changing over time etc. It has an application oriented dimension, i.e. one can define new application specific temporal notions, for example school holidays, financial years, ecclesiastical calendars, Mary's birthday, my own working hours, and a lot more. WEBCAL can deal with fuzzy notions like 'late night' or 'around noon' because it represents time intervals as fuzzy sets.

The location theory for XML is not yet as far developed as the time theory, but the solutions for the location theory will be in the same style as the solutions for the time theory.

We shall integrate these mechanisms into the rule based query and transformation language Xcerpt [7,8,6]. Xcerpt is a declarative (logic-based) query and transformation language for the Web currently developed and tested on web-based systems at the University of Munich. Because of its 'logic bias', Xcerpt appears to be a very convenient 'host' for temporal data types and temporal reasoning. Most of the ideas and methods proposed in this paper, however, are independent of Xcerpt and should work with any query language.

In order to illustrate the problems and approaches, we start with a small introductory example.

2   An Introductory Example

The first example illustrates the problems with temporal reasoning in the Web context. Quite similar problems come up with locational reasoning.

Suppose we have a cinema program as an XML document. The XML document could look like:

```
<cinema_program>
  <cinema name="Atlantis" location="Munich">
    <year year="2003">
      <month month="January">
        <day day="1"> <film>
                        <title>Lampedusa</title>
                        <start>20:00</start>
                        <duration>120min </duration>
                      </film>
                      <film>
                        <title>City of God</title>
                        <start>22:00</start>
                        <duration>121min </duration>
                      </film>
```

```
</day> ... </cinema_program>
```

A reasonable query could now be "give me all films ending before midnight 1/1/2003". None of the currently available query languages can deal with such a query. What are the problems?

1. The end times are not explicitly represented in the XML document.
2. The end times could be computed, but the information needed for this is distributed over parts of the XML document.
3. The used calendar system is not mentioned. It could, however, be deduced from the location "Munich".
4. The notion 'midnight' in the query is not clear. Is midnight in Munich meant, or midnight at the place of the querying person, which could be on another continent.
5. Would we really want to exclude 'City of God' although it ends only one minute after midnight? What kind of relation is to be used to evaluate '24:01 before midnight'? A fuzzy 'before' relation could evaluate this expression to a non-zero fuzzy value, such that this film could also be included in the answer set, maybe at the end of the answer list.

In order to evaluate this query in the user's sense, we need a query language plus quite a number of extra mechanisms:

1. first of all we need a *context detection and managing mechanism*. In the example it must figure out the calendar system from the location 'Munich' (alternatively one could require to specify the calendar system in the XML document). It must also figure out the calendar system used in the query. In addition it must determine the timezone and the daylight savings time regulations – again from the location 'Munich' or from some explicit data in the XML document.
2. in order to compute from start time and duration the end time, we need a *time reasoner* which can compute from "year = 2003", "month = January", "day = 1", "start = 22:00" and "duration = 121min" the end time;
3. since the information to be fed into the time reasoner is distributed over the XML document, we need an *extraction language* with which we can specify where to get the necessary data from and how to transform it to become a valid input for the time reasoner;
4. since 'midnight' is just a string, we need a definition of 'midnight' in terms of concrete time points. To this end, a *specification language* for specifying application or user specific temporal notions is necessary;
5. the relation '24:01 before midnight' must be evaluated by the time reasoner, possibly with a fuzzy version of the 'before' relation.
6. the query language must use the fuzzy values to order the answers.

3   The Top Level Architecture

We propose the following top level architecture:

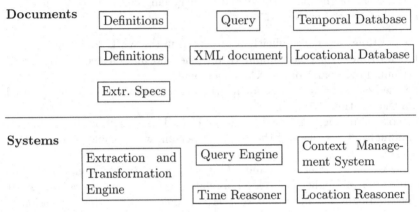

Let us explain each component in more detail.

The Definition Files. Both, the query and the XML document may use application or user specific temporal and locational notions. These notions must be defined in special *definition files*, and loaded into the time and location reasoners before they get invoked. Examples of defined temporal notions which might occur in XML documents are: '3 weeks after Easter', 'the first half of the semester', 'the third school hour', 'weekend', 'the time of the Olympic Games', 'late night', 'around noon' etc. Queries can contain similar expressions, but in addition very user specific expressions. For example, the user may define 'weekend' for himself different to the common notion of 'weekend'. Therefore the query and the XML document may need different definitions.

A few examples of definable *locational* notions which might occur in XML documents and queries are: 'in Munich', 'in the south of Munich', 'close to the station', 'along the A1' 'between Munich and Frankfurt'.

Since locations are 2 or 3-dimensional, there is a much greater variety of locational notions, than of temporal notions. One of the first jobs in the proposed project will therefore be to select classes of locational notions which can be processed in a reasonable way.

The definition files should not be part of the DTD or the XML schema because the notions defined there are not specific to one particular XML document type. With the definition files I can build up libraries of temporal notions which can be used for many different XML-documents. Therefore the definition files are more like style sheet files or JavaScript program files to be loaded together with the XML-document.

The Extraction Specifications. These specify how to extract and transform the data from the XML document to be submitted to the time and location reasoner. In the example of Section 2 we would specify something like: 'in order to calculate the end time, extract the 'year' attribute, the 'month' attribute, the 'day' attribute, the 'start time', turn the 'month' attribute into a number and combine this to a string of the form year/month/day/hour/minute. Then extract the 'duration' element and split it into the duration number and the time unit. Now call the time reasoner to add the duration to the start time. (start hour and minute + duration does not always yield the proper end time, for example when summertime is changed to wintertime. Therefore the complete date and time is needed here.) The preparation of the input to the time reasoner may even require access to external reources. If for example in the cinema example the year is not explicitly stated in the document, one may get the current year as the default from the system clock. This very informal description must of course be put into a formal language. A rule based query language like Xcerpt might be appropriate here.

The Temporal Database. This database contains information which is not specific to any application or user. It need not be one single database, but it can be distributed and hierarchically organized. It must contain in particular mappings from countries and other areas to calendar systems, timezones, daylight savings time regulations. If we want to process XML documents with historical content, we may even need mappings from countries to historical sequences of calendar systems and other time measurement parameters.

It also can contain the dates of public and ecclesiastical holidays, school holidays, the dates of public events, and a lot more.

The Locational Database. This database could be a Geographic Information System with geographic information about the landscape, places, streets, parks, houses etc. It could also contain routes and timetables of public transport systems: buses, underground, trains, taxi stands etc.

Information like 'persons in a wheelchair cannot use bus line 263' could also be there, or heuristics of the kind 'single female persons should avoid Central Park at night'.

The Extraction and Transformation Engine. The Extraction and Transformation Engine processes the extraction specifications. In the example of Section 2 it would collect the relevant data for the start time and duration and turn it into suitable input for the time reasoner.

The Query Engine. processes XML queries almost in the usual way. It moves down the document tree and does string comparisons and maybe evaluate regular expressions over strings. In addition it must also call the time and location reasoners for evaluating expressions like '24:01 before midnight'. If these expressions yield fuzzy values as a result, the query engine must use them to order the answers. This is quite easy if only one expression is involved. But consider the following query 'give me all large cinemas in the south of Munich'. 'large cinemas' is a fuzzy expression and 'in the south of Munich' is a fuzzy expression. The evaluation of this query may yield for each cinema a pair of fuzzy values, and this pair has to be turned into a single total ordering. There may be extra parameters necessary in the query itself, which tell the evaluation engine whether and how to prefer larger cinemas over ones more in the south of Munich, or the other way round. Another alternative is to leave the answers unordered, but return the fuzzy values together with the answers. Then it is up to the application what to do with them. The special theories – time and location and others – should of course not be hardwired into the query language. Instead one should be able to load them as a kind of library into the language evaluator. This is much more flexible and extendible.

The Context Management System. This system is needed to configure the time and location reasoner. In particular, the time reasoner needs to know the calendar system, the timezone, the daylight savings time regulations, in addition to various application specific parameters. For example, on the northern hemisphere the seasons spring, summer, autumn and winter begin and end at different dates than on the southern hemisphere. It is the job of the context management system to turn the information it can get about the document, the application, and the user into corresponding configuration parameters for the time and location reasoner. In the age of mobile computing where the user of a Web Service can move his location (he drives in a car), or even change his device (he switches for the notebook to his PDA or his mobile phone), while accessing the Web service, the context becomes dynamic. It may therefore be necessary for the Context Management System to permanently monitor the query context. Dynamic context need not only come from users changing their location or device. In an ordinary session of a user with some system, for example a tutoring system, the context may change during the course of the session, just by the interactions of the user with the system. Therefore context management has a much wider scope than just tracking times and locations.

The Time Reasoner. The proposed time reasoner is the WEBCAL system, which is explained in more detail in Section 4.

The Location Reasoner. The main purpose of locational notions in XML documents is to relate locational aspects of objects and events to locational aspects of previously introduced objects or events, or to concrete coordinates. Compared to the one-dimensional time axis, there is a much greater variety of relations between 2- or 3-dimensional locational data. The basic relations between 2-dimensional regions have been investigated in the area of qualitative spatial reasoning [10,4,16]. In this area, sophisticated automated reasoning about the spatial relations between physical objects or regions of space has been investigated; and in many cases, this must be done without precise, quantitative information about these relations. Typically, some knowledge of the topological relationships between the entities of interest may be available, along with incomplete and imprecise information about distances, directions and relative sizes; and from this partial information, useful conclusions must be drawn. Examples of the kind of question for which qualitative spatial reasoning is required are: identify the islands in the lake and the largest one. Which parts of the network of tunnels can the robot traverse without getting stuck? Could the collection of objects in the scene fit together to make a spherical or cylindrical shell? When cog A is turned clockwise, will cog B turn and if so, in which direction?

The kind of locational reasoning in the XML-context we want to investigate has a different focus. It is about relations between geographical objects, countries, cities, streets, footpaths, houses etc. which involve a *metric*. The metric on 2- or 3-dimensional locational data comes from the way objects can move from point A to point B. Suppose the query is 'give me the nearest cinema playing Terminator 3'. 'nearest' is here the crucial notion. It is very unlikely that it just refers to the geographical distance to my current location. Instead it very likely refers to the time I will need to get there, and maybe the money it will cost me. But this depends on a lot of different factors: am I walking or driving by bicycle, motorbike or car?; am I sitting in a wheelchair?; can I use public transport?; am I alone or with children or with a pram?; how old am I?; am I male or female?; can I park in a difficult parking lot?; is it advisable for a woman to cross a dark park at night? etc. Evaluating 'nearest' actually amounts to planning a route from my current location to the destination. Route planning for cars is not a difficult issue anymore. The difficulties come up when all the above mentioned possibilities should be taken into account. In particular for people without cars one has to combine quite a number of different networks into a search graph: streets, footpaths, bus lines, underground lines, tram lines etc.

One of the tasks of the location reasoner will be to evaluate 'nearest' in this sense. The location reasoner has to get all the relevant parameters from the context management system, combine the relevant networks into a search graph, and find the shortest path to the potential destinations (the cinemas playing Terminator 3 in the above example).

The XML Document and the Query. We want to put as few restrictions to the structure of an XML document with temporal and locational data as possible, but certain parts need to be stated in a formal language if the data is to be processed automatically. In the cinema program document above, for example, we used the XML element '<start>', but we could also have used '<start_time>' or something else. This freedom is possible because we have the extraction language, where we can specify where to look for the start time in the XML document. The specifications in the extraction language must follow the DTD or XML Schema specification of the XML document. If we want to process two different XML documents, where one uses '<start>' and the other uses '<start_time>', we need two different extraction specifications, which is not a good idea. One could think of an additional abstraction layer, where the difference between '<start>' and '<start_time>' becomes irrelevant, and the matching to the concrete DTD is an extra step, but this has still to be investigated.

The extraction language allows us to leave the structure of the XML document free. The content of the XML elements and attributes with temporal and locational data, however, need to be written in a formal language. In particular we need to agree on formats for date and time strings, but this is only the most simple case. In the general case we may express temporal and locational notions by relating them to other temporal and locational notions. The spectrum of variations for this is almost infinite. Examples for temporal notions are 'three weeks after Easter', 'during my holidays', 'after the Iraq war', 'from around noon until early evening', 'at Mary's birthday' etc. Examples for locational notions are 'in Munich', 'along the A1', 'in the center of London', 'between Picadilly and Trafalgar Square', 'three miles from the river' etc. It would be extremely user friendly if we could put this as strings in natural language into the XML documents, but making the reasoners understanding its meaning is then almost impossible. Therefore we need a formal language to express these facts. The specification language of WEBCAL provides some basics for the temporal part of such a language, but it needs to be considerably extended for this purpose.

Modern designs of formal languages are *typed*. Types and type checking for a language not only help avoiding mistakes. They also can provide useful information for guiding the processing of the expressions. Therefore the formal language for the XML documents and for the queries will be typed. A first proposal for a type system for this purpose has been presented in [9]. Typical types are 'time point', 'time interval', 'duration' etc.

Another problem to be solved is deliberate ambiguity. Consider for example the string 'three weeks after Easter'. First of all, it does not contain the information about the year in which the term 'Easter' is to be evaluated. The year may be listed in another part of the XML document, such that the extraction language can make it precise by turning 'Easter' into for example 'Easter(2003)'. But this is still ambiguous. It is not clear whether the western Easter date or the orthodox Easter date is meant. They may differ by a week. We may want to leave this ambigue in the XML document itself, and resolve the ambiguity by the query context. One querying person may want to interpret Easter as western Easter, and another person may want to interpret it as orthodox Easter.

A similar example with ambigue locational notions could be an XML element <location> capital </location>, where it is left open which capital of which country is meant. Only the query context may make this clear.

Deliberate ambiguity means that the formal language for the time and location dates cannot always refer to concrete events whose data can be taken from the temporal and locational databases or from the definition files. We must allow for an extra level of indirectness. This also means that this indirectness has to be eliminated in an extra step at query time, for example by transforming 'Easter(2003)' into 'Easter(2003,orthodox)'.

The time and location part of the query language is a little bit simpler than the time and location part in the XML documents. Ambiguous queries where it is not clear whether for example the western Easter dates or the orthodox Easter dates are meant, cannot be reasonably evaluated. Therefore we do not need the extra level of indirectness as in the XML document.

4   Temporal Reasoning with WEBCAL

WEBCAL is a computer program which provides advanced calendrical calculations for Web services. WEBCAL has an international dimension: it provides most of the calendar systems world-wide in use, with timezones, daylight savings time regulations, leap years, leap seconds etc. It also has an historical dimension: it models historical sequences of calendrical regulations, for example sequences of calendar systems, sequences of daylight savings time regulations, timezones changing over time etc. It has an application oriented dimension, i.e. one can define new application specific temporal notions, for example school holidays, financial years, ecclesiastical calendars, Mary's birthday, my own working hours, and a lot more. WEBCAL can deal with fuzzy notions like 'late night' or 'around noon' because it represents time intervals as fuzzy sets. The program is based on an algebraic model of basic temporal notions, which gives all the operations a very precise semantics. The main idea behind WEBCAL is to provide a few powerful datastructures, and to offer applications as many operations as possible on these datastructures.

4.1   Fuzzy Time Intervals

All time information which is submitted to WEBCAL is immediately turned into intervals of reference time seconds. For example, the command 'parse 2000' (year in UTC) turns the year 2000 into the interval [946684831 978307231[which corresponds to the time interval from the beginning of the first second in the year 2000 till the end of the last second in the year 2000.

In order to be able to deal with fuzzy notions like 'around noon', WEBCAL represents all intervals as *fuzzy sets*. Even ordinary intervals are in fact fuzzy sets. For example, the above mentioned year 2000 is represented as a rectangular polygon: [946684831,0 946684831,1000 978307231,1000 0,0[. Here the number 1000 stands for the fuzzy value 1.0. We choose an integer representation for fuzzy values instead of a floating point representation because algorithms for polygons with integer coordinates are more efficient and less error prone than algorithms for polygons with floating point coordinates.

Admissible fuzzy intervals in WEBCAL are any polygons of the form $[x_1, y_1$ $x_2, y_2 \ldots x_{n-1}, y_{n-1} x_n, y_n[$ where the x_i are integers in increasing order, and the y_i are integers between 0 and 1000.

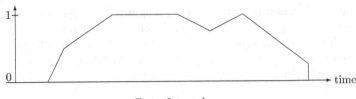

Fuzzy Interval

If y_1 or y_n is not 0 then this represents an infinite fuzzy interval where y_1 or y_n respectively stretch the interval to the infinity. Fuzzy intervals can also be non-convex and therefore represent the union of separate intervals.

WEBCAL provides the following classes of operations on crisp and fuzzy time intervals:

- turning crisp intervals into fuzzy intervals by applying 'fuzzification functions';
- measuring various features of an interval, in particular its size as the integral over the polygon;
- different hull operations (monotone hull, convex hull, crisp hull);
- the usual set theoretic operations on fuzzy intervals, in particular union, intersection, complement, set difference. (For the expert: these operations can be parameterized with t-norms, t-conorms and negation functions);
- some other functions which turn fuzzy sets into fuzzy sets. As an example, consider an XML document about, say, the institute's birthday parties. It may contain the entry that the birthday party for the director took place 'from around noon until early evening' of 20/7/2003. 'Around noon' is a fuzzy notion and 'early evening' is a fuzzy notion. What is now the duration of the birthday party? It must obviously also be a fuzzy set. The fuzzy value of the birthday party duration at a time point x is 1 if the probability that the party started before x is 1 and the probability that the party ended after x is also 1. Therefore the fuzzy value at point x is computed by integrating over the probabilities of the start points and the end points. This is one of the operations the WEBCAL system provides. The resulting fuzzy set is:

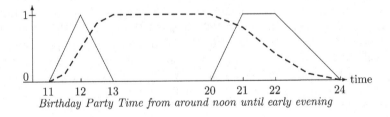

Birthday Party Time from around noon until early evening

The dashed curve may for example represent the percentage of people at the party at a give time.

We can continue this example to illustrate another phenomenon when we reason about time in the XML context. Suppose my diary is also an XML document and it contains the information 'I met this nice girl at the director's birthday party'. If I query the XML document 'did I meet a nice girl between 20 and 21 hours?' the system needs to determine the probability that I met the girl in this time. Since the girl was at the party, the 'meeting the girl' event is correlated with the party time. Therefore the probability that this happened is given by the integral over the party time's fuzzy value during this time period divided by the whole integral. If my diary contained in addition the information 'my mobile phone rang during the director's birthday party', this is an event which is not correlated with the party itself. Therefore the probability that it rang between 20 and 21 hours is just given by 1 hour /(maximal length of the party time).

All these operations are supported by WEBCAL;

– various relations between points and intervals. These relations yield again fuzzy values as results. Therefore a relation '12:01 before midnight', where midnight may for example be represented by a one hour interval, in fact yields a non-zero fuzzy value. In addition to the standard relations 'before', 'starting', 'during' etc. WebCal also provides relations like 'during the first third of the interval' or 'in the middle of the second half' etc.

– Fuzzy versions of Allen's interval relations 'before', 'starts', 'during', 'finishes', 'after', 'equal'. The relations are parameterized. The parameter controls how fuzzy the relation behaves. If the parameter is very large then the relations behave like the ordinary non-fuzzy relations.

4.2   Partitionings

The key notion for modeling calendar systems as well as many repeating events, for example the seasons, is the notion of *a finite partitioning of the real numbers*. A finite partitioning of $\mathbb{R}$ splits the time axis into an infinite sequence of finite intervals, and these intervals can be numbered by integers. Basic time units like seconds, minutes, hours, days, weeks, months, years etc. can all be represented by finite partitions of $\mathbb{R}$. The partitions can be of equal length, but usually they have different sizes. In fact, the only relevant partitioning with equal sized partitions in WEBCAL are the seconds. Already the minutes have different sizes: minutes with added leap seconds are longer than 60 seconds.

Besides the basic time units in calendar systems, there are a lot of other temporal notions which can be modeled as partitions: the seasons, the sequence of Easter dates, financial years, semesters in universities, the sequence of sunrises and sunsets, the sequence of the tides, the sequence of school holidays etc. The WEBCAL interface provides different specification mechanisms for defining temporal notions as partitionings at run time. There are, however, other partitionings which need to be defined with special algorithms. Examples are the sequence of Easter dates, sunsets and sunrises etc. They are built-in.

WEBCAL treats built-in partitions which model time units of calendar systems in the same way as defined partitions representing for example the seasons on the northern or southern hemisphere. All operations working for example with weeks and months work in the same way for the defined partitions. The algorithm for computing the n'th week in a month can therefore also compute for example the n'th week in the summer.

In WEBCAL there are four different methods for defining partitionings. The first method requires a starting point, an average length of the partitions and a correction function. All standard time units, seconds, minutes, hours, weeks, months, years etc. can be defined this way. The correction function for years, for example, has to deal with leap years.

The second method defines a partitioning by giving an anchor date and the length or the partitions. For example, the following command specifies semesters as sequences of 7 months followed by five months, starting in October.

timeUnit semester regular 2000/10 winter 7 summer 5 month

In the third method we provide instead of the lengths of the partitions concrete dates. For example, the following command

timeUnit season calendrical 2000/3/21 spring 6/21 summer 9/23 autumn 12/21 winter +1/3/21 month

specifies the seasons as a partitioning.

Finally, with the fourth method we provide concrete dates. It can for example be used to define holidays.

timeUnit BavarianHolidays finite 2002/10/28 Herbst 2002/11/2 gap 2002/12/23 Weihnachten 2003/1/4 gap 2003/3/3 Winter 2003/3/7 gap 2003/4/14 Ostern 2003/4/26 gap 2003/6/10 Pfingsten 2003/6/21 gap 2003/7/28 Sommer 2003/9/8

In this case the partitioning is preceded by an infinite partition and followed by an infinite partition. In all other cases the sequence of partitions is infinite itself.

Partitions can be labeled, and these labels can be used in various algorithms. 'summer', 'winter' etc. are such labels. 'gap' is a built-in label.

4.3   Calendar Systems

A calendar system in WEBCAL is essentially a collection of time units (seconds, minutes, hours, day, weeks, months, years etc.). Each of these time units is modeled as a partitioning of the reference time line. WEBCAL provides a class **Partitioning**, which allows one to define partitionings by providing the *average length* of a partition and a correction function for the cases that the length of a particular time unit differs from the average length. For example, the Gregorian year is defined by an average length of 31536000 seconds (365 days) and a correction function which adds 86400 seconds (one day) for each leap year. This way, adding a new calendar system is quite easy, and the code to be implemented needs to deal with the calendar specific concepts (leap years, length of months, etc.) only.

Since calendar systems have been changed during the history of countries and societies, WEBCAL allows one to define historical sequences of calendar systems. For example, 'Julian 1582/10/4 Gregorian' in the 'calendarSequence' command specifies that all dates before October, 4th, 1582 (in the Julian calendar) should be interpreted in the Julian calendar, and all later dates should be interpreted in the Gregorian calendar.

4.4   Manipulation of Intervals

With the 'shift' command one can shift intervals by a given number of time units. For example, one can shift forwards by 3 month, 1.5 days, 1 semester, and backwards by 2.6 weeks etc.

Very similar to the shift command is the 'extend' command. Whereas shift always shifts the whole interval, the extend command only shifts the upper or lower part of the (fuzzy) interval. This way intervals can be extended for example by 1 year, by 3.5 minutes, by 1.2 seasons, by 2 holiday periods etc.

The most powerful command is the 'within' command. It models expressions like 'the second day within the week' (Tuesday) or 'the third month within the year' (March) or the 'the last day within the year' (new years eve) or 'the third decade within the century' or 'the second but last winter within the decade' or 'the last week within the summer holiday' etc. Within comes with a number of control parameters which give it an enormous flexibility to compute different things with the same basic algorithm. For example, the version 'first month within day' can be used to cast a smaller interval, for example a day, into a larger interval, in this case a month.

4.5   Definition Language

Many temporal notions are very application or user specific. For example, 'the second school hour' is a temporal notion, which may only be relevant for me and a few other people. Such a notion can't be built into a system. Nevertheless, I may want to ask a TV-program database 'give me all documentations about the Iraq war shown during the second school hour'. To account for this, WEB-CAL provides a specification language for defining new temporal notions. With this language, we may for example define the n'th school hour during the time interval x:

$$school\_hour(x, n) =$$
$$shift(extend(begin\_minute(hour\_within\_day(x, (n <= 5)?8 : 13)),$$
$$45, minute), (n - 1) * 45, minute)$$

This defines a block of 45 minute school hours between 8 o'clock and 11:45, and a second block of 45 minute school hours after 13:00.

4.6   Limits of the Current Version of WEBCAL

There are various things on the agenda to be built-in. Some of them are only a matter of time, but they do not need new concepts: more calendar systems, special time sequences like sunrises, sunset, moonrises, tides, solar and lunar eclipses etc. Although these require special algorithms, they all can be modeled as partitionings, and this fits nicely into the concepts of WEBCAL. The Easter dates (western and orthodox) are already modeled this way.

More serious changes are required to overcome the next restriction: so far, WEBCAL can only deal with concrete time intervals, for example 'one week after Easter'. It cannot deal with notions like 'one week between Christmas and Easter'. This denotes a 'floating interval' which is constrained by concrete dates. In order to deal with such intervals, we need a constraint handling mechanism. Unfortunately things are not so easy that we can take one off the shelf. Consider the following constraints: 'at most one month' and 'at least 29 days'. This means that it cannot be a February, except in a leap year. Obviously these constraints depend very much on the structure of the calendar system. It is currently not clear how to integrate this into WEBCAL.

5   Conclusion

In this paper we tried to give an overview on the various aspects of temporal and locational reasoning in the Web context. We focused on the problem to evaluate queries to XML documents and taking into account the proper semantics of temporal and locational notions. We have shown that there are quite a number of different ideas, methods and systems involved to evaluate even such simple queries like 'give me all films ending before midnight' to an XML cinema program database. Some of the problems have already been solved, in particular for temporal reasoning. Before we can show a first prototype of a complete system, however, many other problems still have to be investigated. For most of them it is not really difficult to find some solution, but all the solutions must fit together in a quite complex system, and the solutions must really be practical, and not only solve simplified abstracted cases.

References

1. *W3C* http://www.w3.org/TR/xmlschema-0/: *XML Schema Part 0: Primer.* 2001.
2. *W3C* http://www.w3.org/TR/xmlschema-1/: *XML Schema Part 1: Structures.* 2001.
3. *W3C* http://www.w3.org/TR/xmlschema-2/: *XML Schema Part 2: Datatypes.* 2001.
4. B. Bennett, A.G. Cohn, F. Wolter, and M. Zakharyaschev.   Multi-dimensional modal logic as a framework for spatio-temporal reasoning. *Applied Intelligence*, 17(3):239–251, 2002.
5. T. Berners-Lee, M. Fischetti, and M. Dertouzos. *Weaving the Web: The Original Design and Ultimate Destiny of the World Wide Web.* Harper, San Francisco, September 1999. ISBN: 0062515861.
6. François Bry, Sacha Berger, and Sebastian Schaffert. Xcerpt and visXcerpt: From Pattern-Based to Visual Querying of XML and Semistructured Data. In *Proceedings of the 29th Intl. Conference on Very Large Databases (VLDB03), Germany*, 2003.
7. François Bry and Sebastian Schaffert. A Gentle Introduction into Xcerpt, a Rule-based Query and Transformation Language for XML. In *International Workshop on Rule Markup Languages for Business Rules on the Semantic Web (invited article)*, http://www.soi.city.ac.uk/~{}msch/conf/ruleml, Italy, June, 2002.

8. François Bry and Sebastian Schaffert. The XML Query Language Xcerpt: Design Principles, Examples, and Semantics. In *Akmal B. Chaudhri, et al. (Eds.), Lecture Notes in Computer Science (LNCS) on Web, Web-Services, and Database Systems*, pages 295–310, 2002.

9. François Bry and Stephanie Spranger. Temporal Constructs for a Web Language. In *Proceedings of the 4th Workshop on Interval Temporal Logics and Duration Calculi during ESSLLI'03, Austria, August, to appear*, 2003.

10. A G Cohn, B Bennett, J M Gooday, and N Gotts. RCC: a calculus for region based qualitative spatial reasoning. *GeoInformatica*, 1:275–316, 1997.

11. Anne Doucet, Stéphane Gançarski, Geneviéve Jomier, and Sophie Monties. Versions of Integrity Constraints in Multiversion Databases. In *Abdelkader Hameurlain, A. Min Tjoa (Eds.): Database and Expert Systems Applications, 8th International Conference, DEXA, Toulouse, Proceedings. Lecture Notes in Computer Science, 1308, Springer*, pages 252–261, 1996.

12. Stéphane Gançarski. Database Versions to represent Bitemporal Databases. In *Trevor J. M. Bench-Capon, Giovanni Soda, A. Min Tjoa (Eds.): Database and Expert Systems Applications, 10th International Conference, DEXA, Florence, Proceedings. Lecture Notes in Computer Science, 1677, Springer*, pages 832–841, 1999.

13. Hans Jürgen Ohlbach. About real time, calendar systems and temporal notions. In H. Barringer and D. Gabbay, editors, *Advances in Temporal Logic*, pages 319–338. Kluwer Academic Publishers, 2000.

14. Hans Jürgen Ohlbach. Calendar logic. In I. Hodkinson D.M. Gabbay and M. Reynolds, editors, *Temporal Logic: Mathematical Foundations and Computational Aspec ts*, pages 489–586. Oxford University Press, 2000.

15. Hans Jürgen Ohlbach and Dov Gabbay. Calendar logic. *Journal of Applied Non-Classical Logics*, 8(4), 1998.

16. J. G. Stell. Part and complement: Fundamental concepts in spatial relations. In *Proceedings 7th International Syposium on AI and Mathematics, Florida, January 2002*. to appear.

Reasoning about Communicating Agents in the Semantic Web

Matteo Baldoni[1], Cristina Baroglio[1], Laura Giordano[2],
Alberto Martelli[1], and Viviana Patti[1]

[1] Dipartimento di Informatica, Università degli Studi di Torino, Torino, Italy
{baldoni,baroglio,mrt,patti}@di.unito.it
[2] Dipartimento di Informatica, Università del Piemonte Orientale, Alessandria, Italy
laura@mfn.unipmn.it

Abstract. In this article we interpret the Semantic Web and Web Service issues in the framework of multi-agent interoperating systems. We will advocate the application of results achieved in the research area of reasoning about actions and change by showing scenarios and techniques that could be applied.

1 Introduction

The fast diffusion of Internet and the World Wide Web has inspired new paradigms for the development of applications distributed over the network, leading to the concept of "web service". We can consider a web service as a program (software) or a device (hardware) accessible through a network, that can be invoked in an automatic way by programs or other web services. This perspective brings along many interesting issues: how to describe the function executed by a web service in a machine-interpretable way? How to advertise web services? How to choose among the providers of apparently identical services? All these questions and many others demand for the definition of tools and languages for handling semantic information, not only ontologies but also information about the functioning of services.

The standardization organizations developed a series of languages for representing the semantic contents of a resource accessible on the web, from the Resource Description Framework (RDF), to OWL and DAML+OIL for ontology description, to WSDL [6] and DAML-S [7] for web service semantic description. DAML-S inherited from the experience of the research community that studies agent systems and their logic formalizations and draws considerably from the action metaphor: a service can be viewed as an action (atomic or complex) with preconditions and effects, that can modify the state of the world and the state of agents that work in the world. Such a semantic characterization of the service as an action is described in the so called DAML-S process model and can be used for accomplishing tasks like automatic identification of a service of interest, automatic invocation, automatic composition of services, and so forth.

In this line, one promising direction of research, that we mean to investigate, consists in exploiting results achieved by the community that studies *logic for AI*

F. Bry et al. (Eds.): PPSWR 2003, LNCS 2901, pp. 84–98, 2003.

and, in particular, *reasoning about actions and change*. Indeed, the availability of semantic information about web resources enables the application of reasoning techniques, such as constraint reasoning, non-monotonic reasoning, and temporal reasoning. The main purpose of adopting reasoning techniques is to allow the design of flexible systems, that can adapt to different users and that are open to interact with one another in ways that cannot be fully foreseen at design time and, thus, require such systems to reason for taking autonomous decisions.

Some work in this direction has already been carried on in [19], where, within the context of the DAML-S project [5], the reasoning techniques supported by GOLOG, an agent language based on the situation calculus, are applied to produce composite and customized services. Actually, when a service is described in terms of the function that it executes, with its preconditions and effects, the use of *agents* that can reason about the consequences of its invocation is a natural choice: a rational agent is by definition characterized by a high-level of autonomy, it has an own internal state containing information about the world and about its goals, it can reason about how to behave for fulfilling them, it can react to alterations of the environment. Agents have also *social capabilities* that enable them to interact both with other agents or devices as well as with human beings. This leads us to claim that there is another fundamental behavior level, currently not addressed by the proposers of DAML-S, that should instead be seriously considered and explicitly incorporated in the high-level service description: the *interaction level*, concerning the *communicative behavior* of a web service, and more specifically the *interaction protocol* that it adopts for communicating with its clients or partners. Our proposal is set in a framework in which the web service is an agent that communicates with other agents in a FIPA-like Agent Communication Language (ACL) using predefined protocols. In this context, the communicative behavior of a service can be expressed as a conversation protocol in a logic language, at high (not at network) level. Having a logic specification of the protocol, it is possible to reason about the effects of engaging specific conversations, and to verify properties of the protocol.

In this paper we introduce two related approaches to reasoning about communicative actions by using as a running example a simple scenario of a web service. Both approaches are based on an action theory where communicative actions are formalized with a set of action and precondition laws. In Section 4 we show how the logic language DyLOG can reason about the changes caused by a communicative action to the beliefs of the involved agents, and how this can be exploited for realizing new forms of personalization in web service fruition. In Section 5 we present a more general action theory which allows to specify systems of communicating agents and to verify properties of such systems containing temporal constraints.

2   Communication between Agents

Communication and dialogue have intensively been studied in the context of formal theories of agency [8]. In particular, a great deal of attention has been devoted to the definition of *standard agent communication languages* (ACL), such as FIPA and KQML. The crucial issue was to achieve interoperability in open agent systems, characterized by the interaction of heterogeneous agents, where it is fundamental to have a universally shared semantic.

Agent communication languages are complex structures because a communicative act must specify many kinds of information, such as its content and the kind of performative. The definition of formal semantics for individual communicative acts has been one of the major topics of research in this field. Most of the proposals are ultimately based on the philosophical theory of speech acts developed by Austin and Searle in the sixties. Following the basic insight of the speech act theory, communications are not just considered as transmitting information but as *actions* that, instead of modifying the external world, affect the mental states of the involved agents. As a consequence, individual speech act semantic has been given in terms of preconditions and effects on mental attitudes, as it is commonly done with action semantic, and standard techniques for reasoning about change have been exploited for proving conversation properties, planning communication with other agents and answer selection. In this line, many approaches in the literature are based on variant of modal logic, in which mental attitudes, such as beliefs, goals and intentions, as well as communicative acts are represented by modalities [4,18,9].

Only recently the attention has been moved to formalize those aspects of communication that are related to the conversational context in which communicative acts occur [21]. The formalization of conversation policies adds a higher semantic level, which improves the interoperability of the various components (often separately developed) and simplifies the verification of compliance to the desired standards. In the area of agent languages based on logic, some examples of definition of protocols for guiding the agent communicative behavior can be found in [26,1]. By working at the level of protocols, agents can more easily be seen as individuals, developed independently, on different platforms and with different approaches, a very attractive view in the applicative field of web applications and web services. For all these reasons we focus on a semantics of communication that supports the specification and reasoning about single speech acts, as well as the specification and reasoning about speech acts in the context of a conversation protocol.

Instead of referring to a mentalistic approach as described above, some authors have proposed a social approach to agent communication [27,14]. The mental approach is not well suited for the verification of an "open" multi-agent system, where the history of communications is observable, but the internal states of the single agents may not be observable. In contrast, in the social approach communicative actions affect the "social state" of the system, rather than the internal states of the agents. The social state records the social facts, like the *permissions* and the *commitments* of the agents, which are created and modified in the interactions among them. The dynamics of the system emerges from the interactions of the agents, which must respect these permissions and the commitments (if they are compliant with the protocol). The social approach provides a high level specification of the protocol, and does not require the rigid specification of all the allowed action sequences by means of finite state diagrams.

3   A Simple Scenario

In this section we will define a simple scenario aimed at showing the advantage of expressing and reasoning about the interaction protocol followed by a web service. Let us consider a software agent (we will refer to it as *pa*) whose task is to crawl the internet for executing specific requests of a given user; indeed, *pa* is a user personal assistant. Let us suppose that *pa* current task is to book a ticket at a cinema where a given movie is shown. In a web service context, it will have to look for a provider of a cinema booking service by consulting a registry, and interact with it accordingly, supplying the requested information. As a further condition, let us imagine that the user requested the personal assistant not to use his credit card number in the upcoming transaction. Suppose also that two cinema booking services are available, called *click_ticket* and *all_cinema* respectively, that apply two different interaction protocols, one permitting both to book a ticket to be paid later by cash (Fig. 1 (a)) and to buy it by credit card (Fig. 1 (b)), the other allowing only ticket purchase by credit card (Fig. 1 (c)). These descriptions would induce a human assistant to choose *click_ticket*, selecting the option to pay cash; this choice can be done because we can reason about the consequences of communicative acts and procedures.

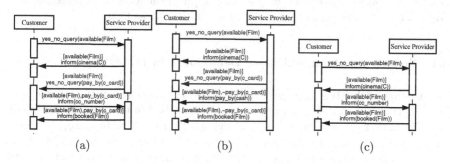

(a)   (b)   (c)

Fig. 1. The three AUML graphs [23] represent the communicative interactions occurring between the customer (*pa*) and the provider; (a) and (b) are followed by *click_ticket*, (c) is followed by *all_cinema*. Formulas among square brackets represent conditions on the execution of the speech act.

4   Interaction Protocols in DyLOG

In the Web service scenario, we are interested in formal languages that support reasoning techniques for proving existential properties of the kind "given a protocol and a set of desiderata, is there a specific conversation, respecting the protocol, that also satisfies the desiderata?". In different words, the scenario demands for some technique that allows the personalization of the interaction. We will show how reasoning methods supported by the agent language DyLOG can be exploited in order to obtain this kind of personalization.

DyLOG is a high-level logic programming language for modelling and programming rational agents [3,24,1]. It is based on a modal theory of actions and mental attitudes where modalities are used for representing actions as well as beliefs for modelling the agent's mental state. It accounts both for atomic and complex actions, or procedures. Atomic actions are either world actions, affecting the world, or mental actions, i.e. sensing and communicative actions which only affect the agent beliefs. Complex actions are defined through (possibly recursive) definitions, given by means of Prolog-like clauses and by making use of action operators like sequence, test and non-deterministic choice. The action theory allows to cope with the problem of reasoning about complex actions with incomplete knowledge and in particular to address the temporal projection and planning problem. Intuitively DyLOG allows to specify the behavior of a rational agent that reasons about its own behavior, chooses a course of actions conditioned on its mental state and can use sensors and communication for obtaining fresh knowledge. In this spirit it has already been used with success for agent programming, in implementing a web application where a *virtual tutor* helps students to build personalized study curricula [2], based on the description of courses viewed as actions (an application that bears many analogies with web service process model description and usage).

Let us recall how to specify and reason about communicative behaviors in DyLOG, by focussing on the web service application scenario depicted above. For a detailed description of the overall agent theory see [3,1].

4.1   Specifying Communicative Behaviours in DyLOG

Let us start with FIPA-like *speech acts*. Following the mentalistic approach, in DyLOG they are considered atomic actions, described in terms of preconditions and effects on the agent mental state, having form $speech\_act(ag_i, ag_j, l)$, where ag_i (sender) and ag_j (receiver) are agents and l (a fluent) is the object of the communication. Since speech acts can be seen as mental actions, affecting both the sender's and the receiver's mental state, we have modelled them by generalizing non-communicative action definitions, so to allow also the representation of the effects of an action executed by some other agent on the current agent mental state, described by a consistent set of *belief fluents*. In fact in our formalization each agent has a twofold, personal representation of the speech act: one is to be used when it is the sender, the other when it is the receiver. Such a representation provides the capability of *reasoning about* conversation effects from the subjective point of view of the agent holding the representation. In the speech act specification that holds when the agent is the sender, the preconditions contain some *sincerity condition* that must hold in its mental state. When it is the receiver, instead, the action is always executable. Let us consider, as an example, a primitive speech act from the standard agent communication language FIPA-ACL, and let us define its semantics within the DyLOG framework: the *inform* speech act (more examples can be found in [24]).

a) $\quad \Box(\mathcal{B}^{Self}l \wedge \mathcal{B}^{Self}\mathcal{U}^{Other}l \supset \langle \mathsf{inform}(Self, Other, l)\rangle \top)$

b) $\quad \Box([\mathsf{inform}(Self, Other, l)]\mathcal{M}^{Self}\mathcal{B}^{Other}l)$

c) $\quad \Box(\mathcal{B}^{Self}\mathcal{B}^{Other}authority(Self, l) \supset [\mathsf{inform}(Self, Other, l)]\mathcal{B}^{Self}\mathcal{B}^{Other}l)$

d) $\quad \Box(\top \supset \langle \mathsf{inform}(Other, Self, l)\rangle \top)$

e) $\quad \Box([\mathsf{inform}(Other, Self, l)]\mathcal{B}^{Self}\mathcal{B}^{Other}l)$

f) $\quad \Box(\mathcal{B}^{Self}authority(Other, l) \supset [\mathsf{inform}(Other, Self, l)]\mathcal{B}^{Self}l)$

Clause (a) states that $Self$ will execute an inform act only if it believes l (we use the modal operator $\mathcal{B}^{ag_i}$ to model the beliefs of agent ag_i) and it believes that the receiver ($Other$) does not know l. It also considers possible that the receiver will adopt its belief (the modal operator $\mathcal{M}^{ag_i}$ is defined as the dual of $\mathcal{B}^{ag_i}$, intuitively $\mathcal{M}^{ag_i}\varphi$ means the ag_i considers φ possible), clause (b), although it cannot be certain about it -autonomy assumption-. If agent $Self$ believes to be considered a trusted *authority* about l by the receiver, it is also confident that $Other$ will adopt its belief, clause (c). Instead, when $Self$ is the receiver, the effect of an inform act is that $Self$ will believe that l is believed by the sender ($Other$), clause (e), but $Self$ will adopt l as an own belief only if it thinks that $Other$ is a trusted authority, clauses (f).

DyLOG agents can be provided with a set of *conversation protocols*, that build on individual speech acts and specify communication patterns guiding the agent communicative behavior during a protocol-oriented dialogue. Reception of a messages is modelled as a special kind of sensing action, what we call *get message actions*. Indeed from the agent perspective receiving a message corresponds to query for an external input, whose outcome is unpredictable. The main difference w.r.t. normal sensing actions is that *get message actions* are defined by means of speech acts performed by the interlocutor. Protocols are expressed by means of a collection of procedure axioms of the action logic, having form $\langle p_0 \rangle \varphi \subset \langle p_1 \rangle \langle p_2 \rangle \ldots \langle p_n \rangle \varphi$, where p_0 is the procedure name the p_i's can be i's communicative acts or special sensing actions for the reception of message. Each agent has a subjective perception of the communication with other agents, for this reason each protocol has as many procedural representations as the possible roles in the conversation. Let us consider for instance the personal assistant introduced in Section 3, its aim is to look for a cinema booking service that satisfies the user's requests. The web service, *click_ticket* follow the interaction protocol **get_ticket_1**, that permits both to book a ticket to be paid later by cash and to buy it by credit card. Let us suppose that such protocol is a part of the DAML-S descriptions of *click_ticket*. Since the protocol is meant to allow the interaction of two agents, it has two complementary views: the view of the web service and the view of the client, i.e. *pa*. Intuitively, if one of the two agents plays the part of the sender of a piece of information, the other should play the part of the receiver. In the following we will report the view –written in DyLOG– that *pa* has of the protocol **get_ticket_1**. We refer to it as **get_ticket_1**$_C$. Notice that it builds on primitive speech acts as well as on procedures for making a

query (yes_no_query$_Q$) or replying to a query (yes_no_query$_I$) according to the
FIPA Query Interaction protocol [9].

(a) $\langle$get_ticket_1$_C$($Self, WebS, Film$)\rangle\varphi \subset$
    $\langle$yes_no_query$_Q$($Self, WebS, available(Film)$);
    $\mathcal{B}^{Self}available(Film)$? ; get_info($Self, WebS, cinema(C)$);
    yes_no_query$_I$($Self, WebS, pay\_by(credit\_card)$);
    $\mathcal{B}^{Self}pay\_by(credit\_card)$? ; inform($Self, WebS, cc\_number$);
    get_info($Self, WebS, booked(Film)$)$\rangle\varphi$
(b) $\langle$get_ticket_1$_C$($Self, WebS, Film$)\rangle\varphi \subset$
    $\langle$yes_no_query$_Q$($Self, WebS, available(Film)$);
    $\mathcal{B}^{Self}available(Film)$? ; get_info($Self, WebS, cinema(C)$);
    yes_no_query$_I$($Self, WebS, pay\_by(credit\_card)$);
    $\neg\mathcal{B}^{Self}pay\_by(credit\_card)$? ; get_info($Self, WebS, pay\_by(cash)$);
    get_info($Self, WebS, booked(Film)$)$\rangle\varphi$
(c) $\langle$get_ticket_1$_C$($Self, WebS, Film$)\rangle\varphi \subset$
    $\langle$yes_no_query$_Q$($Self, WebS, available(Film)$); $\neg\mathcal{B}^{Self}available(Film)$?$\rangle\varphi$
(d) [get_info($Self, WebS, Fluent$)]$\varphi \subset$ [inform($WebS, Self, Fluent$)]φ

Protocol get_ticket_1$_C$ works in the following way: the personal assistant ($Self$)
is supposed to begin the interaction. After checking if the requested movie is
available in some cinema by the yes_no_query$_Q$ protocol, it should wait for an
information (get_info) from the provider ($WebS$) about which cinema shows it.
Then the form of payment is defined: (a) defines the interaction that occurs
when the tickets are paid by credit card (see Fig. 1(i)); (b) is selected when
$\neg\mathcal{B}^{Self}pay\_by(credit\_card)$ is contained in pa mental state, leading to book a
ticket to be paid by cash (see Fig. 1(ii)). In both cases a confirmation of the ticket
booking is returned to the pa. Clause (c) tackles the case in which the movie is
not available. Clause (d) describes get_info, which is a get_message action.

Given a set Π_C of simple action laws defining an agent ag_i's primitive speech
acts, a set Π_{Sget} of axioms for the reception of messages, and a set Π_{CP},
of procedure axioms specifying a collection of conversation protocols, we denote by CKit^{ag_i} (the *communication kit* of a DyLOG agent ag_i), the triple
$(\Pi_C, \Pi_{CP}, \Pi_{Sget})$. CKit^{ag_i} is a part of Π_{ag_i}, i.e. the domain description of the
agent ag_i, including also S_0, i.e the initial set of ag_i's belief fluents, and eventually laws and axioms for specifying the agent non communicative behaviors.

4.2   Reasoning about the Interaction with a Web Service

Given a DyLOG domain description Π_{ag_i} containing a CKit^{ag_i} with the specifications of the interaction protocols and of the relevant speech acts, a *planning*
activity can be triggered by *existential queries* of form $\langle p_1\rangle\langle p_2\rangle \ldots \langle p_m\rangle Fs$, where
each p_k ($k = 1, \ldots, m$) may be an atomic or complex action (a primitive speech
act or an interaction protocol), executed by our agent, or an external[1] speech act,

---

[1] By the word *external* we denote a speech act in which our agent plays the role of
the receiver.

that belongs to CKit^{ag_i}. Checking if the query succeeds corresponds to answering to the question "is there an execution of $p_1, \ldots, p_n$ leading to a state where the conjunction of belief fluents Fs holds for agent ag_i?". Such an execution is a plan to bring about Fs. The procedure definition constrains the search space. During the planning process get_message actions are treated as sensing actions, whose outcome cannot be predicted before the actualexecution: since agents cannot read each other's mind, they cannot know in advance the answers that they will receive. All of the possible alternatives are to be taken into account and, indeed, we can foresee them because of the existence of the protocol. Therefore, the extracted plan will be *conditional*, in the sense that for each get_message and for each sensing action it will contain as many branches as possible action outcomes. Each path in the resulting tree is a linear plan that brings about Fs.

The problem that the personal assistant pa has in the Web service scenario outlined above can be naturally turned into a planning problem in presence of communication, as the one treated by DyLOG. In fact the question pa tries to answer is: "is there some possible conversation, that is an instance of the protocol followed by the Web service provider and satisfies all the conditions posed by the user (e.g. at the and of the interaction the service mustn't know the user's credit card number)?". In a way, pa wonders if it is possible to personalize the interaction with its interlocutor so to achieve certain goals. Let us take a DyLOG domain description containing the description of the get_ticket_1$_C$ protocol reported above, suppose that pa knows the credit card number (cc_number) of the user but it is requested not to use it, and consider the query:

$$\langle\mathsf{get\_ticket\_1}_C(pa, click\_ticket, akira)\rangle\mathcal{B}^{pa}\neg\mathcal{B}^{click\_ticket}cc\_number$$

that amounts to determine if there is a conversation between pa and $click\_ticket$ about the movie $akira$, that is an instance of the conversation protocol get_ticket_1$_C$, after which the service does not know the credit card number of the user. Agent pa works on the behalf of a user, thus it knows the user's credit card number ($\mathcal{B}^{pa}cc\_number$) and his desire not to use it in the current transaction ($\neg\mathcal{B}^{pa}pay\_by(credit\_card)$). It also believes to be an authority about the form of payment and about the user's credit card number and that $click\_ticket$ is an authority about cinema and tickets. This is represented by the beliefs: $\mathcal{B}^{pa}authority(pa, cc\_number)$ and $\mathcal{B}^{pa}authority(click\_ticket, booked(akira))$. The initial mental state will also contain the fact that pa believes that no ticket for $akira$ has been booked yet, $\mathcal{B}^{pa}\neg booked(akira)$, and some hypothesis on the interlocutor's mental state, e.g. the belief fluent $\mathcal{B}^{pa}\neg\mathcal{B}^{click\_ticket}cc\_number$, meaning that the web service does not already know the credit card number. Suppose, now, that the ticket is available; since pa mental state contains the belief $\neg\mathcal{B}^{pa}pay\_by(credit\_card)$, when it reasons about the protocol execution, the test on $\mathcal{B}^{pa}pay\_by(credit\_card)$? fails. Then clause (b) is to be followed, leading pa to be informed that it booked a ticket, $\mathcal{B}^{pa}booked(akira)$, which is supposed to be paid cash. No communication involves the belief $\mathcal{B}^{pa}\neg\mathcal{B}^{click\_ticket}cc\_number$, which persists from the initial state. Even when the ticket is not available or the movie is not known by the provider, the interaction ends without consequences on the fluent $\mathcal{B}^{pa}\neg\mathcal{B}^{click\_ticket}cc\_number$. The briefly described reasoning process lead to find an execution trace of get_ticket_1$_C$, which corresponds to a *personalized conditional dialogue plan* between *pa* and the provider *click_ticket*, always leading to satisfy the user goal of not giving the credit card number.

5   Specifying and Verifying Systems of Communicating Agents

DyLOG is a sequential language which can describe the behavior of a single agent and prove *existential* properties, such as finding a sequence of actions achieving some goal. A more general problem is that of modelling systems of communicating agents, so as to be able to prove properties of the whole system. In this section we present a theory for reasoning about actions which allows to describe the behavior of a network of sequential agents which coordinate their activities by performing common actions together[12,13]. This theory is based on the Product Version of Dynamic Linear Time Temporal Logic (denoted $DLTL^{\otimes}$) [16], a logic which extends LTL, the propositional linear time temporal logic, by strengthening the *until* operator by indexing it with the regular programs of dynamic logic. Regular programs are well suited to model both the agent behaviors and the communication protocols. Moreover, the formulas of the logic are decorated with the names of sequential agents, thus allowing to describe the behavior of a network of sequential agents which coordinate their activities by performing common actions together. Let us first give a quick overview of the logic.

5.1   The Logic $DLTL$ and Its Product Version

First we recall the syntax and semantics of DLTL as introduced in [17]. $DLTL$ is an extension of LTL in which the next state modality is labelled by actions and the until operator is indexed by programs in Propositional Dynamic Logic (PDL) [15].

Let Σ be a finite non-empty alphabet whose members are interpreted as actions. Let $Prg(\Sigma)$ be the set of programs on Σ, defined as regular expressions. A set of finite words, representing computation sequences, is associated with each program by the mapping $[[]] : Prg(\Sigma) \rightarrow 2^{\Sigma^*}$.

Let $\mathcal{P} = \{p_1, p_2, \ldots\}$ be a countable set of atomic propositions. The set of formulas of DLTL(Σ) is defined as follows:

$$\text{DLTL}(\Sigma) ::= p \mid \neg\alpha \mid \alpha \vee \beta \mid \alpha \mathcal{U}^{\pi} \beta$$

where $p \in \mathcal{P}$ and α, β range over DLTL(Σ), and π ranges over $Prg(\Sigma)$.

A model of DLTL(Σ) is a pair $M = (\sigma, V)$ where σ is an infinite sequence of actions and V is a valuation function. Given a model $M = (\sigma, V)$, a finite word $\tau \in prf(\sigma)$ (a finite prefix of σ), and a formula α, the satisfiability of a formula α at τ in M, written $M, \tau \models \alpha$, is defined as usual for the classical connectives. Moreover:

- $M, \tau \models \alpha \mathcal{U}^\pi \beta$ iff there exists $\tau' \in [[\pi]]$ such that $\tau\tau' \in prf(\sigma)$ and $M, \tau\tau' \models \beta$. Moreover, for every τ'' such that $\varepsilon \leq \tau'' < \tau'$, $M, \tau\tau'' \models \alpha$.

The formula $\alpha \mathcal{U}^\pi \beta$ is true at τ if "α until β" is true on a finite stretch of behaviour which is a computation sequence of the program π.

The derived modalities $\langle \pi \rangle$ and $[\pi]$ can be defined as follows: $\langle \pi \rangle \alpha \equiv T\mathcal{U}^\pi \alpha$ and $[\pi]\alpha \equiv \neg\langle \pi \rangle \neg\alpha$. Furthermore $\bigcirc$ (next), $\diamond$ and $\square$ of LTL can be defined as follows: $\bigcirc \alpha \equiv \bigvee_{a \in \Sigma} \langle a \rangle \alpha$, $\diamond \alpha \equiv T\mathcal{U}^{\Sigma^*} \alpha$, $\square \equiv \neg\diamond\neg\alpha$.

Let us now recall the definition of $DLTL^\otimes$ from [16]. Let $Loc = \{1, \ldots, K\}$ be a set of *locations*, the names of the agents. A *distributed alphabet* $\tilde{\Sigma} = \{\Sigma_i\}_{i=1}^K$ is a family of (possibly non-disjoint) alphabets, where Σ_i is the set of actions which require the participation of agent i. If an action a belongs to Σ_i and to Σ_j, the two agents i and j will synchronize on this action. Let $\Sigma = \bigcup_{i=1}^K \Sigma_i$.

Atomic propositions are introduced in a local fashion, by introducing a non-empty set of atomic propositions $\mathcal{P}$. For each proposition $p \in \mathcal{P}$ and agent $i \in Loc$, p_i represents the "local" view of the proposition p at i, and is evaluated in the local state of agent i.

The formulas in $DLTL^\otimes(\tilde{\Sigma})$ are boolean combinations of formulas with the main constraint that no nesting of modalities $\mathcal{U}_i$ and $\mathcal{U}_j$ (for $i \neq j$) is allowed. A model of $DLTL^\otimes(\tilde{\Sigma})$ is a pair $M = (\sigma, V)$, where $\sigma \in \Sigma^\infty$ and $V = \{V_i\}_{i=1}^K$ is a family of functions V_i, where each V_i is the valuation function for agent i. The satisfiability of formulas in a model is defined as in DLTL, except that propositions are evaluated locally and the sequence of actions σ is projected on the alphabet of local actions of each agent.

5.2   Action Theories and Protocols

Given a set of communicating agents, each agent participating in an action execution has its own local description of the action determining the effects on its local state. The global state of the system can be regarded as a set of local states, one for each agent i. The *action laws* and *causal laws* of agent i describe how the local state of i changes when an action $a \in \Sigma_i$ is executed. The underlying model of communication is the synchronous one: the communication action $comm\_act(i, j, m)$ (message m is sent by agent i to agent j) is shared by agent i (the sender) and agent j (the receiver) and executed synchronously by them. Their local states are updated separately, according to their action specification. Though, for simplicity, we adopt the synchronous model, an asynchronous model can be easily obtained by explicitly modelling the communication channels among the agents as distinct locations.

A *protocol* defines the meaning of communicative actions involved in the conversation. In particular, by adopting a social approach, the protocol describes the effects of each action on the social state of the system. These effects, including the creation of new commitments, can be expressed by means of *action laws*. Moreover, the protocol establishes a set of preconditions on the executability of actions (*permissions*), which can be expressed by means of *precondition laws*. Each agent has a local view of the social state and the execution of a communicative action can in general affect both the state of the sender and the state of the receiver. In particular, all agents can see the effects on the social state of the actions to which they participate.

For instance, in the example of Section 3 there are two agents, the personal assistant pa and the web service ws providing ticket booking. The conversation protocol for the two agents will be given through a set of action laws and constraints in the form of permissions or commitments. Since our theory does not allow to express a global states, the protocol will be projected on the local states of the participating agents. Observe that, since the two agents participate in all communicative actions, they have the same local view of the social state, and of the action laws and constraints of the protocol.

Let us assume that pa is the sender of the following actions[2] *queryIf(pa, ws, available(Film))*, *askBooking(pa, ws, Cinema)*, *give_cc(N)*, whereas the actions whose sender is ws are *inform(ws, pa, at(Film, Cinema))*, *inform(ws, pa, ¬ available(Film))*, *makeBooking(ws, pa, Cinema)*, *sendTicket(ws,pa)*. The effects of actions will be described by action laws such as (where $k = pa, ws$):

$$\Box_k([queryIf(pa, ws, available(Film))]_k asked(Film)$$
$$\Box_k([makeBooking(ws, pa, Cinema)]_k booked(Cinema)$$

where $asked(Film)$ and $booked(Cinema)$ are fluents of the social state.

Commitments can be effects of actions and will be represented by special fluents. They can be base-level commitments, of the form $C(ag_1, ag_2, action)$ (agent ag_1 is committed to agent ag_2 to execute the $action$), or they can be conditional commitments of the form $CC(ag_1, ag_2, p, action)$ (agent ag_1 is committed to agent ag_2 to execute $action$, if the condition p is brought about).

For instance, when the web service finds a cinema, it commits to make the booking, if the customer asks it. Furthermore it commits to send a ticket if the customer gives its credit card number.

$$\Box_k([inform(ws, pa, at(Film, Cinema))]_k$$
$$CC(ws, pa, askedBooking(Cinema), makeBooking(ws, pa, Cinema))$$
$$\wedge CC(ws, pa, cc\_given, sendTicket(ws, pa))$$

Some reasoning rules have to be defined for cancelling commitments when they have been fulfilled and for dealing with conditional commitments. For instance we can have the law (where $k = i, j$):

$$\Box_k((CC(i, j, p, a) \wedge \bigcirc_k p) \rightarrow \bigcirc_k (C(i, j, a) \wedge \neg CC(i, j, p, a)))$$

saying that a conditional commitment $CC(i, j, p, a)$ becomes a base-level commitment $C(i, j, a)$ when the condition p has been brought about. This law is a *causal law*.

The protocol can specify constraints (permissions) on the execution of actions by giving precondition to the actions. For instance ws will not send the ticket before the credit card number has been given:

$$\Box_k(\neg cc\_given \rightarrow [sendTicket(ws, pa)]_k \bot)$$

---

[2] This formulation does not correspond exactly to the diagram in Fig. 1.

meaning that $sendTicket(ws, pa)$ cannot be executed in those states in which $\neg cc\_given$ holds, i.e. cc_given is a precondition of the action.

An agent i *satisfies its commitments* when, for all commitments $C(i, j, a)$ in which agent i is the debtor, the formula:

$$\Box_i(C(i, j, a) \rightarrow \Diamond_i \langle a \rangle_i \top)$$

holds. Such a formula says that, when an agent is committed to execute action a, then it must eventually execute a[3].

Note that a protocol specified in this way is less rigid that the one given in Fig. 1, and can have different executions satisfying the action laws, preconditions and commitments. For instance the customer can leave the conversation before asking booking (the web service will have no base-level commitments to fulfill), or after asking booking and receiving confirmation, but before giving the credit card number (in this case the web service will only be committed to make booking, but not to send the ticket).

5.3   Reasoning about Protocols

Given a protocol, we denote with $\mathcal{D}_i$ the *domain description* of agent i, i.e. its action laws and causal laws[4], with $Perm_i$ the set of precondition laws of the actions whose sender is i, and with Com_i the set of all temporal formulas, as the one above, describing the satisfaction of the commitments of agent i.

If we do not know the behavior of any agent, we can only reason on the protocol by proving some properties of it, by assuming that all agents respect their permissions and commitments. This can be formalized as a validity check of the formula:

$$\bigwedge_j (\mathcal{D}_i \wedge Perm_j \wedge Com_j) \rightarrow p$$

where j ranges over all agents.

Following [29] we might also extract from the protocol a plan, that is an execution of the protocol, satisfying some given properties. Planning can be formulated in our theory as a satisfiability problem., i.e. as the problem of finding a model having the plan as a finite prefix. Assume instead that we know the behavior of some agents. For instance we are given a program (regular expression) π which describes the behavior of the web service. In this case we would like to verify that ws always satisfies its social fact, i.e. its permissions and commitments. Since we don't know anything about the behavior of pa, we can only assume that it respects its social facts.

---

[3] Here we assume that an agent cannot change its mind about commitments. However the language allows to define actions for manipulating commitments, for instance for cancelling them, as in [29].

[4] Actually $\mathcal{D}_i$ must also model the frame problem. To deal with it we make use [12] of a completion construction which, given a domain description, introduces frame axioms for all the fluents in the style of the successor state axioms introduced by Reiter [25] in the context of the situation calculus.

If $Prog_{ws}$ is the domain description of the behavior of ws, the following formula:

$$(\mathcal{D}_{ws} \wedge Prog_{ws} \wedge \mathcal{D}_{pa} \wedge Perm_{pa} \wedge Com_{pa}) \rightarrow (Perm_{ws} \wedge Com_{ps})$$

is valid if in all the executions of the system, in which agent ws respects its specification $Prog_{ws}$, and pa (whose internal program is unknown) respects the protocol specification (including its permissions and commitments), the permissions and commitment of agent ws are also satisfied. In general it is possible to prove that an agent is compliant (respects its "social facts") under the assumption that all other agents in the protocol are compliant.

The above verification and satisfiability problems can be solved by extending the standard approach for verification and model-checking of Linear Time Temporal Logic, based on the use of Büchi automata. As described in [17], the satisfiability problem for DLTL can be solved in deterministic exponential time, as for LTL, by constructing for each formula $\alpha \in DLTL(\Sigma)$ a Büchi automaton $\mathcal{B}_\alpha$ such that the language of ω-words accepted by $\mathcal{B}_\alpha$ is non-empty if and only if α is satisfiable. This result has been extended in [16] to $DLTL^\otimes$. The verification of a formula $\alpha \rightarrow \beta$ can be carried out by constructing the two Büchi automata for α and the *negation* of β. If the two automata have a common execution sequence, this sequence provides a counterexample for $\alpha \rightarrow \beta$. Thus $\alpha \rightarrow \beta$ is valid if the language accepted by the product of the two automata is empty. The similarities between the verification approach for LTL and that for $DLTL^\otimes$ suggest the possibility of using techniques and tools which have been developed for LTL. For instance, it is possible to extend to $DLTL^\otimes$ the efficient tableau-based algorithm of [10] for constructing the automaton on the fly.

6   Conclusions

In this paper we have presented various approaches to reasoning about conversation protocols within the framework of logic-based agent languages. We have shown that a theory of communicative actions can be formulated in the DyLOG logical framework, so as to allow the modelling of software agents that can interact with one another by a speech act based communication mechanism. This framework allows an agent to reason about conversation protocols with other agents. We have also presented an action theory based on the logic $DLTL^\otimes$ which provides a unified framework for specifying and verifying systems of communicating agents: Programs are expressed as regular expressions, (communicative) actions can be specified by means of action and precondition laws, properties of social facts can be specified by means of causal laws and constraints, and temporal properties can be expressed by means of the *until* operator.

A related approach is that of ConGolog [11], an extended version of the language Golog, that incorporates a rich account of concurrency, in which complex actions (plans) can be formalized as Algol-like programs in the situation calculus. A substantial difference with ConGolog, apart from the different logical foundation, is that here we model agents with their own local states, while in

Congolog the agents share a common global environment and all the properties are referred to a global state.

Other related proposals for the specification and verification of systems of communicating agents, based on a mentalistic approach, are presented [20] and [28]. The goal of [20] is to extend model checking to make it applicable to multi-agent systems, where agents have BDI attitudes. This is achieved by using a new logic which is the composition of two logics, one formalizing temporal evolution and the other formalizing BDI attitudes. In [28] agents are written in MABLE, an imperative programming language, and have a mental state. MABLE systems may be augmented by the addition of formal claims about the system, expressed using a quantified, linear time temporal BDI logic. [29] presents a social approach based on event calculus to protocol specification and execution. A different approach to specification and verification of web services is presented in [22], which shows how to encode in a Petri Net formalism a service description given in DAML-S, providing decision procedures for web service simulation, verification and composition. Guerin's thesis [14] defines an agent communication framework which gives agent communication a grounded declarative semantics, and defines different languages for agent programming, for specifying agent communication and social facts, and for expressing temporal properties.

References

1. M. Baldoni, C. Baroglio, A. Martelli, and V. Patti. Reasoning about self and others: communicating agents in a modal action logic. In C. Blundo and C. Laneve, editors, *Proc. of ICTCS'2003*, volume 2841 of *LNCS*. Springer, 2003.
2. M. Baldoni, C. Baroglio, and V. Patti. Applying logic inference techniques for gaining flexibility and adaptivity in tutoring systems. In C. Stephanidis, editor, *Proc. of the HCII 2003*, Crete, 2003. Lawrence Erlbaum Associates.
3. M. Baldoni, L. Giordano, A. Martelli, and V. Patti. Reasoning about Complex Actions with Incomplete Knowledge: A Modal Approach. In *Proc. of ICTCS'2001*, volume 2202 of *LNCS*, pages 405–425. Springer, 2001.
4. P. Bretier and D. Sadek. A rational agent as the kernel of a cooperative spoken dialogue system: implementing a logical theory of interaction. In *Intelligent Agents III*, volume 1193 of *LNAI*. Springer-Verlag, 1997.
5. J. Bryson, D. Martin, S. McIlraith, and L. A. Stein. Agent-based composite services in DAML-S: The behavior-oriented design of an intelligent semantic web, 2002.
6. R. Chinnici, M. Gudgin, J. J. Moreau, and S. Weerawarana. Web Services Description Language (WSDL) version 1.2, 2003. Working Draft.
7. The DAML-S coalition. DAML-S: Web service description for the semantic web. In *the 1st Int. Semantic Web Conference (ISWC)*, Sardinia, Italy, 2002.
8. F. Dignum and M. Greaves. Issues in agent communication. In *Issues in Agent Communication*, volume 1916 of *LNCS*, pages 1–16. Springer, 2000.
9. FIPA. FIPA 2000. Technical report, FIPA (Foundation for Intelligent Physical Agents), November 2000.
10. R. Gerth, D. Peled, M.Y.Vardi, and P. Wolper. Simple on-the-fly automatic verification of linear temporal logic. In *Proc. 15th Work. Protocol Specification, Testing and Verification*, Warsaw, 1995. North Holland.

11. G. De Giacomo, Y. Lespèrance, and H.J. Levesque. Congolog, a concurrent programming language based on the situation calculus. *Artificial Intelligence*, 121:109–169, 2000.
12. L. Giordano, A. Martelli, and C. Schwind. Reasoning about actions in dynamic linear time temporal logic. In *J. of the IGPL*, Vol. 9, No. 2, pp. 289-303, March 2001.
13. L. Giordano, A. Martelli, and C. Schwind. Specifying and Verifying Systems of Communicating Agents in a Temporal Action Logic. In A. Cappelli and F. Turini, editors, *Proc. of the 8th Conf. of AI*IA*, volume 2829 of *LNAI*. Springer, 2003.
14. F. Guerin. *Specifying Agent Communication Languages*. Phd thesis, Imperial College, London, April 2002.
15. D. Harel. First order dynamic logic. In D. Gabbay and F. Guenthner, editors, *Extensions of Classical Logic, Handbook of Philosophical Logic*, volume II, pages 497–604. D. Reidel, 1984.
16. J.G. Henriksen and P.S. Thiagarajan. A product version of dynamic linear time temporal logic. In *Proc. of CONCUR'97*, 1997.
17. J.G. Henriksen and P.S. Thiagarajan. Dynamic linear time temporal logic. *Annals of Pure and Applied logic*, 96(1-3):187–207, 1999.
18. A. Herzig and D. Longin. Beliefs dynamics in cooperative dialogues. In *Proc. of AMSTELOGUE 99*, 1999.
19. S.A. Mc Ilraith, T.C Son, and H. Zeng. Semantic web services. *IEEE Intelligent Systems*, pages 46–53, 2001.
20. F. Giunchiglia M. Benerecetti and L. Serafini. Model checking multiagent systems. *Journal of Logic and Computation*, 8(3):401–423, 1998.
21. A. Mamdani and J. Pitt. Communication protocols in multi-agent systems: A development method and reference architecture. In *Issues in Agent Communication*, volume 1916 of *LNCS*, pages 160–177. Springer, 2000.
22. S. Narayanan and S. A. McIlraith. Simulation, verification and automated composition of web services. In *Proc. of the Eleventh International World Wide Web Conference, WWW-11*, May 2002.
23. James H. Odell, H. Van Dyke Parunak, and Bernhard Bauer. Representing agent interaction protocols in UML. In *Agent-Oriented Software Engineering*, pages 121–140. Springer, 2001. http://www.fipa.org/docs/input/f-in-00077/.
24. V. Patti. *Programming Rational Agents: a Modal Approach in a Logic Programming Setting*. PhD thesis, Dipartimento di Informatica, Università degli Studi di Torino, Italy, 2002. Available at http://www.di.unito.it/~patti/.
25. R. Reiter. The frame problem in the situation calculus: a simple solution (sometimes) and a completeness result for goal regression. *Artificial Intelligence and Mathematical Theory of Computation*, pages 359–380, 1991.
26. F. Sadri, F. Toni, and P. Torroni. Dialogues for Negotiation: Agent Varieties and Dialogue Sequences. In *Proc. of ATAL'01*, Seattle, WA, 2001.
27. M. P. Singh. A social semantics for agent communication languages. In *Proc. of IJCAI-98 Workshop on Agent Communication Languages*, Berlin, 2000. Springer.
28. M. Wooldridge, M. Fisher, M.P. Huget, and S. Parsons. Model checking multi-agent systems with mable. In *Proc. of AAMAS'02*, pages 952–959, Bologna, 2002.
29. P. Yolum and M.P. Singh. Flexible protocol specification and execution: Applying event calculus planning using commitments. In *Proc. of AAMAS'02*, pages 527–534, Bologna, Italy, 2002.

A Visual Language for Web Querying
and Reasoning

Sacha Berger, François Bry, and Sebastian Schaffert

Institut für Informatik, Ludwig-Maximilians-Universität München
Oettingenstr. 67, D-80538 München, Germany
{bergers,bry,schaffer}@informatik.uni-muenchen.de

Abstract. As XML is increasingly being used to represent information
on the Web, query and reasoning languages for such data are needed.
This article argues that in contrast to the *navigational* approach taken
in particular by XPath and XQuery, a *positional* approach as used in
the language Xcerpt is better suited for a straightforward visual representation. The constructs of the pattern- and rule-based query language
Xcerpt are introduced and it is shown how the visual representation
visXcerpt renders these constructs to form a visual query language for
XML.

1   Introduction

Five years after its initial specification in 1998, XML [1] has become the de
facto standard for data exchange. It is nowadays increasingly being used for
representing semistructured databases, Web documents, and in particular meta
information like ontological data (as in OWL [2]) or browsing contexts and user
models [3]. There is hence a need for languages that are suitable for both querying
and reasoning with semistructured data.

Many existing query languages, in particular the W3C proposals XPath and
XQuery, are navigational in the sense that their variable binding paradigm requires the programmer to specify path navigations through the document (or
data item). In contrast, some other languages – such as UnQL [4] and Xcerpt
[5] – are pattern-based: their variable binding paradigm is that of mathematical
logics, i.e. the programmer specifies patterns (or terms) including variables. This
difference is discussed in Section 2.

In this article, it is argued that the pattern-based paradigm is particularly
well-suited as a base for a visual query language for semistructured databases.
The reason is that patterns are form-like two dimensional structures that conceptually are very close to two dimensional visual representations. Arguably,
every visual or graphical language for XML and/or semistructured data (such
as XML-GL [6], GraphLog [7], VXT [8], BBQ [9] and Xing [10]) as well as the
veteran language QBE and improvements thereof (such as MS Access and similar products) might be seen as having an (in general implicit) pattern-based
language as an (in general unconscious) foundation.

F. Bry et al. (Eds.): PPSWR 2003, LNCS 2901, pp. 99–112, 2003.

Interestingly, and maybe supporting the last above-mentioned claim, a visual language for a pattern-based textual query and transformation language can be developed simply by specifying a visual rendering (in contrast to a complex transformation) of the textual programs very much like a CSS stylesheet specifies a layout for an HTML document.

Besides the pattern-based nature, another property of the Xcerpt language is of particular interest to visual querying: rule-based queries with a clear separation of condition and result allows for a rather natural visual representation, since an "if ... then ..." is easily conveyed even by novice users.

This article is organised as follows. Section 2 provides a discussion of the navigational and positional approaches for query languages. The basic elements of the declarative, rule- and pattern-based language Xcerpt are then introduced in Section 3. In Section 4 it is shown how semistructured data in general and the Xcerpt constructs in particular are visually represented in the language visX-cerpt. Section 5 finally gives a summary about further and related work.

2   Positional vs. Navigational Data Selection

Essential to querying semistructured data is the selection of data items in a document (i.e. rooted graph). Most widespread query languages for XML – e.g. XQuery – rely on path selections expressed using XPath (or similar approaches). XPath-like languages provide with constructs like regular expressions and wild cards for specifying paths through a rooted graph. For instance, the XPath expression /a[b]//c means "find the document nodes labelled c that can be reached from the document root via a child node labelled a having itself a child node labelled b and having the c-labelled nodes as descendants". Such node selections can be called navigational.

For simple queries and transformations, the navigational approach is very natural and results in simple programs. For more complex queries, especially for queries involving several variables, the navigational approach often leads to intricate programs.

Furthermore, the intertwining of construction and query parts in languages such as XQuery and most of its precursors often yields programs that are difficult to visualise properly.

Also, the possibility to specify forward and reverse axes in path languages like XPath might further increase the complexity of query programs and an equivalent query with only forward axes is often more intuitive.

A further important aspect of navigational node selections is that they do not easily support the selection of several related nodes at once. Such multiple node selections, however, are rather natural and are required by most non-trivial queries. This is e.g. the case when one looks for bibliography entries combining several aspects such as an author's name, a keyword in the title, and a year of publication. Everyone familiar with bibliographies immediately "visualises" the shape or pattern of such a retrieval request and the respective positions of the variables it refers to. Arguably, pattern-based or positional query and transformation languages such as Xcerpt reflect and convey such an intuitive "visualisation".

With the positional query and transformation language Xcerpt the nodes to be selected are specified by variables in patterns called query terms. Query patterns are related to other patterns called construct terms through their common variables. The Xcerpt construct relating a construct term to a query expression consisting of AND and/or OR connected query terms is a rule. These concepts are introduced in the next section.

For querying semistructured data, the positional approach has been suggested first with UnQL [4] and XML-QL [11]. In common programming, the positional approach finds its roots in Functional and Logic Programming. Arguably, both query languages QBE and SQL can be seen as positional languages.

3   Xcerpt's Main Constructs

An Xcerpt program may consist of at least one goal and of some (maybe zero) rules. Goals and rules are built up from database, query and construct terms that are first introduced. Note that besides the "abstract" syntax presented here, Xcerpt also has an XML syntax which is not described here for space reasons.

3.1   Database, Query, and Construct Terms

Common to all terms is that they represent tree-like (or graph-like) structures. Square brackets (i.e. [ ]) denote ordered term specification (as in standard XML), i.e. the matching subterms in the database are required to be in the same order as in the query term. Curly braces (i.e. { }) denote unordered term specification (as is common in databases), i.e. the matching subterms in the database may be in arbitrary order.

Single (square or curly) braces (i.e. [ ] and { }) are used to denote that a matching term must contain matching subterms for all subterms of a term and may not contain additional subterms (total term specification). Double braces (i.e. [[ ]] and {{ }}) are used to denote that the database term may contain additional subterms as long as matching partners for all subterms of the query term are found (partial term specification).

Graph structure is expressed using a reference mechanism. The construct id @ t is used as a defining occurrence of the identifier id and the construct ^id is used as a referring occurrence.

Database Terms are used to represent XML documents and the data items of a semistructured database. They are similar to ground functional programming expressions and logical atoms. Database terms may only contain the single square and curly braces described above.

A database is a (multi-)set of database terms (e.g. the Web). Note, however, that a single database term is often used to represent what is commonly referred to as a "database", as shown in the following example.

Example: a database term representing a bibliography consisting of several books. Note the use of references to share common data. Also note that the author list for a book is ordered while the data in general is unordered:

```
bib {
  authors {
    a1 @ author {
      name { "Serge Abiteboul" }, publications { ^b1, ^b2 } },
    a2 @ author {
      name { "Peter Buneman" }, publications { ^b1 }          },
    a3 @ author {
      name { "Dan Suciu" }, publications { ^b1 }              },
    a4 @ author {
      name { "Richard Hull" },  publications { ^b2 }          },
    a5 @ author {
      name { "Victor Vianu" }, publications { ^b2 }           }
  },
  b1 @ book {
    title { "Data on the Web" },
    authors [ ^a1, ^a2, ^a3 ],
    price { "69.95" }
  },
  b2 @ book {
    title { "Foundations of Databases" },
    editors [ ^a1, ^a4, ^a5 ],
    price { "29.00" }
  }
  ...
}
```

Database terms induce a graph in a straightforward manner. Figure 1 shows a (incomplete) graph representation of the book database of the previous example.

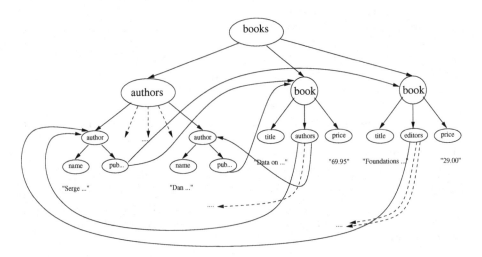

Fig. 1. Graph induced by the book database (incomplete). References to parts not illustrated are shown as dashed arrows.

Note that database terms do not cover all constructs found in XML. Constructs like Attributes or Processing Instructions are intentionally left out because they are either easy to model in the existing database terms or do not add important information to the data represented.

Query Terms are similar to non-ground functional programming expressions and logical atoms. Extending the database terms, query terms have the following properties:

– in a query term, partial specifications omitting subterms irrelevant to the query are possible (indicated by double square brackets or curly braces),
– in a query term, it is possible to specify subterms at arbitrary depth (indicated by the keyword desc).
– a query term may contain term variables and label variables to "select" data from the database (variables are written in upper case letters below)

As Xcerpt queries are pattern-based, a query term should resemble the database as closely as possible, while leaving out such parts that are irrelevant to the query.

The reference mechanism using ^id and id @ t has the same significance as the parent-child edge. In the following example, the right hand side shows a query which matches a parent-child edge with a reference edge in the database.

Example: Left: Select title and author pairs for each book. Right: Select pairs of authors that have written at least one book together.

```
bib {{
  book {{
    var T ~> title {{ }},
    authors {{ var A }}
  }}
}}
```

```
bib {{ authors  {{
  author {{
    var Author ~> name {{ }},
    publications {{
      book {{
        authors {{ var CoAuthor ~> author {{ }} }}
      }} }}
    }}
  }} }}
```

The Xcerpt construct $X \leadsto t$ (read "as") serves to associate a query term to a variable, so as to specify a restriction of its bindings. The Xcerpt construct desc (read "descendant" – not illustrated above) is used to specify subterms at arbitrary depth.

Query terms are unified with database or construct terms using a non-standard unification called simulation unification, which has been investigated in [12]. Simulation unification is based on graph simulation [13] which is similar to graph homomorphisms.

The outcome of unifying a query term with a database term are bindings for the variables in the query term. Applying these bindings to the query term results in a ground query term which is simulated (in the sense of [13]) in the database term.

Construct Terms serve to reassemble variable (the bindings of which are specified in query terms) so as to construct new database terms. They may only contain single brackets and variables, but no partial specification or variable restrictions. The rationale of this is to keep variable specifications within query terms, ensuring a strict separation of purposes between query and construct terms.

Example: Create an Author-Title pair wrapped in a "result" element:

```
result {
  var A, var T
}
```

In a construct term, the Xcerpt construct *all t* serves to collect (in the construct term) all instances of *t* that can be generated by different variable bindings for the variables in *t* (returned by the associated query terms in which they occur). Likewise, *some n t* serves to collect at most *n* instances of *t* that can be generated in the same manner.

Example: Create a list publications for each author and a list of authors for each publication:

```
results {            results {
  result {             result {
    var A,                 all var A,
    all var T              var T
  }                     }
}                    }
```

Example: The following construct term collects all title/author pairs for the previous query:

```
results { all result { var A, var T } }
```

The constructs *all* and *some n* may be nested to form more complex results. The following example shows the usefulness of nesting:

Example: Assuming the previous query, the following construct term collects all titles for each author:

```
results { all result { var A, all var T } }
```

Positioning the nested *all* around the *A* yields "all authors for each title" as a result:

```
results { all result { all var A, var T } }
```

3.2   Queries

A query is a connection of zero or more query terms using the n-ary connectives and and or. A query is always (implicitly or explicitly) associated with a resource. A resource may be the program itself, an external Xcerpt program or an (XML or other) document specified by a URI (uniform resource identifier).

Variables occurring in more than one query terms in an and connected query evaluate similar to an equijoin in relational databases.

Example: Query for the prices of books in two different book stores (specified by the resource identifier A and B).

```
and {
  bib {{
    book {{ var T ↝ title{{ }}, var Pa ↝ price{{ }} }}
  }} in http://www.a.com,
  reviews {{
    entry {{ var T ↝ title{{ }}, var Pb ↝ price{{ }} }}
  }} in http://www.b.com
}
```

If a query does not explicitly have an associated resource, the resource specification is implicit and inherited from the parent. If none of the parents have a resource specification, or the query does not have a parent, the queried resource is the program itself (i.e. the heads of the rules and possibly database terms contained in the program – see "Rule Chaining" below).

Note that it is possible to use curly and square braces in *and* and *or* connections to specify that the evaluation order is of importance or not. This may serve as an indication to the evaluation engine whether certain optimizations are applicable or not.

3.3   Construct-Query Rules, Goals

An Xcerpt program consists of zero or more construct-query rules, one or more goals and zero or more database terms. Both rules and goals have the form

$$\text{Construct Term} \leftarrow \text{Query Part}$$

where a construct term is constructed depending on the evaluation of a query part.

Example: A rule that creates a price summary for the books in the two databases A and B:

```
rule {
  cons {
    summary {
      all book { var T, price-at-A { var Pa }, price-at-B { var Pb } }
    }
  },
  query {
    and {
      bib {{
        book {{ var T ↝ title{{ }}, price{{ var Pa }} }}
      }} in A,
      reviews {{
        entry {{ var T ↝ title{{ }}, price{{ var Pb }} }}
      }} in B
    }
  }
}
```

A rule can be seen as a "view" specifying how t^c-shaped documents can be obtained by evaluating the query part against a Web resource (e.g. an XML document or a database).

In addition to the form above, goals are always (explicitly or implicitly) associated with an output resource. This resource specifies where to "write" the resulting database terms. If not explicitly specified, the output resource defaults to stdout, writing all output to the console.

Rule Chaining. In addition to querying external resources, a query may also be evaluated against the program. In such a case, the heads of the program rules (but not of the goals) are queried and the associated rule is evaluated. Both forward and backward chaining are feasible.

Forward Chaining. In a forward chaining approach, rules are evaluated iteratively against the current set of database terms until saturation is achieved. Forward Chaining is useful for instance for materializing views and for view maintenance.

Backward Chaining. Backward Chaining is a goaldriven approach. Beginning with the query part of the goal, program rules are selected if they are relevant for "proving" a query term. The query term in question is then replaced by the query part of the selected rule. Backward Chaining is useful when the expected result is small in comparison with the number of possible results of the program.

Backward Chaining in Xcerpt following the SLD resolution used in e.g. Prolog, with some major modifications to cover constructs like all and some and to cope with multiple results of a simulation unification.

4   visXcerpt: A Visual Rendering of Xcerpt

The main goal of visual languages in general is to ease the use of a technology especially among novice users since it avoids many common errors by abstracting from the textual syntax. The Web context in particular demands for query technology that is easy to use even by non-programmers, since there are always queries not forseen by developers. Hence, a visual language would likely be well accepted among many Web users.

For visual query languages it is considered to be important to have a strong visual relationship between queries and queried data or query results. A natural approach is to provide some sort of example of a valid result as query as first presented in QBE. Xcerpt query patterns with positional variables can be seen as samples of valid source data items, where some parts are left out and others represented by variables. Construction patterns can be seen as samples or templates of result data items.

The syntax and semantics of Xcerpt as a whole is well suited as foundation for a visual language. As a consequence, textual Xcerpt's visual counterpart visXcerpt can be conceived as a mere rendering instead of a fully novel language. This rendering might be seen as an advanced (because of the dynamic features) layout.

In the following, it is illustrated how the textual Xcerpt constructs have their visual counterparts in visXcerpt. A generic term representation is introduced first, followed by the rule- and query constructs used to form Xcerpt programs and by dynamic aspects of the visual representation.

4.1 Visual Representation of Terms

Xcerpt **terms** (i.e. elements) are visualised as boxes. A term label (or tag) is attached as a tab on the top of its associated box. visXcerpt has features for handling attributes and text. Attributes are placed in a two-column table with names in the left column and values in the right column. The attribute table appears first in a box and is omitted if there are no attributes. Direct subterms (i.e. children) are visualised the same way as sub- or child boxes. Child boxes are arranged vertically in a parent box. For better distinction, they are coloured differently. Figure 2 on the right illustrates this nesting on the Xcerpt term $f[[a\{"TextA"\}, b["TextB"], c[["TextA"]]]]$.

Different box borders are used as visual counterparts to the **Xcerpt parentheses** $\{\{~\}\}$, $[[~]]$, $\{~\}$, and $[~]$. Ordered or unordered children are indicated graphically by an icon (ascending bars represent ordered, random bars unordered) at the top right corner of a box. Optionally, partial and total matching can also be indicated graphically by an icon (see also Figure 2 on the right).

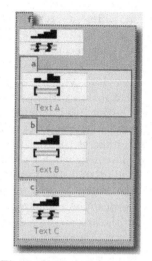

Fig. 2. visXcerpt representation of a term using different combinations of ordered/unordered and partial/total.

Visual Identifiers and References. Beyond the hierarchical structure that terms can express, Xcerpt provides a reference mechanism based on IDs associated to terms (like $id@t$) and references (like $\uparrow id$).

Figure 3 on the right illustrates the visual representation of a database term containing references and both ordered and unordered content. The references are represented with an icon resembling a pointer and referenced terms carry the anchor name in the title tab.

Note that visXcerpt also provides navigational support for references by representing those constructs as hyperlinks (see dynamic aspects below).

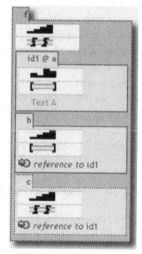

Fig. 3. identifiers appear in the tab, references are visualised by icons.

Visual Query and Construction Patterns.
The constructs presented so far are the foundation of visXcerpt database terms. They can be used to visualise any XML data as well as any Xcerpt data. Visualisation of further Xcerpt constructs are irrelevant for pure data and are distinguished visually from the former constructs – they use reserved colours (black, white and gray) and in some cases textual adornment with a reserved text style (italic font). Those textual extensions always match to the corresponding Xcerpt keywords.

- variables are represented as black boxes with the variable name written in white in the box. If a variable is restricted to a term (by the ~> construct), this term appears within the box of the variable. The variable A in Figure 4 illustrates this representation on the example f[[desc var A -> a{{ }}]]. The variable A is restricted to such terms that match with desc a{{ }}.
- The desc (descendant) construct is rendered as gray box with strong bevelled border (a visual metaphor for depth) and the keyword descendant is written in italic at the top (see Figure 4).
- The constructs all, and and or are rendered as white boxes with black border and textual adornment. To further distinguish disjunctions and conjunctions the content of or is arranged horizontally while the content of and is arranged vertically. A visual representation of all and and can be seen in Figure 5 (left of the arrow).

4.2 visXcerpt Programs

Visual Construct-Query Rules and Goals are visualized in visXcerpt by connecting a query part with a construct term by means of an arrow, so as to emphasize the fact that in an Xcerpt rule a result follows from a query. As can be seen in Figure 5, the construct term is positioned left of the arrow while the query part is positioned right of the arrow.

Query and/or construct parts may contain resource specifications. Since a resource specification has a scope, it is indicated as a box containing all parts for which they are valid. The resource itself is specified in the title of this box (see Figure 5).

Fig. 4. descendant as bevelled box, variables as black box with white text.

Visual Programs are seen as documents of visXcerpt construct-query rules. They are arranged vertically as a list of rules.

4.3 Dynamic Features

A static visualisation as described above is not sufficient for an interactive query system that should provide features which enhance the usability and allow for editing visXcerpt programs. The visXcerpt prototype provides features that allow for easier navigation and improved comprehension (browsing aspects). Furthermore, an editor is provided as well as the possibility to "try out" programs while developing them.

Browsing Aspects. When viewing (and editing) documents, an important aspect are properties that allow navigation and different views upon the data. In visXcerpt, such properties are referred to as browsing aspects. In particular, visXcerpt provides means for:

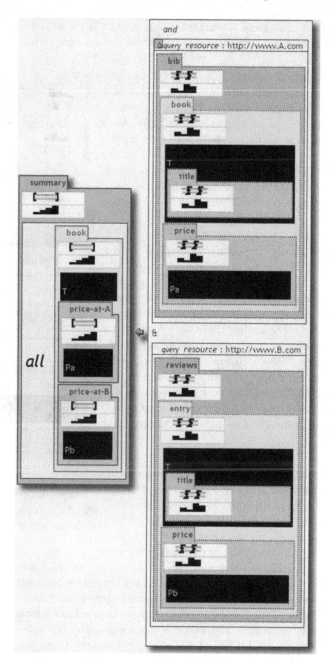

Fig. 5. A visual representation of the Xcerpt rule from Section 3.3. The construct term is left of the arrow while the query part – consisting of an *and* connection of two query terms – is right of the arrow. Note that the Xcerpt-specific constructs not found in database terms (e.g. variables) are always displayed in shades of black and white.

PartialViewing. For large documents, only a part is displayed in the viewer. Vertical and horizontal scrollbars allow to move the current view.

Information Hiding. In large documents, it is desirable to be able to hide such information that is irrelevant for the current task. In visXcerpt, clicking on the title tab of an element "folds" the element together with all its contents such that only the title tab remains (in a shaded color). Any subsequent element boxes below the same parent element move upwards such that their title tab is besides the hidden elements (Illustrated in Figure 6 on the right).

Fig. 6. information hiding: element "b" is folded.

References. Visually depicting references with icons and identifiers only (as described above) is dissatisfactory, since it does not model the graph structure appropriately. Instead of further depicting references visually, visXcerpt "moves them into hyperspace" by representing them as hyperlinks. That is, by clicking on a reference the visualisation scrolls or focuses on the occurence of the referenced element. Hovering with the pointer above a term with ID highlights all occurrences of references to it. Backward navigation to references is supported through a popup menu of elements containing an ID.

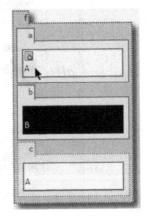

Fig. 7. variable highlighting of the variable "A".

Variable Highlighting. In (vis)Xcerpt rules, all variables that appear in the head of a rule are also required to appear in its body. Moreover, the same variable may occur in several parts of the body, even several times within the same query term. To support the user in designing visXcerpt rules, all occurrences of a variable are highlighted by inverting its color when the mouse hovers over one occurrence of the variable (see Figure 7 on the right). This eases the comprehension of term equality in positional queries and thus allows the user to recognize connections between different parts of a rule or within a term.

The reference visualisation and variable handling is similar indeed and future implementations of variable visualisation may rely on the more general reference mechanism.

Editing Capabilities. As visXcerpt is an editor for tree structured data, many of the editing capabilities commonly found in plain text editors have only limited applicability. Thus, in addition to common text editing primitives (like "cut", "paste"), the visXcerpt editor provides primitives that are suitable for insertion of subtrees and nodes (e.g. "paste into at beginning/end" or "paste before/after", illustrated in Figure 8 on the right).

When build documents, the visXcerpt editor follows a "copy and paste" paradigm with a template area where templates of common elements like "element" or "variable" can be copied from and inserted into the edited document. A "drag and drop" paradigm has also been considered but is not yet implemented due to technical reasons.

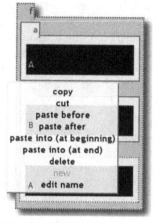

Interactive Queries. When designing programs, it is often necessary to be able to run the program for test purposes as well as restrict the test to certain parts of the program. The visXcerpt interface allows both:

Fig. 8. Editing capabilities: context menu.

- A program can be evaluated at any time, provided its semantics is meaningful (the visual interface ensures that the syntax is always correct). For a program to be evaluated, it must contain at least one goal. Depending on the output resource specified for the goal, the result of the evaluation is either displayed in a new windows in the generic visXcerpt term representation or written to the specified output resource.

- A single query term can be evaluated against the program to test only specific parts. This query term is evaluated against all rules and the result is displayed as a disjunction of alternative variable bindings in a new window.

5   Related and Future Work

There is a large number of XML query languages available on the Web, most of them based on a navigational selection of nodes. Most notably, the W3C has issued the XQuery, XSLT and XPath recommendations [14]. The pattern-based approach to querying semistructured data has first been presented in the language UnQL [4]. However, UnQL rules may not be connected by chaining and lack many of the constructs found in Xcerpt. Several publications concerning the language design and semantics of Xcerpt are available, in particular[5, 15, 12, 16].

Visual XML query languages that the authors are aware of are XML-GL [6], GraphLog [7], VXT [8], BBQ [9] and Xing [10]. Most of these languages visualize the XML document as a tree (i.e. nodes connected with arrows or similar). While on first look this appears to be very concise, it does not scale well to larger documents and queries. Thus, visXcerpt uses the concept of nested boxes as visual representation, which is borrowed from the language Xing and enhanced in many ways in the visXcerpt viewer/editor.

Work on Xcerpt is currently conducted to formally provide a model-theoretic semantics (see [16]) and a reasoning calculus. Future work will investigate Xcerpt as a reasoning language in a Web environment and add additional language features like arithmetics, basic and complex types, constraints, etc.

The visXcerpt prototype will be extended by adding improved browsing facilities, like browsing from an element to such elements that refer to it. Furthermore, investigating suitable commands for editing tree- and graph-structured data is of major interest. As the current visXcerpt editor is implemented prototypically in HTML and JavaScript, a more efficient implementation is also sought for, possibly by extending already-existing XML editors.

References

1. W3 Consortium http://www.w3.org/TR/REC-xml: Extensible Markup Language (XML) 1.0, Second Edition. (2000)
2. W3 Consortium http://www.w3.org/TR/owl-ref/: OWL Web Ontology Language Reference. (2003) W3C Working Draft, 31 March 2003.
3. Bry, F., Kraus, M.: Position Paper: Style Sheets for Context Adaptation. In: W3C Delivery Context Workshop. (2002)
4. Buneman, P., Fernandez, M., Suciu, D.: UnQL: A Query Language and Algebra for Semistructured Data Based on Structural Recursion. VLDB Journal **9** (2000)
5. Bry, F., Schaffert, S.: A Gentle Introduction into Xcerpt, a Rule-based Query and Transformation Language for XML. In: Proc. Int. Workshop on Rule Markup Languages for Business Rules on the Semantic Web. (2002) (invited article).
6. Ceri, S., Damiani, E., Fraternali, P., Paraboschi, S., Tanca, L.: XML-GL: A Graphical Language for Querying and Restructuring XML Documents. In: Sistemi Evoluti per Basi di Dati. (1999)
7. Consens, M., Mendelzon, A.: Expressing Structural Hypertext Queries in GraphLog. In: Second ACM Hypertext Conf. (1989) 269–292
8. Pietriga, E., Quint, V., Vion-Dury, J.Y.: VXT: A Visual Approach to XML Transformations. In: ACM Symp. on Document Engineering. (2001)
9. Munroe, K.D., Papakonstantinou, Y.: BBQ: A Visual Interface for Integrated Browsing and Querying of XML. In: VDB. (2000)
10. Erwig, M.: A Visual Language for XML. In: IEEE Symp. on Visual Languages. (2000) 47–54
11. Deutsch, A., Fernandez, M., Florescu, D., Levy, A., Suciu, D.: A Query Language for XML. In: Proc. of Eighth Int. WWW Conf. (1999)
12. Bry, F., Schaffert, S.: Towards a Declarative Query and Transformation Language for XML and Semistructured Data: Simulation Unification. In: Proc. Int. Conf. on Logic Programming (ICLP). LNCS 2401, Springer-Verlag (2002)
13. Abiteboul, S., Buneman, P., Suciu, D.: Data on the Web. From Relations to Semistructured Data and XML. Morgan Kaufmann (2000)
14. World Wide Web Consortium (W3C) http://www.w3.org/. (2002)
15. Bry, F., Schaffert, S.: The XML Query Language Xcerpt: Design Principles, Examples, and Semantics. In: Proc. 2nd Int. Workshop "Web and Databases". LNCS 2593, Erfurt, Germany, Springer-Verlag (2002)
16. Bry, F., Schaffert, S.: An Entailment for Reasoning on the Web. Technical Report PMS-FB-2003-5, Institute for Computer Science, University of Munich (2003)

XML Document Adaptation Queries (XDAQ): An Approach to Adaptation Reasoning Using Web Query Languages

Michael Kraus[1,2], François Bry[1], and Kazuhiro Kitagawa[2]

[1] Institute of Computer Science, University of Munich
{michael.kraus,francois.bry}@informatik.uni-muenchen.de
[2] Graduate School of Media and Governance, Keio University

Abstract. Adaptive web applications combine data retrieval on the web with reasoning so as to generate context dependent contents. The data is retrieved either as content or as context specifications. Content data is, for example, fragments of a textbook or e-commerce catalogue, whereas context data is, for example, a user model or a device profile. Current adaptive web applications are often implemented using ad hoc and heterogeneous techniques. This paper describes a novel approach called "XML Document Adaptation Queries (XDAQ)" requiring less heterogeneous software components. The approach is based on using a web query language for data retrieval (content as well as context) and on a novel generic formalism to express adaptation. The approach is generic in the sense that it is applicable with all web query and transformation languages, for example with XQuery and XSLT.

1 Introduction

Adaptive web applications combine data retrieval on the web with reasoning so as to generate context dependent contents. Data is retrieved either as content (for example fragments of a textbook or e-commerce catalogue), or as context specifications (for example a user model or a device profile). For example, the presentation of learning material for students (content) may be adapted to the student's estimated knowledge about the topics (context) [16]. Current adaptive web applications [8,6] are often implemented using ad hoc and heterogeneous techniques.

This paper describes a novel approach called "XML Document Adaptation Queries (XDAQ)" requiring less heterogeneous software components. The approach is based on using a web query language for (content as well as context) data retrieval and on a (novel) generic formalism to express adaptation. The approach is generic in the sense that it is applicable with all web query and transformation languages, for example with XQuery and XSLT.

F. Bry et al. (Eds.): PPSWR 2003, LNCS 2901, pp. 113–127, 2003.

The benefits and contributions of XDAQ are as follows:

- The goal is not to implement a single or several adaptive web applications, but to provide a framework that can be used to implement a wide variety of adaptive web applications, ranging from educational hypermedia to e-commerce systems and device-independent web applications for desktop and mobile computers. Sample applications, however, will be implemented to test and improve the XDAQ approach.
- XDAQ does not rely on a single, fixed query language. XDAQ can be used with a wide variety of web query languages, among other with XQuery and XSLT. XDAQ can also be applied with more than one query language simultaneously.
- XDAQ is a generic formalism for expressing adaptation of arbitrary XML documents such as XML data and databases, HTML documents, XSLT transformations, XSL documents, or XLink linkbases.
- Non-intrusive adaptation rules separate between web contents and adaptation rules. This greatly improves modularity of adaptive web application modeling and helps to avoid unwanted redundancy.
- XDAQ defines a formal model of how to process XML documents together with adaptation rules, third-party links and style rules, thus avoiding existing ambiguities when combining these approaches.

There are also two extensions which further broaden the application spectrum of XDAQ. The first extension allows XDAQ adaptation rules not only to be used with XML documents, but also with non-XML data like CSS style sheets, XPath expressions, or URIs. The approach is based on the idea of separating data model and syntax of those languages, and providing a data model based on XML while keeping the original syntax.

The second extension is a processing model which allows processing of adaptation rules to be distributed between client, server and proxy. The distribution is determined by the user's privacy settings, and device characteristics like network bandwidth and processing power. This approach allows XDAQ to be used for both typical client-side adaptations like in educational hypermedia [8], as well as typical server-side adaptations like in tourist information systems [6]. Furthermore, this approach enables a single adaptive web application to be used both in desktop environments (fast network, powerful clients) and mobile environments (slow network, slim clients). For simplicity, these two extensions are not described in the present paper.

The rest of this paper is organized as follows: The next four sections introduce step by step the concepts of XDAQ. Section 6 then discusses how the XDAQ framework can be used to model complex adaptive web applications. Finally, section 7 briefly presents an XDAQ prototype and future research issues.

2   Modeling Context Information

Adaptation is based on *context information*. XDAQ assumes context information to be stored in one or more *context documents*. These documents are referenced by URIs (see section 3), therefore they can be located not only on the client or the server of the adaptive web application, but anywhere on the web. Context documents can be modeled using XML, RDF, or any other web modeling language.

The following is an example of a (freely shaped) XML context document which will be used by the examples in the rest of the paper:

```
<context>
  <knowledge topic="html">beginner</knowledge>      <!-- User Data -->
  <language>en</language>
  <language>ja</language>
  <interest field="music">Pop</interest>
  <device type="large"/>                             <!-- Device Data -->
  <device pixel_width="1024"/>
  <device pixel_height="768"/>
  <time value="12:56"/>                              <!-- Environment Data -->
  <date>30 June 2003</date>
  <temperature value="24C"/>
  <location value="Yokohama"/>
  <situation>meeting</situation>
  <history>                                          <!-- Browsing History -->
    <page uri="http://xyz.com/index.html">
      <page uri="http://xyz.com/page1.html">
        <page uri="http://xyz.com/page2.html"/>
      </page>
      <page uri="http://xyz.com/page3.html"/>
    </page>
  </history>
</context>
```

Context information considered in this paper covers the following (the list does not preclude further context information that is not explicitly mentioned in this paper to be used with the XDAQ approach):

- User: knowledge about certain topics (beginner about HTML), language competence (speaks English and Japanese), or interests (pop music).
- Device: type ("large" device), resolution (1024x768 pixels).
- Environment: date and time, temperature, location, situation (meeting).
- Browsing history

The term *context information,* as it is used in this paper, is an abstraction of notions like user profile and device profile, which are used in other approaches for adaptive (web) applications [2,17]. Context information subsumes these notions, and even goes beyond them: Any data found on the web can be used as context information, not only data about the user or his device.

Context documents are typically administered by the adaptive web application itself, but this could also be done by the web browser or by the operating system. Maintaining and updating context information can be done in three ways. Most information, like device data, environment data, the browsing history and part of the user data can be updated automatically. Information like the *situation* can be explicitly set by the user. Data like test results and the user's knowledge or interest on certain topics can be updated by the adaptive web application. The user's interests could also be deduced from the browsing history, for example.

The definition of suitable standard vocabularies describing context information for certain domains has been identified as one of the most urgent tasks within the web context adaptation community [17,11]. There is a common need for a standardized and simple vocabulary which ensures interoperability, and which allows for proprietary extensions for domain-specific or application-specific context information. In spite of this, it is a major goal of XDAQ to provide adaptation methods that are independent from the actual vocabulary of the context information, and thus can be used with a wide variety of adaptive web applications. XDAQ makes no further assumption about context information than that it is represented in a language like XML or RDF. While the examples in this paper only use XML as language to represent context information, the XDAQ approach can also be used with the existing CC/PP or UAProf [18] vocabularies, which are based on RDF.

Context information may be modeled flat (like the *user*, *device*, and *environment* sections), or structured (like the *browsing history* section). Many traditional adaptive hypermedia systems [8,16], as well as the CC/PP framework [13], which is targeted at device independence, simply use flat lists of property/value pairs for representing context information. In contrast to this, XDAQ also allows to model complex structured context information. In conjunction with XDAQ's approach of modeling adaptation based on web query languages, this enables adaptation not only to rely on the actual content of the context information, but also on structural information. For example, adaptation could rely on certain browsing patterns of the user, which can be queried from the structure (not the contents) of the browsing history.

An advantage of allowing for freely shaped contexts is that the roles of context and content can be exchanged, if the application requires it. Consider for example the browsing history information from above. This information can be used by an educational hypermedia application to make recommendations to the user about the suitability of yet unvisited pages, like it is done in [8]. In this case, the browsing history serves as context information. Another application, for example the history function of a web browser, might use the same information but present it directly to the user. In this case, the browsing history serves as content. Not requiring a fixed shape or vocabulary for context information makes it possible to change the angle from which information is looked at, context or content.

3   Expressing Adaptation with Query Languages

With XDAQ, adaptation is expressed through *adaptation rules* of the form:

```
<rule>
  <href>URI</href>
  <if context="URI" type="language">query</if>
  <copy context="URI" type="language">query</copy>
</rule>
```

There are two kinds of adaptation rules: *if-rules* and *copy-rules*. These rules each consist of a set of *target node bindings* and a set of *queries*. The target node bindings attach an adaptation rule to a set of nodes of one or more XML documents, called the *target nodes* of that rule. The documents containing the target nodes are called *target documents* of that rule. The queries each consist of a reference to a context document, called the *context document* of that query, and an expression of a web query language like XPath, XSLT, or XQuery. It is possible to use more than one query language within a set of adaptation rules and even within a single rule. This section discusses the queries of an adaptation rule, and the following section discusses the target node binding.

An if-rule consists of one or more if-queries. The semantics is as follows: Each query is evaluated against its context document, which is given by the `context` attribute. If the result of at least one query is empty, that is, if there aren't any nodes in the context document that match the query, then each target node of the rule is deleted from its containing document. Put the other way round, the target nodes of an if-rule are remain in their containing document if and only if the results of all the if-queries are not empty. The nodes are deleted together with their all their children and descendants.

The following example illustrates the use of if-rules in conjunction with an HTML document. As the queries do not specify their context document, the default of the application is used, for example the context document maintained by a web browser.

```
<rule>
  <href>#paragraph1</href>
  <if type="xpath">//knowledge[@topic='html'][.='beginner']</if>
</rule>

<rule>
  <href>#paragraph2</href>
  <if type="xpath">//knowledge[@topic='html'][.='expert']</if>
</rule>

<html>
  ...
  <p>This page gives an explanation of HTML.</p>
  <p id="paragraph1">Very <em>simple</em> introduction to HTML, in
  addition to the following standard explanation.</p>
  <p><em>Standard</em> explanation of HTML.</p>
  <p id="paragraph2">Additional <em>advanced</em> aspects of HTML.</p>
  ...
</html>
```

The two rules can be used to adapt the HTML document to the user's knowledge about HTML:

– By default, the document contains a "standard explanation" of HTML. If the user is neither classified as *beginner* nor as *expert*, then only the standard explanation will be displayed.

- If the user is classified as *beginner* about the topic *HTML*, then an additional "simple introduction" to HTML will be displayed before the standard explanation.
- If the user is classified as *expert*, then additional "advanced aspects" of HTML will be displayed after the standard explanation.

Actually, the HTML document contains both the standard explanation as well as the simple introduction and the advanced aspects. According to the context information, however, either the simple introduction or the advanced aspects or both are deleted from the document by an XDAQ processor before it is displayed by the browser.

A copy-rule consists of one copy-query and zero or more if-queries. The semantics is as follows: The copy-query is evaluated against its context document, given by the **context** attribute. Then the children of each of the rule's target nodes are replaced by the result of the query. Thus, if the rule has n target nodes, then n copies of the query result are inserted into the target documents of that rule. If the rule also contains if-queries, then first the if-queries are evaluated against their context documents. Only if the results of all if-queries are not empty (similar as with if-rules), then the copy-query is evaluated, otherwise the copy-rule has no effect.

The following example illustrates the use of a copy-rule in conjunction with an XML document and an XSLT transformation:

```
<rule>
  <href>#xpointer(//recommendation)</href>
  <if type="xpath">//interest[@field='music']</if>
  <copy type="xpath">//interest[@field='music']/text()</copy>
</rule>

<library>
  <recommendation>Rock</recommendation>
  <album title="Radio Musicola" artist="Nik Kershaw" genre="Pop"/>
  <album title="Calling All Stations" artist="Genesis" genre="Rock"/>
  <album title="Script From A Jester's Tear"
         artist="Marillion" genre="Progressive Rock"/>
  <album title="The Works" artist="Nik Kershaw" genre="Pop"/>
</library>

<xsl:template match="library">
<html>
  ...
  <p>Recommended Albums:</p>
  <ul><xsl:apply-templates select="album[@genre=//recommendation]"/></ul>
  <p>Other Albums:</p>
  <ul><xsl:apply-templates select="album[@genre!=//recommendation]"/></ul>
  ...
</html>
</xsl:template>
```

The copy-rule is used to adapt the XML document by copying the user's preferred music genre into the document. The result of the copy-query is only copied if the result of the if-query is not empty, that is, if the context document specifies the user's preferred music genre. Without the if-query, the contents of the rule's target node would be deleted (set to empty) if the context document did not specify such information. The XSLT transformation generates an HTML document containing two lists: The first is a list of *recommended* albums, based on the user's interest that has been copied from the context document. The second list contains all other albums.

Obviously, instead of XPath, any other query and transformation language, for example XQuery, could be used. Thus, XDAQ does not rely on a single, fixed query language. The only, obvious requirement is that the query language can be used with the query's context document, for example, using an RDF query language for CC/PP documents.

4   Binding Adaptation Rules to Document Nodes

This section describes how adaptation rules are attached to nodes in an XML document. The approach of XDAQ is non-intrusive, that is, adaptation rules can be attached to nodes in a document without having to change to document itself. This is important because it makes it possible to non-proprietary build an adaptive system referring to contents collected from the web.

Non-intrusively binding is done by using references that point from an *adaptation pool* document, that is, a document containing a set of adaptation rules, into the rules' target documents, for example the HTML and XML documents from the examples in the previous section. A single adaptation rule may have more than one target node as well as more than one target document, that is, the target nodes may be contained in more than one XML document. For example:

```
<rule>
  <href>http://xyz.com/page1.html#xpointer(//p[@class='beginner'])</href>
  <href>http://xyz.com/page2.html#paragraph11</href>
  <href>http://xyz.com/page2.html#paragraph12</href>
  <if type="xpath">//knowledge[@topic='html'][.='beginner']</if>
</rule>
```

This if-rule is attached to a class of p elements in document page1.html, as well as to two single elements in document page2.html.

As reference mechanism URIs together with XPointer fragment identifiers are used. XPointer allows not only to select arbitrary nodes from an XML document, but also a set of locations, that is, simply speaking, substrings of the content of a node [12]. Thus it is possible to model not only coarse adaptation like deletion of elements, but also very fine-grained adaptation using attributes and even substrings of nodes as targets. A single XPointer fragment identifier may select more than one location, as in the example above.

Because the adaptation rules are separated from the documents that they affect, both documents can be created and maintained by different persons and be stored in different locations, even on different servers. In a large adaptive web application which is created and maintained by a number of people, the task of adaptation modeling can be performed simultaneously to other tasks. The goal is that, once the overall structure of an XML document (HTML document, XSLT style sheet and so on) is fixed, it should be possible for one person to fill the document with data, while another person may work on the adaptation rules, without interfering each other. It is even possible for a third party to define adaptation rules for a set of documents without having write access to those documents.

Note that the same approach, that is, pointing from an external document into the main document, is also used by CSS and XSLT style sheets as well as XLink linkbases. Defining adaptation rules non-intrusively, both improves modularity and avoids unwanted redundancy in adaptive web applications.

In contrast, an intrusive approach, that is, an approach that is attaching the adaptation rules directly to nodes in an XML document, introduces redundancy, as adaptation rules queries have to be copied for each target node. With an intrusive approach, the example from above may look like the following (note that adaptation queries in real applications might be much more complex than those used in the examples in this paper):

```
<p class="beginner" xdaq:if="//knowledge[@topic='html'][.='beginner']">...</p>
<p class="beginner" xdaq:if="//knowledge[@topic='html'][.='beginner']">...</p>
<p class="expert">...</p>

<p id="paragraph10">...</p>
<p id="paragraph11" xdaq:if="//knowledge[@topic='html'][.='beginner']">...</p>
<p id="paragraph12" xdaq:if="//knowledge[@topic='html'][.='beginner']">...</p>
```

Even if the queries are not directly inserted into the document, but only pointers to them, the document has still to be altered if it is to be equipped with adaptation, thus hindering modularity:

```
<p class="beginner" xdaq:href="http://adapt.org/adaptation-pool1.xml#rule1">...</p>
<p class="beginner" xdaq:href="http://adapt.org/adaptation-pool1.xml#rule1">...</p>
<p class="expert">...</p>

<p id="paragraph10">...</p>
<p id="paragraph11" xdaq:href="http://adapt.org/adaptation-pool1.xml#rule1">...</p>
<p id="paragraph12" xdaq:href="http://adapt.org/adaptation-pool1.xml#rule1">...</p>
```

Furthermore, using an intrusive approach as above, it is not possible to attach an adaptation rule to attributes or substrings of the contents of an element, because XML does not allow to let attributes have attributes themselves, for example. Thus, in contrast to XPointer fragment identifiers, only coarse adaptation, based on full elements, can be modeled.

A system using intrusive adaptation rules like above is [7]. Also CSS media queries [15] use an intrusive approach by attaching *media queries* (adaptation queries) directly to CSS document nodes. Therefore both of these approaches suffer from unwanted redundancy and a lack of modularity.

Absolute vs. Relative Pointers

XDAQ allows the use of both absolute and relative URIs [1] for the target node bindings of an adaptation rule. This allows to define adaptation rules for either a specific document or for a class of documents.

The example at the beginning of this section uses absolute URIs as target node bindings, while the examples in section 3 all use relative URIs.

Relative URIs are relative to the document that is processed by an XDAQ processor, called the *main document*. For example, if a set of adaptation rules is used to adapt document A, then all relative URIs used as document node bindings for adaptation rules are resolved using the URI of document A as base URI. If the same rules are used to adapt another document B, then the URI of document B is used as base URI.

The right use of absolute and relative URIs allows a single adaptation pool document, that is, a single set of adaptation rules, to be used for a whole website, even if some pages use different adaptation rules that all the others. Relative URIs are used to describe the default adaptation, that is used by almost all pages of the web site, while absolute URIs are used to describe exceptions from that, for example to use different adaptation rules for the title page.

Note that while XLink also allows the use of both absolute and relative URIs [9], there is no absolute referencing in CSS or XSLT style sheets. Therefore, if a single page of a web site, is meant to be styled different than all the other pages, either a different style sheet has to be used for that page, or the nodes in that page have to be identified by id and class attributes that are not used elsewhere on the web site.

5   Adaptive Web Document Processing

In an adaptive web application, adaptation rules exist together with links and style rules, which both can change the structure and contents of the main document. This may lead to ambiguous situations like this:

- A link inserts an image after element e1
- An adaptation rule deletes element e1 from the document

There are two possible semantics for this set of rules: Either the image is inserted after e1 and then e1 is deleted, keeping the image. Or first e1 is deleted, then there is nothing that is referenced by the link, resulting in the image not being inserted. Adding style rules, things can get even more complicated. To avoid such ambiguities, XDAQ defines a formal processing model for adaptive web documents. A *web document* is referenced by a URI and consists of the following parts:

- The *main document*, which is the XML document actually referenced by the URI of the web document. The main document might be the result of an XSLT transformation, a XQuery query of a database and so on. This step, however, lies out of the scope of the XDAQ processing model.
- A set of *processing information* documents, that is, XDAQ adaptation pool documents, XLink linkbases and CSS style sheets. These documents are either referenced by the main document, recursively referenced by other processing information documents that already have been referenced, or they are known to an XDAQ processor by any other means.

– Links from the main document to processing information documents are in-line (intrusive) links. They may also contain inline (intrusive) adaptation rules, in order to prevent unnecessary transfers of unused documents. Otherwise, the main document contains no other intrusive links, style rules or adaptation rules.

The XDAQ processing model considers adaptation rules, links and certain style rules as transformations of the main document. Such style rules include CSS pseudo-selectors like :before, or the display property with a value of none. Properties that affect fonts, colors and similar are not considered to be transformations, of course.

An XDAQ processor, for example contained in a web browser, performs the following steps in order to process an adaptive web document:

1. Parse the main document m.
2. Recursively parse all processing information documents linked by m, after evaluating each link's adaptation rule. This leads to a set of adaptation pool documents $\mathcal{A}$, a set of linkbases $\mathcal{L}$, and a set of style sheets $\mathcal{S}$. Accordingly, there exist sets of adaptation rules $\mathcal{R}(\mathcal{A})$, links $\mathcal{R}(\mathcal{L})$, and style rules $\mathcal{R}(\mathcal{S})$.
3. Process $\mathcal{R}_\mathcal{A}(\mathcal{A}) = \{r \in \mathcal{R}(\mathcal{A}) \mid T \cap \mathcal{A} \neq \emptyset, T = target\_documents(r)\}$. In other words, process all adaptation rules which have adaptation pool documents as target nodes. The rule r is not processed as a whole, but only those target nodes contained in adaptation pool documents. This step ensures that all adaptation rules, which are subject to adaptation, are adapted themselves before they are applied to their target nodes in the next step (see section 6).
4. Process $\mathcal{R}_\mathcal{L}(\mathcal{A}) = \{r \in \mathcal{R}(\mathcal{A}) \mid T \cap \mathcal{L} \neq \emptyset, T = target\_documents(r)\}$ and $\mathcal{R}_\mathcal{S}(\mathcal{A}) = \{r \in \mathcal{R}(\mathcal{A}) \mid T \cap \mathcal{S} \neq \emptyset, T = target\_documents(r)\}$. This step applies all remaining adaptation rules except those affecting the main document, as the main document can still be changed by links and style rules in the next step.
5. Process $\mathcal{R}(\mathcal{L})$ and $\mathcal{R}(\mathcal{S})$.
6. Process $\mathcal{R}_m(\mathcal{A}) = \{r \in \mathcal{R}(\mathcal{A}) \mid T \ni m, T = target\_documents(r)\}$, resulting in m', the adapted main document. This step finally applies all remaining adaptation rules to the main document, after is has been modified by links and style rules, thus giving adaptation rules the lowest priority in the adaptation process.

This processing model avoids ambiguities like the one described at the beginning of this section. The lack of a formal processing model for XLink is considered the main reason why major web browsers still do not support more than XLink simple links, despite being the XLink specification a recommendation for more than two years [10]. Several implementations have reported problems when combining XLink with other mechanisms that alter the XML document structure, for example XSLT transformations [14]. The combined processing model for XLink and CSS described in [19], however, is much more complicated than the XDAQ processing model and still lacks the concept of adaptation.

6   Adaptation Reasoning

After the previous sections introduced the technical aspects of XDAQ (modeling context information, definition of adaptation rules, binding of adaptation rules to document nodes and the outline of a formal processing model), this section takes a look at *adaptation reasoning*, that is, how adaptive applications can be modeled using the XDAQ framework. By applying if-rules and copy-rules to certain nodes of web pages, databases, or transformations, various adaptation technologies like adaptive presentation and adaptive navigation support [2] can be modeled. Two aspects of adaptation are important here: adaptation *actions*, for example, deletion of a node from a document, and the query part of adaptation rules.

The kind of adaptation that can be modeled using if-rules is very similar to the approach of *Author's Views* described in [4]. With Author's Views, certain parts of an XML document (for example paragraphs in an HTML document) are labelled with identifiers. A *view* corresponding to one of those identifiers then deletes all parts of the document not labelled with that identifier. Author's Views can be implemented using the `display` property of CSS with a value of `none`, and the user can choose between different views by selecting different style sheets. The concept of if-rules is based on that approach, but extends the simple notion of identifiers as labels to queries over a set of context documents, thus allowing to implement *conditional text* [2]. This means that the *views* are selected automatically based on the context information.

The metaphor of *variables* in programming languages can be used to illustrate adaptation modeling with copy-rules. As in the example from section 3, the target node of a copy-rule can be considered a variable, whose value is set by a copy-rule. If the copy-rule also contains if-queries, then the original content of the target node can be considered the default value of the variable. If the conditions expressed by the if-queries do not apply, the variable keeps its default value.

If-rules used to model Author's View-like adaptation in conjunction with copy-rules providing variables, are considered to be able to cover a large variety of adaptive web applications, namely technical documents like educational hypermedia or manuals. Such documents can be adapted to *beginner* users and *expert* users, or to *small* devices and *large* devices, as illustrated by the examples in the previous sections. However, adaptation may consist of more than just deleting nodes, for example:

- inserting nodes into a document
- replacing node contents
- ordering
- splitting and merging of documents
- disabling of hyperlinks

In order to provide such functionality, one could introduce new types of rules, one for each functionality: *insert-rule*, *replace-rule*, and so on. This, however, would yield a complete XML transformation language equipped with adaptation facilities, for example an XSLT/XQuery-like language with if/copy/insert/replace-rules.

The approach of XDAQ is different: take an existing, non-adaptive language like XLink, and attach adaptation rules from the outside (non-intrusive). The result is a two-step approach in many cases: XLink models for example insertion of nodes into the main document, and an attached if-rule models the adaptation:

```
<link id="link1" xlink:type="extended">
  <locator xlink:type="locator" xlink:href="a.xml#paragraph11-short"/>
  <locator xlink:type="locator" xlink:href="b.xml#paragraph11-long"/>
  <arc xlink:type="arc" xlink:actuate="onLoad" xlink:show="embed"/>
</link>

<rule>
  <href>linkbase.xml#link1</href>
  <if type="xpath">//device[@type='large']</if>
</rule>
```

The link inserts a long version of *paragraph11* from document b.xml into document a.xml, at the place of the short version of *paragraph11*. The if-rule, however, deletes the link if the device is not "large". This has the effect that the long version is only inserted on large devices, whereas on other devices, the short version of the paragraph is used as it is.

XDAQ adaptation rules can be used to directly adapt HTML documents, or to adapt XML data, which is then transformed into an HTML document, for example, or to adapt XML transformations, linkbases, style sheets, and any combination of these. For example, by applying adaptation rules to hyperlinks (as opposed to the actual content of a web page), adaptive navigation methods like hyperlink sorting, hiding, and annotation [2] can be modeled. Finally, XDAQ allows adaptation rules to be applied to other adaptation rules, which could be called *second-order* adaptation. A detailed investigation of these issues within the scope of sample applications remains to be done in the future (see section 7).

Adaptation may not only rely on "typical" context information, which is stored in context documents, but also on properties of the main document. For example:

> If the document is displayed on a small device, then cut of all long paragraphs (more than 200 characters) after 200 characters and add "..." at the end.

Something like this can be modeled using an XSLT transformation, for example, which checks the condition based on the main document (paragraph longer than 200 characters) and performs the adaptation action (cut off paragraph and add "..."). The condition based on context information is modeled by an attached if-query. Thus again a two-step approach is used: conditions based on the main document are modeled using a non-adaptive transformation mechanism, while conditions based on context information is attached via adaptation rules.

The same example could also be implemented using CSS, with an appropriate if-rule attached to the following set of style rules:

```
p[``length>200''] { ``cut: 200'' }
p[``length>200'']:after { content: "..." }
```

The current CSS specification is both unable to express the notion of the length of a paragraph as well as cutting off text. These two features, however, could easily be introduced, as well as other, similar functionalities desirable for adaptive web applications like ordering, splitting and merging of documents, and hyperspace disabling.

The question whether such functionalities are considered as transformations in the sense of XSLT and similar transformation or query languages, or simply as style properties in the sense of CSS, cannot be answered unambiguously. Both approaches are applicable, but the differences are as follows:

- A general-purpose transformation language like XSLT can be used to implement any desired functionality, whereas a style sheet language like CSS has to be extended each time a new functionality is added.
- Using a transformation language, authors have to write an algorithm, that is, *how* the adaptation action is to be performed. In the above example, this could be done using either a loop or recursive templates together with the strlen function of XPath. With CSS, authors only have to define the result of the adaptation action, that is, *what* should be performed. The algorithm itself is part of the CSS processors and has to be implemented only once (and not by the author of the web application).
- Even if the CSS approach can only provide a limited set of functionalities, a web application can combine it with a general-purpose transformation language. Functionalities not covered by CSS can still be implemented using the transformation language.

The idea of considering certain kinds of adaptation actions as style/layout instead of transformations is described in more detail in [3]. Future research will further investigate this issue and combine XDAQ with an extended version of CSS, that is able to perform adaptation actions like splitting and merging documents.

Query Languages for Adaptation

When used to express adaptation, query languages face different requirements than when used within other applications.

In addition to simply retrieve values from context documents (content queries), for example screen resolution, it must also be possible to express complex structural queries. Using structural queries, certain kinds of browsing behaviour can be detected from the history data in the context document, for example. According to the browsing behaviour, users can be classified into groups like beginner or expert, which is important for educational hypermedia systems.

Educational hypermedia typically also makes use of various stochastic functions. For example, adaptation might be based on the standard deviation of a series of test results. Query languages used for adaptation should provide a wide range of such functions.

Another feature widely used in adaptive hypermedia systems is ranking of list items. Ranking can be performed on both contents, like a list of news headlines, or on navigation (links), like a list of keyword search results. It is sufficient for the query language to generate rank values, for example by adding a rank attribute to list elements. The ordering itself is considered as a style/layout issue, which can be expressed by a CSS rule like this:

```
ul.recommendation li { sort-key: @rank; order: descending }
```

Furthermore, query languages used for adaptation must be able to perform reasoning based on ontologies. For example, it should be possible to model something like $small \subset medium \subset large$, that is, everything that can be displayed on a small device can also be displayed on a medium sized device, and that can be displayed on a large device. Also, ontologies can be used to provide interoperability between different context vocabularies.

7   XDAQ Prototype and Future Research

A prototype implementing the XDAQ framework has been developed in Java. At present, it exists only as a stand-alone tool, but it is being integrated into a web browser, a web server and a proxy, thus implementing the extended processing model described in the introduction. The prototype includes processing of adaptation rules as defined in sections 3 and 4, the processing model of section 5, as well as processing of non-XML data (CSS) as described in the introduction.

Future research will concentrate on the issues discussed in section 6. Especially the combination of XDAQ with the web query language Xcerpt [5] is promising, as Xcerpt is meant to be extended with functionalities needed for adaptation reasoning. Also, further investigation of the difference between adaptation considered as *transformation* and adaptation considered as *style/layout* is on the way. At present, the development of two adaptive web applications is planned to investigate these topics and the issues discussed in section 6, adaptive student learning material and an access-anywhere organizer.

Acknowledgements

The authors are thankful to Nobuo Saito and Keita Matsuyama, Keio University, for useful suggestions, and to Epson and DAAD for financial support.

References

1. T. Berners-Lee et al. Uniform Resource Identifiers (URI): Generic Syntax. RFC 2396, August 1998. http://www.ietf.org/rfc/rfc2396.txt.
2. P. Brusilovsky. Methods and techniques of adaptive hypermedia. *User Modeling and User-Adapted Interaction*, 6(2-3):87–129, 1996. http://www.contrib.andrew.cmu.edu/~plb/UMUAI.ps.
3. F. Bry and M. Kraus. Adaptive Hypermedia made simple using HTML/XML Style Sheet Selectors. In *Proceedings of the 2nd International Conference on Adaptive Hypermedia and Adaptive Web Based Systems (AH 2002)*, number 2347 in LNCS, pages 472–475. Springer, May 2002. http://www.pms.informatik.uni-muenchen.de/publikationen/#PMS-FB-2002-1.

4. F. Bry and M. Kraus. Advanced Modeling and Browsing of Technical Documents. In *Proceedings of the 17th ACM Symposium on Applied Computing (SAC 2002)*, pages 520–524. ACM Press, March 2002. http://www.pms.informatik.uni-muenchen.de/publikationen/#PMS-FB-2001-11.

5. F. Bry and S. Schaffert. A Gentle introduction into Xcerpt, a Rule-based Query and Transformation Language for XML. In *International Workshop on Rule Markup Languages for Business Rules on the Semantic Web*, June 2002. http://www.pms.informatik.uni-muenchen.de/publikationen/#PMS-FB-2002-11.

6. K. Cheverst, K. Mitchell, and N. Davies. The role of adaptive hypermedia in a context-aware tourist guide. *Communications of the ACM*, 45(5):47–51, 2002.

7. The Consensus Project. http://www.consensus-online.org/.

8. P. De Bra et al. AHA! The Next Generation. In *ACM Conference on Hypertext and Hypermedia*, May 2002. http://wwwis.win.tue.nl/~debra/ht02.pdf.

9. S. DeRose et al. XML Linking Language (XLink) Version 1.0. W3C Recommendation, June 2001. http://www.w3.org/TR/xlink/.

10. B. DuCharme. XLink: Who Cares?, March 2002. http://www.xml.com/pub/a/2002/03/13/xlink.html.

11. R. Gimson. Using Delivery Context to Achieve Device Independence: Outstanding Issues. In *W3C Delivery Context Workshop*, March 2002. http://www.w3.org/2002/02/DIWS/submission/gimson-issues.html.

12. P. Grosso et al. Xpointer framework. W3C Working Draft, July 2002. http://www.w3.org/TR/2002/WD-xptr-framework-20020710/.

13. G. Klyne et al. Composite apability/Preference Profiles (CC/PP): Structure and Vocabularies. W3C Working Draft, March 2003. http://www.w3.org/TR/2003/WD-CCPP-struct-vocab-20030325/.

14. M. Kraus. A Toolkit for Advanced XML Browsing Functionalities. Diploma thesis, Institute for Computer Science, University of Munich, November 2000. http://www.pms.informatik.uni-muenchen.de/publikationen/#DA_Michael.Kraus.

15. H. W. Lie et al. Media queries. W3C Candidate Recommendation, July 2002. http://www.w3.org/TR/2002/CR-css3-mediaqueries-20020708.

16. W. Nejdl. Adaptivity in the KBS Hyperbook System. In *2nd Workshop on Adaptive Systems and User Modeling on the WWW*, 1999. http://www.kbs.uni-hannover.de/~henze/paperadaptivity/Henze.html.

17. L. Suryanarayana and J. Hjelm. Profiles for the Situated Web. In *The Eleventh International World Wide Web Conference (WWW2002)*, 2002. http://www2002.org/CDROM/refereed/214/index.html.

18. Wireless Application Group User Agent Profile Specification, November 1999. http://www1.wapforum.org/tech/documents/SPEC-UAProf-19991110.pdf.

19. N. Walsh. XML Linking and Style. W3C Note, June 2001. http://www.w3.org/TR/xml-link-style/.

On Types for XML Query Language Xcerpt

Artur Wilk[1] and Włodzimierz Drabent[1,2]

[1] IDA, Linköping University, 581-83 Linköping, Sweden
{g-artwi,wdr}@ida.liu.se
[2] IPI PAN, Polish Academy of Sciences, Warszawa, Poland

Abstract. Our intention is to provide a type system for rule languages used in web applications. In this work we deal with an XML query language Xcerpt. Our types are sets of documents. We represent XML data as so called data terms and propose a formalism to define sets of data terms. The formalism is a generalization of tree automata; the defined sets roughly correspond to sets of documents definable by means of XML schema languages, like DTD and XML Schema. The main contribution of this paper is an algorithm for computing the type of possible results of an Xcerpt rule, given the type of the database. The algorithm can be used to automatically check correctness of Xcerpt programs with respect to type specifications. For non recursive Xcerpt programs it can also be used to compute the type of program results.

1 Introduction

A long range objective of this work is to develop analysis techniques for rules used in web applications. A main intended application is locating errors in (programs consisting of) rules. The rules we deal with can be seen as transformers of sets of XML documents. To begin with, we have chosen XML query language Xcerpt [6,7,5,1] as an example rule language. We show how to automatically prove correctness of Xcerpt rules and how to compute (approximations of) the sets of rule results. To make this possible, a restriction to some class of recursive sets is necessary, together with a fixed formalism of defining sets. The sets from the chosen class approximate the actual ones, in the sense that the latter are subsets of the former.

XML (eXtensible Markup Language) has become a dominant standard for data encoding and exchange on the Internet. It has been designed to create more structured and adaptable documents and document systems. Sets of documents, often called types, can be specified using various schema languages, like DTD [12], XML Schema [13], or RELAX NG [8]. Applications which deal with many different DTD's or XML Schemas require mechanisms for comparing such specifications; in other words to compare types. This includes comparing types given by different schema languages. For this purpose a common view of them is necessary.

As XML data are essentially tree structured, a natural approach is to view XML documents as trees (or, equivalently, terms), and types as sets of trees. So we need a formalism to describe decidable sets of trees. It should be able

F. Bry et al. (Eds.): PPSWR 2003, LNCS 2901, pp. 128–145, 2003.
© Springer-Verlag Berlin Heidelberg 2003

to describe sets corresponding to those specified by major schema languages for XML. Our intended application requires that basic operations on sets expressed in the formalism (like intersection and checks for membership, emptiness and inclusion) are decidable and efficient algorithms for them exist. A well known such formalism is tree automata [9] (or tree grammars, which are just another view of tree automata). However tree automata deal with terms where each symbol has a fixed arity. This is not compatible with XML, where the number of elements between a given pair of a start-tag and end-tag is not fixed. One can adjust the view of XML data to the tree automata formalism, by representing sequences of arbitrary length as lists (this means terms built using two symbols of fixed arities 2 and 0). In this way n children of a tree node can be replaced by one child, which is a list of length n. Such an approach is used in [15]. We follow here another approach – extending the tree automata formalism.

As abstraction of XML data we employ data terms. Data terms can be seen as mixed trees, which are labelled trees where children of a node are either linearly ordered or unordered. Our formalism for defining sets of data terms combines tree grammars with regular expressions. The latter are used to describe the possible sequences (or sets) of children of a single node in a tree. Similar formalism is used in [16], the novelty of our approach is that we deal with mixed trees.

There exist various rule languages related to XML documents (like RuleML [2] or Xcerpt). Usually rules are (intended to be) applied to documents of a certain type. An obvious question arises about the set of possible results of such a rule (or of a set of rules). One would like to express the type of rule results in terms of the types of documents to which the rule is applied. A variant of this question is checking whether the rule is type correct – one requires that any result of the rule is of certain type and wants to prove (or disprove) this fact. Ability to perform such checks automatically, or to compute the type of results, is instrumental for discovering errors in the rules. Experience with programming languages shows how crucial static typing has been for quick discovering of certain kinds of errors in programs and thus for improving efficiency of programmers and quality of programs. On the other hand, experience with untyped programming languages, like Prolog, shows how lack of typing makes many simple errors difficult to discover.

Providing algorithms for checking correctness of programs w.r.t. type specifications, or for deriving types, is sometimes called descriptive typing. This can be seen as adding types to an untyped programming language, without modifying its semantics. In this way one can combine advantages of typed and untyped programming languages. See [10] for an example of such approach for (constraint) logic programming, and for further references.

In this paper we present descriptive typing for (a large subset of) XML query language Xcerpt [6,7,5,1]. Xcerpt stems from logic programming. It uses patterns instead of paths to navigate the database. The mechanism of matching a pattern against a database resembles unification. We present a method of computing the type of results for an Xcerpt program, given a type of the database. To simplify the presentation, our method is introduced for programs consisting of a single rule of a rather restricted form. Abandoning this restriction is however discussed informally. The method applies to checking of type correctness of arbitrary programs and to finding the result type for non recursive programs. It also subsumes checking whether a given data term is a member of a given type.

The paper is organized as follows. The next section introduces data terms and their correspondence to XML data. Section 3 presents the formalism of type definitions. Section 4 discusses certain restrictions on type definitions, their purpose is to obtain simpler and more efficient algorithms. As an example, Section 5 discusses an algorithm for checking type inclusion. Other basic algorithms employed in this work are presented in an appendix available from the Web. Section 6 presents Xcerpt and introduces the algorithm for computing query answer types.

2   Modelling XML Data

We model XML data using a formalism of data terms similar to that defined in [6]. Data terms can be seen as mixed trees which are labelled trees where children of a node are either linearly ordered or unordered. This is related to existence of two basic concepts in XML: *tags* which are nodes of an ordered tree and *attributes* that attach attribute-value mappings to nodes of a tree. These mappings are represented as unordered trees. Unordered children of a node may also be used to abstract from the order of elements, when this order is inessential. We assume that there is no syntactic difference between XML tag names and attribute names and they both are labels of nodes in our mixed trees (and symbols of our data terms). The infinite alphabet of labels will be denoted by $\mathcal{L}$.

A content of an element is a sequence of other elements or **basic constants**. Basic constants are basic values such as attribute values and all "free" data appearing in an XML document – all data that is between start and end tag except XML elements. Basic constants occur as strings in XML documents but they can play a role of data of other types depending on an adequate definition in DTD (or other schema languages) e.g. IDREF, CDATA,. . . . The set of basic constants will be denoted by $\mathcal{B}$. In our notation we will enclose all basic constants in quotation marks "".

XML documents are represented as *data terms*.

Definition 1. *A* **data term** *is an expression defined inductively as follows:*

- *Any basic constant is a data term,*
- *If l is a label and $t_1, \ldots, t_n$ are $n \geq 0$ data terms, then $l[t_1 \cdots t_n]$ and $l\{t_1 \cdots t_n\}$ are data terms.*

The linear ordering of children of the node with label l is denoted by enclosing them by brackets [], while unordered children are enclosed by braces {}.

A *subterm* of a data term t is defined inductively: t is a subterm of t, and any subterm of t_i ($1 \leq i \leq n$) is a subterm of $l'[t_1, \ldots, t_n]$ and of $l'\{t_1, \ldots, t_n\}$.

To show how XML elements are represented by data terms, consider an XML element

$$E = <tag \ attr_1=value_1 \cdots attr_k=value_k>E_1 \cdots E_n</tag>,$$

$(k \geq 0, n \geq 0)$ where each E_i (for $i = 1, \ldots, n$) is an element or the text occurring between two elements or before the first element or after the last element. E is represented as a data term $tag[attributes\ child_1 \cdots child_n]$, where the data terms $child_1, \ldots, child_n$ represent $E_1, \ldots, E_n$, and the data term

$$attributes = \&\{attr_1[value_1] \cdots attr_k[value_k]\}$$

represents the attributes of E. If E has no attributes then $attributes$ is the data term $\&\{\}$, which will be usually abbreviated as $\&$. Subterms representing attributes are not ordered and this is denoted by enclosing them by braces.

Example 1. This is an XML element and the corresponding data term.

```
<CD price="9.90" year="1985">     CD[&{price["9.90"] year["1985"]}
    Empire Burlesque                  "Empire Burlesque"
    <subtitle></subtitle>             subtitle[&]
    <artist>Bob Dylan</artist>        artist[& "Bob Dylan"]
    <country>USA</country>            country[& "USA"]
</CD>                               ]
```

The *root* of a data term t, denoted $root(t)$, is defined as follows . If t is of the form $l[t_1, \ldots, t_n]$ or $l\{t_1, \ldots, t_n\}$ then $root(t) = l$; for t being a basic constant we assume that $root(t) = \$$.

3   Type Definitions

Here we introduce a formalism for specifying a class of decidable sets of data terms representing XML documents. It is a certain simplification of the formalism of [4]. First we specify a set of **type names** $\mathcal{T} = \mathcal{C} \cup \mathcal{S} \cup \mathcal{V}$ which consist of

- **type constants** from the alphabet $\mathcal{C}$
- **special type names** from the alphabet $\mathcal{S}$
- **type variables** from the alphabet $\mathcal{V}$

We associate each type name T with a set $[\![T]\!]$ (the *type denoted by T*) of data terms which are allowed values assigned to T. For T being a type constant or a special type name, the elements of $[\![T]\!]$ are basic constants.

Type constants corresponds to an XML schema language base types. The set of type constants is fixed and finite. In our examples we will use a type constant # assuming that $[\![\#]\!]$ is the set of non empty strings of characters. This is similar to #PCDATA in DTD.

For a special type name T the corresponding set $[\![T]\!]$ is a finite set of basic constants $\{c_1, \ldots, c_m\}$ ($m \geq 0$). This set is specified by a rule of the form $T \to c_1 | \ldots | c_m$. In our notation, type constants and special type names are sequences of letters beginning with character #.

Each type variable T is associated with a set of data terms $[\![T]\!]$ which is specified in a way similar to that of [4] and described below. First we introduce some auxiliary notions. The empty string will be denoted by ϵ. A *regular expression* over an alphabet Σ is ε, ϕ, any $a \in \Sigma$ and any $r_1 r_2$, $r_1 | r_2$ and r_1^*, where r_1, r_2 are regular expressions. A language $L(r)$ of strings over Σ is assigned to each regular expression r in the standard way (see e.g. [14]). In particular, $L(\phi) = \emptyset$, $L(\varepsilon) = \{\epsilon\}$ and $L(r_1 | r_2) = L(r_1) \cup L(r_2)$.

Definition 2. *A* **regular type expression** *is a regular expression over the alphabet of type names* $\mathcal{T}$. *We abbreviate a regular expression* $r^n | r^{n+1} | \cdots | r^m$, *where* $n \leq m$, *as* $r(n : m)$, $r^n r^*$ *as* $r(n : \infty)$, rr^* *as* r^+, *and* $r(0 : 1)$ *as* $r^?$. *A regular type expression of the form*

$$W_1 \cdots W_k$$

where $k \geq 0$, *each* W_i *is* $T_i(n_{i,1} : n_{i,2})$, $0 \leq n_{i,1} \leq n_{i,2} \leq \infty$ *for* $i = 1, \ldots, k$, *and* $T_1, \ldots, T_k$ *are distinct type names, will be called a* **multiplicity list**.

Multiplicity lists will be used to specify multisets of type names.

Definition 3. *A* **type definition** *for type variables* $T_1, \ldots, T_n$ *is a set of rules* $\{R_1, \ldots, R_n\}$ *where each rule* R_i $(i = 1, \ldots, n)$ *is of the form*

$$T_i \to G_i,$$

$T_1, \ldots, T_n$ *are distinct, and each* G_i *is an expression of the form* $l_i[r_i]$ *or* $l_i\{q_i\}$ *where* l_i *is a label,* r_i *is a regular type expression over* $\{T_1, \ldots, T_n\} \cup \mathcal{C} \cup \mathcal{S}$, *and* q_i *is a multiplicity list over* $\{T_1, \ldots, T_n\} \cup \mathcal{C} \cup \mathcal{S}$.

A type definition for type variables together with a set of rules defining special type names will be called a **type definition**. A rule of the form $T \to G$ (occurring in a type definition D) will be called the *rule for* T (in D). We require that for any special type name S the definition contains at most one rule for S.

Example 2. Consider type definition D:

$$Cd \to cd[\textit{Title Artist}^+ \, \#Category^?]$$
$$Title \to title[\# \; Subtitle^?]$$
$$Subtitle \to subtitle[\#]$$
$$Artist \to artist[\#]$$
$$\#Category \to \text{pop} \mid \text{rock} \mid \text{classic}$$

D contains a rule for each of type variables: Cd, $Title$, $Subtitle$, $Artist$ and a rule for special type name $\#Category$. Labels occurring in D are: *cd*, *title*, *subtitle*, *artist*, and pop, rock, classic are basic constants.

Type definitions are a kind of grammars, they define sets by means of derivations over data patterns.

Definition 4. *A* **data pattern** *is inductively defined as follows*

- *a type name and a basic constant are data patterns,*

– if $d_1, \ldots, d_n$ $(n \geq 0)$ are data patterns and l is a label then $l[d_1 \cdots d_n]$ and $l\{d_1 \cdots d_n\}$ are data patterns.

Thus, data terms are data patterns, but not necessarily vice versa, since a data pattern may include type names in place of data terms. Given a type definition D we use it to define a rewrite relation $\rightarrow_D$ on data patterns.

Definition 5. *Let d, d' be data patterns. $d \rightarrow_D d'$ iff one of the following holds:*

1. *d' is obtained from d by replacing an occurrence of a type variable T in d by $l[s]$, for some rule $T \rightarrow l[r]$ in D and some $s \in L(r)$ (so s is a string of type names).*
2. *d' is obtained from d by replacing an occurrence of a type variable T in d by $l\{s\}$, for some rule $T \rightarrow l\{r\}$ in D and a permutation s of some $s_0 \in L(r)$.*
3. *d' is obtained from d by replacing an occurrence of a type constant C by a basic constant in $[\![C]\!]$.*
4. *There exists in D a rule $S \rightarrow c_1 | \ldots | c_m$ for a special type name S, and d' is obtained from d by replacing an occurrence of S by one of the basic constants $c_1, \ldots, c_m$.*

Example 3. For the type definition D from the previous example it holds: $Cd \rightarrow_D$ $cd[\textit{Title Artist \#Category}] \rightarrow_D^* cd[\textit{title}[\#] \textit{ artist}[\#] \text{ "pop"}] \rightarrow_D^* cd[\textit{title}[\text{"Stop"}]$ $\textit{artist}[\text{"Sam Brown"}] \text{ "pop"}]$.

Iterating the rewriting steps we may eventually arrive at a data term. This gives a semantics for type definitions.

Definition 6. *Let D be a type definition. The type $[\![T]\!]_D$ associated with a type name T by D is the set of the data terms that can be obtained from T*

$$[\![T]\!]_D = \{\, t \mid T \rightarrow_D^* t \text{ and } t \text{ is a data term}\,\}$$

Notice that if T is a type constant then $[\![T]\!]_D = [\![T]\!]$. If it is clear from the context which type definition is considered, we will often omit the subscript in the notation $[\![\ ]\!]_D$ and similar ones.

4   Proper Type Definitions

For our analysis of Xcerpt rules we need algorithms computing intersection of sets defined by type definitions, and performing emptiness and inclusion checks for such sets. To obtain efficient algorithms we impose certain restrictions on type definitions. They are discussed in this section.

Consider a type definition D. If $T \rightarrow G$ is the rule for a type variable T in D, where G is of the form $l[r]$ or $l\{q\}$, then l will be called the **label** of T (in D) and denoted $label_D(T) = l$. For T being a type constant or a special type name we define $label_D(T) = \$$. So if $d \in [\![T]\!]$ then $root(d) = label(T)$.

For any regular type expression r in D we have the **corresponding regular expression over labels** that is r with each type name S replaced by $label_D(S)$.

We assume that alphabet of labels $\mathcal{L} \cup \{\$\}$ is totally ordered by a relation $\leq$; we call this ordering *alphabetic ordering*. A multiplicity list $W_1 \ldots W_k$, where each $W_i = T_i(n_{i,1} : n_{i,2})$ and T_i is a type name, is **sorted** w.r.t D if $label_D(T_1) \leq \ldots \leq label_D(T_k)$. For practical reasons we assume that the multiplicity lists occurring in our type definitions are sorted.

We say that a type definition D is **proper**, if for each regular expression r in D all distinct type names occurring in r have different labels. Thus given a term $l[c_1 \ldots c_n]$ and a rule $T \rightarrow l[r] \in D$ or a term $l\{c_1 \ldots c_n\}$ and a rule $T \rightarrow l\{r\} \in D$ for each c_i, the root of c_i determines at most one type name S such that S occurs in r and $label_D(S) = root(c_i) = l_i$. Such type name S will be denoted $type_D(l_i, r)$. If any type occurring in r does not have label l_i we assume that $type_D(l_i, r) = NULL$. We use $types_D(r)$ to denote the set of all type names occurring in the regular expression r.

Notice that, for a proper type definition D, at most one type constant or special type name occurs in any regular expression of D since all type constants and special type names have the same label $\$$.

Restriction to proper type definitions results in simpler and more efficient algorithms. Unless stated otherwise, we assume that the considered type definitions are proper. The class of proper type definitions, when restricted to ordered terms (i.e. without $\{\}$), is essentially the same as single-type tree grammars of [16]. Dealing only with proper definitions seems reasonable, as the sets defined by main XML schema languages (DTD and XML Schema) can be expressed by such definitions [16].

Example 4. Type definition $D_1 = \{A \rightarrow a[A|B|C], B \rightarrow b[D], C \rightarrow b[\#], D \rightarrow c[\#]\}$ is not proper because type names B, C have the same label b and occur in one regular expression. In contrast, $D_2 = \{A \rightarrow a[A|B|D], B \rightarrow b[CD], C \rightarrow b[\#], D \rightarrow c[\#]\}$ is proper and e.g. $type_{D_2}(b, A|B|D) = B$ and $type_{D_2}(b, CD) = C$.

Our algorithms employ inclusion and equality checks for languages described by given regular expressions, and computing intersection of such languages. This can be done by transforming regular expressions to deterministic finite automata (DFA's) and using standard efficient algorithms for DFA's.

In the general case the number of states in a DFA may be exponentially greater than the length of the corresponding regular expression [14]. Notice that the XML definition [12] requires (Section 3.2.1) that content models specified by regular expressions in element type declarations of a DTD are *deterministic* in the sense of Appendix E of [12]. It seems that the formal meaning of this requirement is that the regular type expressions are 1-unambiguous in a sense of [3]. For such regular expressions a corresponding DFA can be constructed in linear time.

5   Inclusion Subtyping

Due to lack of space we discuss only checking type inclusion. Algorithms for type intersection and emptiness check are presented in [17]. Let T_1, T_2 be type names defined in type definitions D_1, D_2, respectively. T_1 is an *inclusion subtype* of T_2 iff $[\![T_1]\!]_{D_1} \subseteq [\![T_2]\!]_{D_2}$. We present an algorithm which checks this fact. It is not required that D_1 is proper.

The first part of the algorithm constructs a set $C(T_1, T_2)$ of pairs of types to be compared. It is the smallest set such that

- if $label(T_1) = label(T_2)$ then $(T_1, T_2) \in C(T_1, T_2)$,
- if
  - $(T_1', T_2') \in C(T_1, T_2)$,
  - D_1, D_2 contain, respectively, rules $T_1' \to l[r_1]$ and $T_2' \to l[r_2]$, or $T_1' \to l\{r_1\}$ and $T_2' \to l\{r_2\}$ (with the same label l), and
  - type names T_1'', T_2'' occur respectively in r_1, r_2, and $label_{D_1}(T_1'') = label_{D_2}(T_2'')$

  then $(T_1'', T_2'') \in C(T_1, T_2)$. As D_2 is proper, for every T_1'' in r_1, there exists at most one T_2'' in r_2 satisfying this condition.

The second part of the algorithm checks whether $[\![T_1']\!] \subseteq [\![T_2']\!]$ for each $(T_1', T_2') \in C(T_1, T_2)$:

> IF $C(T_1, T_2) = \emptyset$ THEN return false
> ELSE for each $(T_1', T_2') \in C(T_1, T_2)$ do the following:
> > IF T_1', T_2' are special type names or type constants
> > > THEN check whether $[\![T_1']\!] \subseteq [\![T_2']\!]$ and return the result
> > Let $T_1' \to l[r_1]$ and $T_2' \to l[r_2]$, or $T_1' \to l\{r_1\}$ and $T_2' \to l\{r_2\}$
> > > be rules of D_1, D_2, respectively
> > Let s_1 and s_2 be the regular expressions over labels
> > > corresponding to r_1 and r_2
> > Check whether $L(s_1) \subseteq L(s_2)$
> IF for all pairs from $C(T_1, T_2)$ the answer is true THEN return true
> ELSE return false

The algorithm employs a check if $[\![T_1']\!] \subseteq [\![T_2']\!]$, where each of T_1', T_2' is either a special type name or a type constant. This check is based on recorded information about inclusion of the sets defined by type constants and about which constants are members of these sets.

If the algorithm returns *true* then $[\![T_1]\!]_{D_1} \subseteq [\![T_2]\!]_{D_2}$. If it returns *false* and D_1 has no nullable symbols (i.e. $[\![T]\!]_{D_1} \neq \emptyset$ for each type name T in D_1) then $[\![T_1]\!]_{D_1} \not\subseteq [\![T_2]\!]_{D_2}$. The main fact used in the proof of this property is that a positive answer of the algorithm means the following. For any (S, U), $(S_1, U_1), \ldots, (S_n, U_n) \in C(T_1, T_2)$ if $S \to_{D_1} l[S_1 \cdots S_n]$ then $U \to_{D_2} l[U_1 \cdots U_n]$. A similar fact holds for terms with $\{\}$ (remember that in this case the regular expressions in the applied rules are sorted multiplicity lists).

Example 5. Consider type definitions: $D = \{A \to l[B|C], B \to l[A^+], C \to m[]\}$ and $D' = \{A' \to l[A'^*|C'], C' \to m[C'^*]\}$. To check whether $[\![A]\!]_D \subseteq [\![A']\!]_{D'}$, first we construct set $C(A, A')$ which is $\{(A, A'), (B, A'), (C, C')\}$. Then the second part of the algorithm checks if $L(l|m) \subseteq L(l^*|m)$, $L(l^+) \subseteq L(l^*|m)$ and $L(\epsilon) \subseteq L(m^*)$. Since all the checks give positive results, we conclude that $[\![A]\!]_D \subseteq [\![A']\!]_{D'}$.

Notice that for a proper D_2 and 1-unambiguous regular expressions [3] in D_1, D_2 the algorithm is polynomial. In the general case a polynomial algorithm does not exist, as inclusion for a less general formalism of tree automata is EXPTIME-complete [9].

6   Typing of Xcerpt Query Results

In this section we first introduce XML query language Xcerpt. Then we discuss objectives of computing types of query results and present an algorithm.

6.1   Xcerpt – Introduction

Xcerpt is a rule-based query and transformation language for XML (see [5,6,7,1]). It employs patterns instead of paths to query XML and semistructured data. This approach stems from logic programming. A query term is matched against a data term from a database. A successful matching results in binding the variables in the query term to certain subterms of the data term. This operation is called simulation unification.

We consider here a somehow simplified version of Xcerpt. The main difference is that our data terms represent trees while in full Xcerpt terms are used to represent graphs (by adding unique identifiers to some tree nodes and introducing nodes which are references to identifiers).

We assume that a database is a data term or a multiset of data terms. There are two other kinds of terms in Xcerpt: query terms and construct terms. A **construct term** is a data term possibly with some subterms replaced by variables. We define query terms later on. Any data term is a construct term, and any construct term is a query term. The role of query terms is to be matched against a database. Construct terms are used in constructing data terms which are query results. Queries in Xcerpt are (sets of) rules; the premise of a rule is a query term and the conclusion of a rule is a construct term.

Definition 7. Query terms *are inductively defined as follows:*

- *Any basic constant is a query term.*
- *A variable X is a query term.*
- *If q is a query term, then desc q is a query term.*
- *If X is a variable and q is a query term, then $X \rightsquigarrow q$ is a query term.*
- *If l is a label and $q_1 \ldots q_n$ $(n \geq 0)$ are query terms, then $l[q_1 \ldots q_n]$, $l\{q_1 \ldots q_n\}$, $l[[q_1 \ldots q_n]]$ and $l\{\{q_1 \ldots q_n\}\}$ are query terms (called* rooted *query terms).*

For a rooted query term $q = l\alpha q_1, \ldots, q_n\beta$, where $\alpha\beta$ are parentheses $[\,], [[\,]], \{\}$ or $\{\{\}\}$, $root(q) = l$ and $q_1, \ldots, q_n$ are the child subterms of q. If q is a basic constant then $root(q) = \$.

To informally explain the role of query terms, consider a query term $q = l\alpha q_1 \ldots q_m\beta$ and a data term $d = l'\alpha' d_1 \ldots d_n\beta'$, where $\alpha, \beta, \alpha', \beta'$ are parentheses. In order to q match d it is necessary that $l = l'$. Moreover the child subterms

$q_1, \ldots, q_m$ of q should match certain child subterms of d. Single parentheses in d ([] or {}) mean that $m = n$ and each q_i should match some (distinct) d_j. Double parentheses mean that $m \leq n$ and $q_1, \ldots, q_m$ are matched against some m terms out of $d_1, \ldots, d_n$. Curly brackets ({} or {{}}) in q mean that the order of the child subterms in d does not matter; square brackets in q mean that $q_1, \ldots, q_m$ should match (a subsequence of) $d_1, \ldots, d_n$ in the same order.

A variable matches any data term, $desc\, q$ matches a data term d whenever q matches some subterm of d. A query term $X \rightsquigarrow q$ matches any data term matched by q. A side effect of a query term X or $X \rightsquigarrow q$ matching a data term d is that variable X obtains a value d.

Now we formally define which query terms match which data terms and what are the resulting assignments of data terms to variables. We do not follow the original definition of simulation unification. Instead we define a notion of answer substitution for a query term q and a data term d.

Definition 8. *A substitution θ (of data terms for variables) is an answer substitution (shortly, an **answer**) for a query term q and a data term d if q and d are of one of the forms below and the corresponding condition holds. (In what follows $m, n \geq 0$, X is a variable, l is a label, $q, q_1, \ldots$ are query terms, and $d, d_1, \ldots$ data terms; set notation is used for multisets, for instance $\{d, d\}$ and $\{d\}$ are different multisets).*

q	d	condition on q and d
c	c	c is a basic constant
$l[q_1 \cdots q_n]$	$l[d_1 \cdots d_n]$	θ is an answer for q_i and d_i, for each $i = 1, \ldots, n$
$l[[q_1 \cdots q_m]]$	$l[d_1 \cdots d_n]$	for some subsequence $d_{i_1}, \ldots, d_{i_m}$ of $d_1, \ldots, d_n$ (i.e. $0 < i_1 < \ldots < i_m \leq n$) θ is an answer for q_j and d_{i_j}, for each $j = 1, \ldots, m$,
$l\{q_1 \cdots q_n\}$	$l\{d_1 \cdots d_n\}$ or $l[d_1 \cdots d_n]$	for some permutation $d_{i_1}, \ldots, d_{i_n}$ of $d_1, \ldots, d_n$ (i.e. $\{d_{i_1}, \ldots, d_{i_n}\} = \{d_1, \ldots, d_n\}$) θ is an answer for q_j and d_{i_j} for each $j = 1, \ldots, m$,
$l\{\{q_1 \cdots q_m\}\}$	$l\{d_1 \cdots d_n\}$ or $l[d_1 \cdots d_n]$	for some $\{d_{i_1}, \ldots, d_{i_m}\} \subseteq \{d_1, \ldots, d_n\}$ θ is an answer for q_j and d_{i_j} for each $j = 1, \ldots, m$,
X	d	$\theta X = d$
$X \rightsquigarrow q$	d	$\theta X = d$ and θ is an answer for q and d
$desc\, q$	d	θ is an answer for q and some subterm d' of d

We say that q matches d if there exists an answer for q, d.

Thus if q is a rooted query term (or a basic constant) and $root(q) \neq root(d)$ then no answer for q, d exists. If $q = d$ then any θ is an answer for q, d. A query $l\{\{\}\}$ matches any data term with the label l. If θ, θ' are substitutions (of data terms for variables) and $\theta \subseteq \theta'$ then if θ is an answer for q, d then θ' is an answer for q, d. If a variable X occurs in a query term q then queries $X \rightsquigarrow q$ and $X \rightsquigarrow desc\, q$ match no data term, provided that $q \neq X$ and q is not of the form $desc \cdots desc\, X$.

Example 6. Query term $q_1 = a[\, c\{\{d[\,]\, "e"\}\}\, f[[g[\,]\, h\{"i"\}]]\,]$ matches data terms $a[\, c\{"e"\, d[\,]\, g[\,]\}\, f[g[\,]\, l[\,]\, h["i"]]\,]$ and $a[\, c[d[\,]\, g[\,]\, "e"]\, f[g[\,]\, h["i"]]\,]$. In contrast, data terms $f[h["i"]\, g[\,]]$ and $f\{g[\,]\, h["i"]\}$ are not matched by $f[[g[\,]\, h\{"i"\}]]$. Query term $q_2 = desc\, w\{\{\}\}$ matches data terms $a[b[w[\,]]]$ and $w\{"s"\}$ and query term $q_2 = a[[\, X_1 \rightsquigarrow c[[d\{\}]]\, X_2\, "p"\,]]$ matches $a["s"\, c[d\{\}\, "r"]\, h\{j[\,]\}\, "p"]$, with an answer which binds X_1 to $c[d\{\}\, "r"]$ and X_2 to $h\{j[\,]\}$.

Each answer for a query term q binds all the variables of the query to some data terms. For any such answer θ' (for q and d) there exists an answer $\theta \subseteq \theta'$ (for q and d) binding exactly these variables. We will call such answers *non redundant*. Out of Definition 8 one can derive an algorithm which produces non redundant answers for a given q and d. Construction of the algorithm is rather simple, due to lack of space we skip the details.

An Xcerpt program is a set of construct-query rules. We restrict ourselves to a simple kind of rules and to programs consisting of a single rule.

Definition 9. *A* **construct-query rule** *(shortly,* query rule *or* query*) is an expression of the form $t \leftarrow q$, where t is a construct term, q is a query term and every variable occurring in t also occurs in q. t will be sometimes called the* head *and q the* body *of the rule. If θ is an answer for q and a data term d then $t\theta$ is a* **result** *for query $t \leftarrow q$ and d.*

Each result of a query rule is a data term, as an answer for a query term binds all the variables of the rule to data terms.

Example 7. Consider a database:

$catalogue[\, cd[\, title["Empire Burlesque"]\, artist["Bob Dylan"]\, year["1985"]\,]$
$cd[\, title["Hide your heart"]\, artist["Bonnie Tyler"]\, year["1988"]\,]$
$cd[\, title["Stop"]\, artist["Sam Brown"]\, year["1988"]\,]\,]$

Here is a rule which extracts titles and artists for the CDs issued in 1988 and presents the results in a changed form (title as name and artist as author). *TITLE* and *ARTIST* are variables.

$result[\, name[TITLE]\, author[ARTIST]\,] \leftarrow$
$\qquad catalogue\{\{\, cd\{title[TITLE]\, artist[ARTIST]\, year["1988"]\,\}\}\}$

The results returned by the rule are:

$result[\, name["Hide your heart"]\, author["Bonnie Tyler"]\,]$
$result[\, name["Stop"]\, author["Sam Brown"]\,]$

6.2 Reasoning about Types of Xcerpt Query Results

In this section we study the relation between types of databases and types of query results. Assume that the only information available about the database is that it is a data term (or a set of data terms) of a given type $[\![T_{\mathrm{DB}}]\!]$. One may want to know what query results are possible for such database. We show how to compute (a superset of) the set of such results. The set will be expressed as a type, specified by a type definition. We will usually call it the query result type.

Computing the query result type may serve some additional purposes. 1. If this type is empty, then the query will never give an answer for a data term from $[\![T_{\mathrm{DB}}]\!]$. An algorithm checking this property is obtained by combining computing query result type with checking emptiness of a type. 2. If some specification of the intended type of results exists, one may check if the query is correct w.r.t. the specification, by checking whether the computed type of the results is included in the specified one. 3. If we use a data term d as the body of the query, then computing the result type is also a check whether $d \in [\![T_{\mathrm{DB}}]\!]$. Namely $d \in [\![T_{\mathrm{DB}}]\!]$ iff the result type is not empty. 4. The algorithm computing the query result type produces as a side effect the types of the variables of the queries. For each variable from the query it gives a set containing every value that can be assigned to the variable (when querying a data term from type $[\![T_{\mathrm{DB}}]\!]$). This provides additional information about the behaviour of the query. We may consider specifications of the types of the query variables. A query is correct w.r.t. such a specification if for every variable the computed type is a subset of the specified type.

Example 8. Consider the type definition D from Example 2 and a construct-query rule Q:

$$result[\,name[\mathit{TITLE}]\ author[\mathit{ARTIST}]\,] \leftarrow$$
$$cd\{\{\ \mathit{TITLE}\ \mathit{ARTIST} \leadsto artist\{\{\}\}\ \text{"rock"}\ \}\}$$

The intention of the rule is to collect titles and authors of all the cd's of the rock category. When the query term of the rule is matched against a database of type Cd, the variables $\mathit{TITLE}, \mathit{ARTIST}$ are bound to data terms of types, respectively, *Title, Artist* or *Artist, Artist*. As the variable TITLE is intended to take values only of type *Title*, the query is incorrect w.r.t. our expectations. The type *Result* of the query result can be described by the following type definition $D' = D \cup \{\ Result \rightarrow result[Name\ Author],\ Name \rightarrow name[\,Title\,|\,Artist\,],\ Author \rightarrow author[Artist]\,\}$.

In what follows we assume a fixed proper type definition D (describing the type of the database).

To represent a set of answers (for a query term and a set of data terms) we will use a mapping $m\colon V \to \mathcal{E}$, where V is the set of variables occurring in the considered query rule and $\mathcal{E}$ is a set of expressions. $\mathcal{E}$ contains 0, 1, the type names from D, and expressions of the form $T_1 \cap T_2$, where $T_1, T_2 \in \mathcal{E}$. Each expression E from $\mathcal{E}$ denotes a set $[\![E]\!]$ of data terms. $[\![1]\!]$ denotes the set of all data terms, $[\![0]\!] = \emptyset$, $[\![T]\!] = [\![T]\!]_D$ for any type name T, and $[\![T_1 \cap T_2]\!] =$

$\llbracket T_1 \rrbracket \cap \llbracket T_2 \rrbracket$. The set of substitutions corresponding to a mapping $m \colon V \to \mathcal{E}$ is $substitutions_D(m) = \{\, \theta \mid \forall_{X \in V}\, \theta X \in \llbracket m(X) \rrbracket \,\}$.

We define $\bot, \top \colon V \to \mathcal{E}$ by $\bot(X) = 0$ and $\top(X) = 1$ for every $X \in V$. For $Y_1, \ldots, Y_k \in V$, $T_1, \ldots, T_k \in \mathcal{E}$, mapping $[Y_1 \mapsto T_1, \ldots, Y_k \mapsto T_k] \colon V \to \mathcal{E}$ is defined as

$$[Y_1 \mapsto T_1, \ldots, Y_k \mapsto T_k](X) = \begin{cases} T_i & \text{if } X = Y_i \\ 1 & \text{otherwise.} \end{cases}$$

We will not distinguish between expressions $T \cap 1$ and T, and between $T \cap 0$ and 0 (where $T \in \mathcal{E}$). For any $m_1, m_2 \colon V \to \mathcal{E}$ we introduce $m_1 \cap m_2 \colon V \to \mathcal{E}$ such that

$$(m_1 \cap m_2)(X) = m_1(X) \cap m_2(X).$$

Notice that $m \cap \bot = \bot$ and $m \cap \top = m$ for any $m \colon V \to \mathcal{E}$.

For a particular query term there may be many possible assignments of types for variables. That is why we will use sets of mappings from $V \to \mathcal{E}$. For such sets M_1 and M_2 we define:

$$M_1 \sqcap M_2 = \{m_1 \cap m_2 \mid m_1 \in M_1, m_2 \in M_2\}$$
$$M_1 \sqcup M_2 = M_1 \cup M_2$$

Hence $M \sqcap \{\bot\} = \{\bot\}$, $M \sqcap \{\top\} = M$, for any set of mappings M. We will not distinguish between $M \sqcup \{\bot\}$ and M, and between $M \sqcup \{\top\}$ and $\{\top\}$.

Computing the Set of Answers for a Query Term. A first step of computing the types of results of query rules is computing the set of answers for a given query term q and the data terms from a given $\llbracket T \rrbracket_D$. We begin presentation of our algorithm from its auxiliary procedure, called *match_seq*.

The input for *match_seq* are parentheses $\alpha\beta$, a type variable T, and a string of type names $T_1 \cdots T_n$. It checks whether some query term of the form $q = l\alpha q_1 \cdots q_n \beta$, where $l = label(T)$ and $root(q_i) = label(T_i)$ for $i = 1, \ldots, n$, matches a data term from $\llbracket T \rrbracket_D$ of the form $l[d_1, \ldots, d_n]$ or $l\{d_1, \ldots, d_n\}$. This is done by treating type names as basic constants and checking whether query term $l\alpha T_1 \cdots T_n \beta$ matches some data term $l\alpha' U_1 \cdots U_l \beta'$, where the rule for T in D is $T \to l\alpha' r \beta'$ and $U_1 \cdots U_l \in L(r)$. (We cannot simply check if $T_1, \ldots, T_n \in L(r)$ because the brackets of q must also be considered.)

$match\_seq(\alpha\beta, T_1 \ldots T_n, T)$:
    IF the rule for T in D is of the form $T \to l[r]$ THEN
        let s be r with every type name U replaced by $U|\epsilon$
        IF $\alpha\beta = [\,]$ THEN   check whether $T_1 \ldots T_n \in L(r)$ and return the result
        IF $\alpha\beta = [[\,]]$ THEN   check whether $T_1 \ldots T_n \in L(s)$ and return the result
        IF $\alpha\beta = \{\}$ THEN
            check whether there exist a permutation $S_1 \ldots S_n$ of $T_1 \ldots T_n$
                such that $S_1 \ldots S_n \in L(r)$ and return the result
        IF $\alpha\beta = \{\{\}\}$ THEN
            check whether there exist a permutation $S_1 \ldots S_n$ of $T_1 \ldots T_n$
                such that $S_1 \ldots S_n \in L(s)$ and return the result
    ELSE (the rule for T in D is $T \to l\{r\}$ where r is a sorted multiplicity list)

let $S_1 \ldots S_n$ be a permutation of $T_1 \ldots T_n$
   such that $label(S_1) \leq label(S_2) \leq \ldots \leq label(S_n)$
let s be r with every type name U replaced by $U|\epsilon$
IF $\alpha\beta = [\,]$ or $\alpha\beta = [[\,]]$ THEN return false
IF $\alpha\beta = \{\}$ THEN
  check whether $S_1 \ldots S_n \in L(r)$ and return the result
IF $\alpha\beta = \{\{\}\}$ THEN
  check whether $S_1 \ldots S_n \in L(s)$ and return the result

This algorithm employs a check whether some permutation x of a given string y is in a given regular language L. This can be done by constructing a DFA M' for the language L' of all permutations of y and then checking emptiness of $L \cap L'$. The states of M' are multisets of symbols (subsets of the multiset Y of the symbols of y); there is also an error state $\bot$. State Y is the start state, $\emptyset$ is the final state. For each symbol $S \in Y$ there is a transition labelled S from Y to $Y \setminus \{S\}$. If $S \notin Y$ then the transition goes to $\bot$.

Now we are ready to present an algorithm which computes the set of answers for a given query term q and the data terms from a given type $[\![T]\!]_D$ of a database.

We will say that a type name T' is *reachable* from T if $T \to_D t$ for a data pattern t in which T' occurs.

$match(q, T)$:
  IF q is a variable X THEN
     return $\{[X \mapsto T]\}$
  IF q is of the form $X \leadsto q'$
    return $\{[X \mapsto T]\} \sqcap match(q', T)$
  IF q is of the form $desc\, q'$ THEN
    let $W = \{\, T' \mid T'$ reachable from $T \,\}$
    return $\bigsqcup_{T' \in W} match(q, T')$

(Now q is a rooted query term or a basic constant).

IF $root(q) \neq label(T)$ THEN return $\emptyset$

IF T is a type constant or a special type name THEN
  IF q is a basic value in $[\![T]\!]$ THEN return $\{\top\}$ ELSE return $\emptyset$

let r be the regular type expression in the rule for T in D
let $q = l\alpha q_1 \cdots q_n \beta$ $(n \geq 0)$,

$$ \text{let } S = \left\{ T_1 \ldots T_n \;\middle|\; \begin{array}{ll} T_i = type(root(q_i), r) & \text{if } q_i \text{ is a rooted query term} \\ & \text{or a basic constant,} \\ T_i \in types(r) & \text{otherwise} \end{array} \right\} $$

(so $|S| > 1$ only if some q_i is of the form X, $X \leadsto q'$, or $desc\, q'$)
let $S' = \{\, T_1 \ldots T_n \in S \mid match\_seq(\alpha\beta, T_1 \ldots T_n, T) \,\}$
return $\bigsqcup_{T_1 \ldots T_n \in S'} \bigsqcap_{i=1}^{n} match(q_i, T_i)$

Notice that any mapping $m \in match(q, T)$ has a property that $m(X)$ is neither 1 nor 0 for any variable X occurring in q, and $m(X) = 1$ for any X not occurring in q. (It is however possible that $m(X) = T_1 \cap T_2$, where $[\![T_1]\!] \cap [\![T_2]\!] = \emptyset$.)

The set of mappings $match(q, T)$ produced by the algorithm describes the possible answers for q. If q does not contain $\rightsquigarrow$ then the description is exact.

Proposition 1. *Let q be a query term and $S = \bigcup_{m \in match(q,T)} substitutions_D(m)$. If θ is an answer for q and a data term $d \in [\![T]\!]_D$ then $\theta \in S$. If q does not contain $\rightsquigarrow$ then each $\theta \in S$ is an answer for q and some $d \in [\![T]\!]$.*

To avoid technical complications, we do not attempt here to compute more precise descriptions for queries with $\rightsquigarrow$.

The values of the mappings from $M = match(q, T)$ may be expressions of the form $T_1 \cap \ldots \cap T_n$, where each T_i is a type name. Consider the set W_M of all such expressions

$$W_M = \left\{ T_1 \cap \ldots \cap T_n \,\middle|\, \begin{array}{l} T_1 \cap \ldots \cap T_n = m(X),\ m \in M,\ X \in V \\ n > 1,\ \text{each } T_i \text{ is a type name} \end{array} \right\}.$$

For any expression $E \in W_M$, $[\![E]\!]$ is the intersection of types defined by D. Using the algorithm of the appendix [17] we can construct a type definition D_M such that for each $E \in W_M$ there exists a type variable T_E for which $[\![T_E]\!]_{D_M} = [\![E]\!]$. Moreover, $[\![T]\!]_{D_M} = [\![T]\!]_D$ for all type variables occurring in D (hence for those occurring in M). If D is proper then D_M is proper.

So without lack of generality we can assume that $match(q, T)$ returns a set of mappings M such that $m(X)$ is a type name, for each $m \in M$ and for each variable X occurring in q.

Computing the Type of Query Results. Given a proper type definition D and a set $match(q, T)$ of mappings describing answers to a query term q, the set of results for a query $t \leftarrow q$ and data terms from $[\![T]\!]_D$ is a subset of

$$R = \bigcup_{m \in match(q,T)} R(m) \qquad \text{where } R(m) = \{\, t\theta \mid \theta \in substitutions_D(m) \,\}$$

(by Proposition 1). If q does not contain $\rightsquigarrow$ then R is the set of results. We first show how to compute $R(m)$. We construct a type definition with a type name T_u for each subterm u of the query head t. If u is a variable X then T_X is $m(X)$. The type names T_u corresponding to the basic constants occurring in t are new distinct special type names. For the remaining subterms of t the corresponding variables of t are new distinct type variables. We construct a set of rules

$$\begin{aligned} rules(t, m) = &\{\, T_c \rightarrow c \mid c \text{ is a basic constant and a subterm of } t \,\} \\ &\cup \{\, T_u \rightarrow l\alpha T_{u_1} \cdots T_{u_n}\beta \mid u = l\alpha u_1 \cdots u_n\beta \text{ is a subterm of } t \,\}. \end{aligned}$$

Type definition $D_m = D \cup rules(t, m)$ describes $R(m)$:

$$[\![T_t]\!]_{D_m} = \{\, t\theta \mid \theta \in substitutions(m) \,\}$$

Let us find out whether D_m is proper. For each subterm u of t consider a corresponding label. If u is a variable then the corresponding label is $label_D(T_u) =$

$label_D(m(u))$. Otherwise it is $root(u)$. The type definition D_m is proper iff for each subterm u of t the labels corresponding to distinct child subterms of u are distinct. (Repeated occurrences of the same child subterm are allowed.)

Computing $rules(t,m)$ for each $m \in match(q,T)$ completes our algorithm. The union R of the sets $[\![T_t]\!]_{D \cup rules(t,m)}$ contains all the results for query $t \leftarrow q$ and any database which is a data term (or a set of data terms) from $[\![T]\!]$.

If t is a variable then R may contain data terms with distinct roots; such a set is not a type in our sense (i.e. is not $[\![T]\!]_D$ for any type definition D). If t is not a variable then one may express R by a single type definition, possibly non proper. Assume that for no type name there exist rules in two distinct sets $rules(t,m)$ (in other words, all the newly introduced type names are distinct). If t is a basic constant then R is defined by an obvious definition $\{T_R \rightarrow t\}$ or $\emptyset$. So assume that t is a term $l\alpha t_1 \cdots t_n \beta$. For each $m \in match(q,T)$, let T_t^m be the type variable corresponding to t in $rules(t,m)$ and let r_m be the regular expression in the rule for T_t^m. Let T_R be a new type variable and r be the union of the regular expressions r_m, for $m \in match(q,T)$. For the type definition

$$D' = \{T_R \rightarrow l\alpha r\beta\} \cup D \cup \bigcup_{m \in match(q,T)} rules(t,m)$$

we have $R = [\![T_R]\!]_{D'}$.

In general, the type definition D' is not proper. It may be impossible to describe R by a proper type definition. Instead one may consider constructing a proper type definition defining a superset of the given set. This topic is however outside of the scope of this paper.

Example 9. Consider the type Cd from Example 2 and the construct-query rule Q from Example 8. When we apply our algorithm to obtain the type of the results for Q and a database from $[\![Cd]\!]$, we will get two type definitions: $D' = D \cup \{Result \rightarrow result[Name\ Author], Name \rightarrow name[Artist], Author \rightarrow author[Artist]\}$, $D'' = D \cup \{Result \rightarrow result[Name\ Author], Name \rightarrow name[Title], Author \rightarrow author[Artist]\}$. Thus every query result is a member of $[\![Result]\!]_{D'} \cup [\![Result]\!]_{D''}$. The latter set is equal to that described by the proper type definition of Example 8.

Analysis of Xcerpt Programs. It is easy to generalize the method presented in this section to query rules containing more than one query term. The method applies also to Xcerpt programs containing many query rules, provided they are not recursive and the constructed type definitions are proper. If a query term q from a rule R_2 is matched against the results of a query rule R_1 then the algorithm applied to R_1 gives a type definition which is an input to the algorithm applied to R_2. The algorithm requires that the type definition is proper. It is however sufficient that each D_m, treated separately, is proper (for a condition under which this happens, see above). The algorithm for R_2 can be executed repetitively, for each D_m as an input. Each run of the algorithm produces some description of a result set, the union of these sets is the set of results of query rule R_2.

Applying this idea to a recursive set of rules may result in a non terminating sequence of applications of the algorithm. Here one needs an approach similar to abstract interpretation or set constraints solving. (For related work in the area of logic programming see e.g. [10] and references therein.) However our approach can still be used to check correctness of recursive sets of rules w.r.t. type specifications. Consider a set P of Xcerpt rules and a specification S describing a set of allowed database terms and sets of allowed query results. A sufficient condition for correctness of P w.r.t. S is that each rule of P applied to allowed data terms produces an allowed result. This is an inductive proof method, similar to those used for partial correctness of programs. (For such a method for logic programs see [11] and references therein.) If specification S is given by a proper type definition then the sufficient condition can be checked by means of algorithms described in this paper. For each rule of P one can compute the set of results, using the algorithm described above; it is not necessary that the obtained type definition is proper. Then, using the algorithm of Section 5, one can check if the computed set is included in that given by S.

7   Conclusions and Topics for Future Work

We introduced an abstraction of XML data by data terms and a formalism of type definitions to specify sets of data terms. To simplify our algorithms, we restrict this formalism to proper type definitions. The restriction seems acceptable, as the sets defined by main XML schema languages (DTD and XML Schema) can be expressed by proper type definitions. (Here we neglect some special features of these languages, like non context-free conditions of DTD on uniqueness of identifiers). Our algorithms are more efficient when the regular expressions in the type definitions are 1-unambiguous in a sense of [3]. Restriction to such regular expressions seems not unnatural; for instance the regular expressions in DTD are required to be 1-unambiguous.

The main contribution of this paper is an algorithm for computing (approximations of) the sets of results of Xcerpt rules, given (approximations of) the sets of databases. This makes it possible to prove correctness of Xcerpt programs w.r.t. specifications expressed by type definitions, and to compute approximations of the sets of results of non recursive Xcerpt programs. Computing approximations for recursive programs is a subject for future work.

The presented algorithm requires a prototype implementation; the work is in progress (we have e.g. a translator from DTD to type definitions and a type inclusion checker). Another subject for future work is studying how much the restriction to proper definitions may be relaxed. (A slightly more general class of definitions is considered in [4].) A compromise has to be found between the descriptive power of the formalism, and efficiency and simplicity of algorithms using it. In this context a study should be done on how much expressive power is actually needed in practice.

We have chosen Xcerpt as an example rule language; we expect that the ideas of this paper are applicable to other rule languages used in web applications.

References

1. S. Berger, F. Bry, S. Schaffert, and C. Wieser. Xcerpt and visXcerpt: From pattern-based to visual querying of XML and semistructured data. In *Proceedings of the 29th Intl. Conference on Very Large Databases (VLDB03) – Demonstrations Track*, Berlin, Germany, 2003.

2. H. Boley, S. Tabet, and G. Wagner. Design rationale of RuleML: A markup language for semantic web rules. In *Proc. Semantic Web Working Symposium (SWWS'01)*, Stanford, 2001. http://www.dfki.uni-kl.de/ruleml.

3. A. Brüggemann-Klein and D. Wood. One-unambiguous regular languages. *Information and Computation*, 142(2):182–206, May 1998.

4. F. Bry, W. Drabent, and J. Maluszynski. On subtyping of tree-structured data. Technical report, IDA, Linköpings universitet, 2003. http://www.ipipan.waw.pl/~drabent/types.winter.03/.

5. F. Bry and S. Schaffert. A gentle introduction into Xcerpt, a rule-based query and transformation language for XML. Technical Report PMS-FB-2002-11, Computer Science Institute, Munich, Germany, 2002. Invited article at International Workshop on Rule Markup Languages for Business Rules on the Semantic Web.

6. F. Bry and S. Schaffert. Towards a declarative query and transformation language for XML and semistructured data: Simulation unification. In *Proc. of the International Conference on Logic Programming*, LNCS. Springer-Verlag, 2002.

7. F. Bry and S. Schaffert. The XML query language Xcerpt: Design principles, examples, and semantics. In *Proc. 2nd Int. Workshop "Web and Databases"*, LNCS 2593, Erfurt, Germany, October 2002. Springer-Verlag.

8. J. Clark and M. Murata (editors). RELAX NG specification, Dec. 2001. http://www.oasis-open.org/committees/relax-ng/spec-20011203.html.

9. H. Common, M. Dauchet, R. Gilleron, F. Jacquemard, D. Lugiez, S. Tison, and M. Tommasi. Tree automata techniques and applications. http://www.grappa.univ-lille3.fr/tata/, 1999.

10. W. Drabent, J. Maluszynski, and P. Pietrzak. Using parametric set constraints for locating errors in CLP programs. *Theory and Practice of Logic Programming*, 2(4–5):549–610, 2002.

11. W. Drabent and M. Miłkowska. Proving correctness and completeness of normal programs — a declarative approach. In P. Codognet, editor, *Logic Programming, 17th International Conference, ICLP 2001, Proceedings*, volume 2237 of *LNCS*, pages 284–299. Springer-Verlag, 2001.

12. Extensible markup language (XML) 1.0 (second edition), W3C recommendation 6 October 2000. http://www.w3.org/TR/REC-xml.

13. D. C. Fallside (ed.). XML Schema part 0: Primer. W3C Recommendation, http://www.w3.org/TR/xmlschema-0/, 2001.

14. J. E. Hopcroft and J. D. Ullmann. *Introduction to Automata Theory, Languages and Computation*. Addison-Wesley, 1979.

15. H. Hosoya, J. Vouillon, and B. C. Pierce. Regular expression types for XML. In *Proceedings of the International Conference on Functional Programming (ICFP)*, pages 11–22, 2000. Full version under submission to TOPLAS.

16. M. Murata, D. Lee, M. Mani, and K. Kawaguchi. Taxonomy of XML schema languages using formal language theory. Submitted, 2003.

17. A. Wilk and W. Drabent. On Types for XML Query Language Xcerpt, Appendix. http://www.ida.liu.se/g-artwi/TypesForXML/appendix.pdf, 2003.

Integrating Description Logics and Answer Set Programming

Stijn Heymans and Dirk Vermeir*

Dept. of Computer Science
Vrije Universiteit Brussel, VUB
Pleinlaan 2, B1050 Brussels, Belgium
{sheymans,dvermeir}@vub.ac.be

Abstract. We integrate an expressive class of description logics (DLs) and answer set programming by extending the latter to support inverted predicates and infinite domains, features that are present in most DLs. The extended language, conceptual logic programming (CLP) proves to be a viable alternative for intuitively representing and reasoning nonmonotonically, in a decidable way, with possibly infinite knowledge. Not only can conceptual logic programs (CLPs) simulate finite answer set programming, they are also flexible enough to simulate reasoning in an expressive class of description logics, thus being able to play the role of ontology language, as well as rule language, on the Semantic Web.

1   Introduction

Description logics (DLs) [2] and answer set programming [10, 19] are well-established knowledge representation mechanisms. We integrate them by adding predicate inverses to disjunctive logic programs (DLPs) and extending the answer set semantics by allowing for an infinite domain, without introducing function symbols. Both extensions to answer set programming are inspired by their presence in most DLs, effectively integrating the flexible and intuitive way of representing knowledge in logic programming with DLs features, making elegant reasoning with infinite knowledge possible.

However, simply extending answer set programming leads to undecidability, notably of satisfiability checking. We therefore restrict the syntactic structure of DLPs, obtaining conceptual logic programs (CLPs). Satisfiability checking can then be decided by reducing it to checking satisfiability w.r.t. simpler DLPs with finite answer set programming techniques.

CLPs can simulate (disjunction-free) logic programs as well as expressive classes of DLs, such as $\mathcal{SHIQ}^*$. $\mathcal{SHIQ}^*$ is a slight modification of $\mathcal{SHIQ}$ [15] with transitive closure of roles instead of transitivity of roles. $\mathcal{SHIQ}$ is regarded as the formal specification of the ontology language OIL [17, 8], which can be used to express ontologies[1] on the Semantic Web [4]. Other, more expressive, ontology languages are, for

---

* This work was partially funded by the Information Society Technologies programme of the European Commission, Future and Emerging Technologies under the IST-2001-37004 WASP project.

[1] Like DL knowledge bases or database schema's, ontologies are models of a domain, providing an *agreed* and *shared* understanding [20].

F. Bry et al. (Eds.): PPSWR 2003, LNCS 2901, pp. 146–159, 2003.

example, DAML+OIL [3] and, more recently, OWL [21] which also include support for data types and individuals.

Although, satisfiability checking w.r.t. a $\mathcal{SHIQ}^*$ knowledge base can be intuitively reduced to satisfiability checking w.r.t. a CLP the reverse is not true, i.e. there are CLP rules that cannot be translated to $\mathcal{SHIQ}^*$. Moreover, we believe that, in many cases, CLPs are more intuitive, modular and easier to use than description logics.

Consider the following example,

$$restore(X) \leftarrow crash(X), yest(X, Y), BackupSucceeded(Y) \quad (1)$$
$$BackupSucceeded(X) \leftarrow \neg crash(X), yest(X, Y), not(BackupFailed(Y)) (2)$$
$$BackupFailed(X) \leftarrow not(BackupSucceeded(X)) \quad (3)$$
$$\leftarrow yest^-(X, Y_1), yest^-(X, Y_2), Y_1 \neq Y_2 \quad (4)$$
$$\leftarrow yest(X, Y_1), yest(X, Y_2), Y_1 \neq Y_2 \quad (5)$$
$$yest(X, Y) \vee not(yest(X, Y)) \leftarrow \quad (6)$$
$$crash(X) \vee not(crash(X)) \leftarrow \quad (7)$$
$$\neg crash(X) \vee not(\neg crash(X)) \leftarrow \quad (8)$$

where a system that has crashed on a particular day, can be restored on that day if a backup of the system on the day before succeeded. Backups succeed, if the system does not crash and it cannot be established that the backups at previous dates failed.

Rules (1) and (2) express the above knowledge, and are called tree rules, due to their tree-like structure, i.e. a tree with root X and leaf Y connected trough *yest*. Rules (4) and (5) ensure that for a particular today there can be only one yesterday and only one tomorrow, where $yest^-$ denotes the inverse of *yest*. Both rules also have a tree structure (with root X and leafs Y_1 and Y_2), and, since the conclusion part of the rule is empty, we call them tree constraints. The last three rules are so-called free rules and express that on any day a crash may or may not have occurred. In general, free rules express that certain facts may freely be added to the model, subject to restrictions implied by other rules.

The main point of attention in this example is that all answer sets, claiming a restore on a particular date, should also assure that on all previous dates the backup succeeded, explicitly demanding for an infinite domain, and an infinite domain only. Furthermore, reasoning with CLPs is clearly nonmonotonic due to the presence of *negation as failure*, i.e. the "not" in front of literals.

The attempt to integrate DLs with logic programming is not new. [1] presents, without considering decidability issues, a translation from the DL $\mathcal{ALCQI}$ to answer set programs, using, unlike in the present approach, artificial function symbols to accommodate for an infinite Herbrand universe. [11] simulates reasoning in DLs through simple datalog programs. This necessitates heavily restricting the usual DL constructors: e.g. negation or number restrictions cannot be expressed. While our approach can express those constructions and, as such, makes the possible interweaving of ontologies and rules more complete, the approach in [11] has the advantage that existing LP-reasoning engines can be used. An alternative approach is to simply add datalog-like programs to coexist with DL theories, as in [6, 7], thus exploiting the strengths of both knowledge representation mechanisms. This contrasts with our approach which aims to import the advantages of DLs into an extension of answer set programming.

Other approaches that connect rules to ontologies are, for example, [9], where a mapping of a set of descriptions in the languages RDF, RDF-S or DAML+OIL to first-order predicate calculus is specified, or [18], where DAMLJessKB enables the querying of information in DAML files, by using Jess as a forward chaining production system.

The remainder of this paper is organized as follows: Section 2 extends the answer set programming semantics to support inverses and infinite domains. Section 3 restricts the programs to DLPs with a tree structure in order to enforce the tree-model property and decidability of reasoning with CLPs. A simulation of finite answer set programming and a particular expressive DL can be found in Sect. 4. Sect. 5 contains conclusions and directions for further research.

2   Answer Set Programming with Infinity

We give some basic definitions about disjunctive logic programs (DLPs) and answer sets [10, 19], and extend them to take into account infinite domains and inverses.

We call individual names *constants* and write them as lowercase letters, *variables* will be denoted with uppercase letters. Variables and constants are *terms*. *Atoms* are defined as being of the form $p_1(t_1)$, $p_2(t_1, t_2)$, $p_2^-(t_1, t_2)$, with p_1 a unary predicate, and p_2 a binary predicate, t_1 and t_2 are terms. We assume p^{--} to be defined as p for a binary predicate p, and for atoms a, we assume a^- is a with the predicate and the arguments inverted in case of binary (possibly inverted) predicates, i.e. $p(t_1, t_2)^- = p^-(t_2, t_1)$, and $p(t_1)^- = p(t_1)$ for unary predicates. Note that we restrict to unary and binary predicates; inverting atoms does not seem to make sense for predicates of greater arity.

Ground atoms are atoms without variables. A *literal* is an atom or an atom preceded by $\neg$, i.e. l is a literal if $l = a$ or $l = \neg a$ for an atom a. We define $(\neg a)^-$ as $\neg(a^-)$ for an atom a. A *ground literal* is a literal without variables. An *extended literal* is a literal l or something of the form $not(l)$, with l a literal. A *ground extended literal* is an extended literal without variables. For a set X of literals, $\neg X = \{\neg l \, | l \in X\}$, where we define $\neg\neg a$ as a. A set of ground literals X is *consistent* if $X \cap \neg X = \emptyset$. For a set X of extended literals, we define $X^- = \{l \, | not(l) \in X\}$, i.e. the set of underlying literals.

We use Greek letters to represent sets of (unary or binary, possibly negated and/or inverted) predicates. Attaching variables then allows us to write e.g. $\alpha(X)$ for $\{a(X)|a \in \alpha\}$, $\beta(X, Y)$ for $\{b(X, Y)|b \in \beta\}$, or $not(\alpha)(X)$ for $\{not(a(X))|a \in \alpha\}$. Furthermore, we assume the existence of a binary predicate $\neq$, with the usual interpretation.

A *disjunctive logic program* (DLP) is a finite set of rules $\alpha \leftarrow \beta$ where α and β are finite sets of extended literals. We call programs where for each rule $\beta^- \cup \alpha^- = \emptyset$, *programs without negation as failure* (naf). Programs without naf such that for all rules β contains at most one element, i.e. no disjunction in the head, are called *simple programs*. Programs that do not contain variables are ground. For a program P and a (possibly infinite) non-empty set of constants $\mathcal{H}$, such that every constant appearing in P is in $\mathcal{H}$, we call $P_{\mathcal{H}}$ the *grounded program* obtained from P by substituting every variable in P by every possible constant in $\mathcal{H}$. Note that $P_{\mathcal{H}}$ may contain an infinite number of rules (if $\mathcal{H}$ is infinite). An infinite DLP must be a grounded version of a finite one.

The *universe* of a grounded program $P_{\mathcal{H}}$ is the (possibly infinite) non-empty set of constants $\mathcal{H}_{P_{\mathcal{H}}}$ appearing in $P_{\mathcal{H}}$. Note that $\mathcal{H}_{P_{\mathcal{H}}} = \mathcal{H}$. The *base* of a grounded program $P_{\mathcal{H}}$ is the (possibly infinite) set $\mathcal{B}_{P_{\mathcal{H}}}$ of ground atoms that can be constructed using the predicates in $P_{\mathcal{H}}$ and their inverses, with the constants in $\mathcal{H}$.

An *interpretation* I of a grounded DLP P is any consistent set of literals that is a subset of $\mathcal{B}_P \cup \neg \mathcal{B}_P$. An interpretation I of a grounded DLP P without naf *satisfies* a rule $\alpha \leftarrow \beta$ if $\alpha \cap I \neq \emptyset$ whenever $\beta \subseteq I$. Or, intuitively, if the conjunction of literals in the body of a rule is true, the disjunction of the literals in the head must be true. An interpretation I is a *model* of a grounded DLP P without naf if it satisfies every rule in P and $p(t_1, t_2) \in I \iff p^-(t_2, t_1) \in I$ for all literals $p(t_1, t_2)$ in $\mathcal{B}_P \cup \neg \mathcal{B}_P$. Furthermore, it is a *minimal model* if there is no model $J \subset I$ of P.

For a grounded DLP P and an interpretation I, the Gelfond-Lifschitz transformation [19], is the program P^I, obtained by deleting in P

- each rule that has $not(l)$ in its body with $l \in I$,
- each rule that has $not(l)$ in its head with $l \notin I$, and
- all $not(l)$ in the bodies and heads of the remaining rules.

An *interpretation* of a DLP P (not grounded) is a tuple $(I, \mathcal{H}_I)$, such that I is an interpretation of the grounded $P_{\mathcal{H}_I}$. An interpretation $(I, \mathcal{H}_I)$ of a DLP P is an *answer set* of P if I is a minimal model of $P^I_{\mathcal{H}_I}$.

A DLP P is *consistent* if P has an answer set. For a unary p (p possibly negated), appearing in P, we say that p is *satisfiable* w.r.t. P if there exists an answer set $(I, \mathcal{H}_I)$ of P such that $p(a) \in I$ for an $a \in \mathcal{H}_I$; if $\mathcal{H}_I$ is finite we call p *finitely satisfiable*. Checking this satisfiability for a (possibly negated) unary predicate is called *satisfiability checking*.

Although we allow for infinite domains, we can motivate the presence of literals in a minimal model of a simple program in a finite way. We express the motivation of a literal more formally by means of an operator T that computes the closure of a set of literals w.r.t. a program P.

For a DLP P and an answer set $(M, \mathcal{H}_M)$ of P such that $P^M_{\mathcal{H}_M}$ is a simple program, we define the operator $T_{P^M_{\mathcal{H}_M}} : \mathcal{B}_{P^M_{\mathcal{H}_M}} \cup \neg \mathcal{B}_{P^M_{\mathcal{H}_M}} \rightarrow \mathcal{B}_{P^M_{\mathcal{H}_M}} \cup \neg \mathcal{B}_{P^M_{\mathcal{H}_M}}$ [2] as follows.

$$T_{P^M_{\mathcal{H}_M}}(B) = B \cup \{a, a^- | a \leftarrow \beta \in P^M_{\mathcal{H}_M} \wedge \beta \subseteq B\}$$

We define $T^0(B)$ as B, and $T^{n+1}(B)$ as $T^n(T(B))$. The operator gives the immediate consequences of a set B according to $P^M_{\mathcal{H}_M}$.

Theorem 1. *Let P be a DLP and $(M, \mathcal{H}_M)$ an answer set of P, with $P^M_{\mathcal{H}_M}$ a simple program. Then $\forall a \in M \cdot \exists n < \infty \cdot a \in T^n(\emptyset)$*

Proof Sketch. Assume $\exists a \in M \cdot \forall n < \infty \cdot a \notin T^n(\emptyset)$. We write down all $r : a' \leftarrow \beta \in P^M_{\mathcal{H}_M}$ with $a' = a$ or $a' = a^-$ such that $\beta \subseteq M$ and such that there exist $a_2 \in \beta$

---

[2] We omit the subscript if it is clear from the context.

such that $\forall n < \infty \cdot b \notin T^n(\emptyset)$. Since such r can always be chosen, we can repeat this procedure for all b ad infinitum. This way we can define a strict subset M' of M, i.e. M without a, a^- and all b with their inverses (intuitively, we throw away all the literals that are causing a to be not finitely deducible). It can be shown that M' is a model of $P^M_{\mathcal{H}_M}$. A contradiction with the minimality of M.   □

The previous theorem allows to find a finite foundation for a literal in an answer set $(M, \mathcal{H}_M)$. It proves useful in the decidability proof of satisfiability checking, as well as in the DLs simulation.

3   Conceptual Logic Programs

Satisfiability checking in the above context of answer set programming with infinity is undecidable[3]. Hence we will restrict arbitrary DLPs, such that we regain the decidability of satisfiability checking while being careful so as to maintain a sufficient degree of expressiveness.

Inspired by modal logics (and DLs in particular), we restrict arbitrary DLPs to *conceptual logic programs* as to obtain DLPs such that if a unary predicate is satisfied by an answer set, it can be satisfied by an answer set with a tree structure, i.e. CLPs have the *tree-model property*. In [22] this tree-model property is held responsible for the robust decidability of modal logics. Confirming this, the tree-model property proves to be of significant importance to the decidability of satisfiability checking in CLPs.

A CLP is defined as a collection of several kinds of rules: *free rules*, i.e. rules that express that it does not matter whether a literal is in the answer set or not, provided there are no other rules prohibiting or enforcing the presence of that literal, a collection of *tree constraints*, and *tree rules*, both general rules, that are suitably restricted to ensure the tree-model property, i.e. they have a tree structure.

Formally, a *(finite) tree* T is a (finite) subset of $\mathbb{N}_0^*$ [4] such that if $x \cdot c \in T$ for $x \in \mathbb{N}_0^*$ and $c \in \mathbb{N}_0$, we have that $x \in T$. Elements of T are called nodes and the empty word ε is the root of T. For a node $x \in T$ we call $x \cdot c$, $c \in \mathbb{N}_0$, *successors* of x. By convention, $x \cdot 0 = x$ and $(x \cdot c) \cdot -1 = x$ ($\varepsilon \cdot -1$ is undefined). If every node x in a tree has k successors we say that the tree is k-*ary*. We call the maximum number of successors for a node in a tree, the *rank* of that tree. A *labeled tree* over an alphabet Σ is a tuple (T, V) where T is a tree and $V : T \to \Sigma$ is a function, labeling the nodes of T with elements from the alphabet. We extend the definitions of free tree DLPs from [13] by allowing for more general occurrences of inequalities, as well as the general tree structure also for constraints and rules with a binary literal in the head, instead of only for rules with a unary literal in the head.

Definition 1. *A conceptual logic program (CLP) is a set of rules that does not contain constants and such that every rule is of one of the following types:*

---

[3] Similar to the simulation in Section 4, it can be shown that satisfiability checking in the DL $\mathcal{SHIQ}$ [15], extended such that arbitrary roles, i.e. roles that are transitive or have transitive subroles, are allowed in number restrictions, can be reduced to checking satisfiability in an extended DLP. Since satisfiability checking for the former is undecidable [15], it remains so for the latter.

[4] $\mathbb{N}_0 = \mathbb{N} \setminus \{0\}$

- free rules $a \vee not(a) \leftarrow$ with a a (binary or unary) literal. E.g. a rule such as $p(X) \vee not(p(X)) \leftarrow$ indicates that ground literals of the form $p(c)$ can be accepted (or rejected) without further motivation, subject to restrictions imposed by the other rules in the program.
- tree rules $a(X) \leftarrow \beta$ with $a(X)$ a unary literal and β a finite set of extended literals with the following restrictions:
  - there exists a finite tree T such that there is a bijection $\phi : T \to \mathrm{Vars}$, with Vars the variables in $a(X) \leftarrow \beta$, such that y is a successor of x in T iff there exists a literal $f(\phi(x), \phi(y))$ in β,
  - if β contains a literal of the form $not(f(U, Z))$ then β must also contain a positive (without "not") literal $g(U, Z)$,
  - there may be inequalities $Y_i \neq Y_j$ in β if $\phi^{-1}(Y_1)$ and $\phi^{-1}(Y_2)$ have the same predecessor in T (they are siblings). We call T the tree representation of the rule.
- tree rules $f(X, Y) \leftarrow \beta$ with the same tree restrictions on β as above, and additionally at least one positive $g(X, Y)$ in β,
- tree constraints $\leftarrow \beta$ with the same tree restrictions on β as for tree rules with a unary literal in the head.

Consider for example the following tree rule, expressing that a top film is a film that did well at the box office and received a good review of an expert magazine.

$$topFilm(Film) \leftarrow film(Film), boxOffice(Film, Number), high(Number),$$
$$goodReview(Film, Reviewer), writes(Reviewer, Magazine), expert(Magazine)$$

Graphically, one sees that this rule has indeed a tree structure.

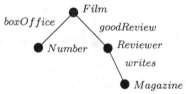

Note that we also allow rules of the form $a(X) \leftarrow$ in CLPs, since they can be replaced by $a(X) \vee not(a(X)) \leftarrow$ and $\leftarrow not(a(X))$. Furthermore, one does not need to have that the X in the head of a tree rule is the root of the tree representation.

In a rapidly evolving environment such as the Semantic Web, it is important to be able to revise or withdraw conclusions when additional information becomes available. Such nonmonotonicity is provided by *negation as failure*, i.e. the allowance for "not" in front of literals. Assume, for example, that we have that top films for which we cannot establish that they are released in the US are low budget films.

$$lowBudget(Film) \leftarrow topFilm(Film), not(releasedInUS(Film))$$

If x is then a top film, with nothing known about its release status, all answer sets will indicate that x is a low budget production. However, if we learn that all top films get a chance to make it also in the US, i.e. our knowledge gets enriched with

$$releasedInUS(Film) \leftarrow topFilm(Film)$$

we are no longer able to deduce that x is a low budget film.

An important factor in the decidability of satisfiability checking is the assessment of the tree-model property for CLPs. We define *tree-satisfiability* as satisfiability such that the involved answer set has a tree structure. Formally, a unary predicate p (possibly negated) in a DLP P is *tree-satisfiable* w.r.t. P if there exists an answer set $(M, \mathcal{H}_M)$ and a labeling function V such that $(\mathcal{H}_M, V : \mathcal{H}_M \to 2^{\text{Pred}(P)})$, with $\text{Pred}(P)$ the predicates in P, is a tree with bounded rank such that

- $p \in V(\varepsilon)$, and
- $p_1 \in V(x)$ iff $p_1(x) \in M$, for a unary predicate p_1 (possibly negated), and
- $p_2 \in V(xi)$ iff $p_2(x, xi) \in M$ or $p_2^-(xi, x) \in M$, for a binary predicate p_2 (possibly inverted and/or negated).

A DLP P then has the *tree-model property* if the following property holds: if a unary predicate p (possibly negated) is satisfiable w.r.t. P then p is tree-satisfiable w.r.t. P. For example the predicate *restore* from the example program in the introduction is tree-satisfiable w.r.t. that program, since it has an answer set

$$\{restore(x), crash(x), BackupFailed(x), yest(x, y), yest^-(y, x),$$
$$BackupSucceeded(y), \neg crash(y), yest(y, z), yest^-(z, y),$$
$$BackupSucceeded(z), \neg crash(z), yest(z, u), yest^-(u, z), \ldots\}$$

and this answer set has a tree-structure:

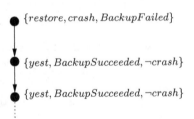

Furthermore, this is the case for every CLP.

Theorem 2. *Every CLP has the tree-model property.*

Proof Sketch. Assume P is a CLP. We can assume that P is such that every X in the head of a rule is the root of the tree representation of that rule, and such that the tree representation is a tree of one level deep [14]. We show that P has the tree-model property, from which we can deduce that every (general) CLP has the tree-model property [14].

Take a unary predicate p (possibly negated) of the CLP P to be satisfiable, i.e. there exists an answer set $(M, \mathcal{H}_M)$ of P such that $p(a) \in M$.

First note that every tree rule in P has a tree representation that is of bounded rank, let m be the maximum rank of the tree representations of all rules, and define n to be the product of m with the number of unary predicates (possibly negated) in P, We define a $\theta : \{1, \ldots, n\}^* \to \mathcal{H}_M$, such that $(\text{dom}(\theta), t : \text{dom}(\theta) \to 2^{\text{Pred}(P)})$ is a labeled tree of bounded rank. We define t such that

$$t(xi) = \{p_1 | p_1(\theta(xi)) \in M\} \cup \{p_2 | p_2(\theta(x), \theta(xi)) \in M \vee p_2^-(\theta(xi), \theta(x)) \in M\}$$

Define $\theta(\varepsilon) = a$ and assume we have already considered, as in [23], every member of $\{1, \ldots, n\}^k$, as well as $xi1, \ldots, xi(j-1)$ for $xi \in \{1, \ldots, n\}^k$.

For every $p_1 \in t(xi)$, p_1 not free, $xi \in \text{dom}(\theta)$, p_1 unary, we have that $p_1(\theta(xi)) \in M$ and, since M is minimal, there is a rule

$$r_1 : p_1(\theta(xi)) \leftarrow \alpha(\theta(xi)), \gamma_l(\theta(xi), e_l), \epsilon_l(e_l) \ ,$$

such that $\text{body}(r_1) \subseteq M$. In the case that $\gamma_l \neq 0$ we proceed as follows.

If there exists a rule[5] (either a tree constraint or a tree rule) with a body

$$\alpha(X), not(\beta(X)), \gamma_1(X, Y_1), \ldots, \gamma_n(X, Y_n),$$
$$not(\delta_1(X, Y_1)), \ldots, not(\delta_n(X, Y_n)), Y_k \neq Y_l, \epsilon_1(Y_1), \ldots, \epsilon_n(Y_n)$$

such that there exist $n - 1$ nodes y_i corresponding to Y_i, with $y_i \in \{xi1, \ldots, xi(j-1), xij, \ldots, xi(j+(l-1))\}$ or $y_i = x$ such that

- $y_i \neq y_j$ if $Y_i \neq Y_j$ in the body,
- $\alpha \subseteq t(xi)$,
- $\beta \cap t(xi) = \emptyset$,
- for all y_i,
  - if $y_i = x$, then $\overline{\gamma_i} \subseteq t(xi)$, $\overline{\delta_i} \cap t(xi) = \emptyset$, and $\epsilon_i \subseteq t(y_i)$, where $\overline{\gamma_i}$ is γ_i with all binary literals inverted,
  - if $y_i \neq x$, then $\gamma_i \subseteq t(y_i)$, $\delta_i \cap t(y_i) = \emptyset$, and $\epsilon_i \subseteq t(y_i)$,
- for the one remaining Y_j, $j \neq i$, we have that $\gamma_j \subseteq \{f | f(\theta(xi), e_l) \in M\}$, $\delta_j \cap \{f | f(\theta(xi), e_l) \in M\} = \emptyset$, and $\epsilon_j \subseteq \{q | q(e_l) \in M\}$

and we have that the body cannot be made true w.r.t. M and $\theta(xi)$ corresponding to X, $\theta(y_i)$, $i \neq j$ corresponding to Y_i and e_l corresponding to Y_j, then $\theta(xi(j+l))$ is undefined, else $\theta(xi(j+l)) = e_l$.

Define $M' = \{p_1(x) | p_1 \in t(x)\} \cup \{p_2(x, xi), p_2{}^-(xi, x) | p_2 \in t(xi)\}$ and $\mathcal{H}_{M'} = \text{dom}(\theta)$. This model clearly makes p tree-satisfiable, if $(M', \mathcal{H}_{M'})$ is an answer set of P, which is the case. $\qquad\square$

The decidability proof of satisfiability checking of unary predicates w.r.t. a CLP uses then a reduction to a finite number of simple CLPs for which satisfiability can be checked with normal finite answer set programming. The details can be found in [14].

4   Simulating Description Logics and Finite Answer Set Programming

CLPs can simulate several expressive DLs as well as answer set programming with a finite (Herbrand) universe and without disjunction in the head (i.e. *datalog programs*, where $not()$-literals may appear in the body of a clause). E.g. the program $q(X) \leftarrow f(c, b, c)$ has $\{b, c\}$ as its Herbrand universe. This universe is finite (if it is assumed that a DLP consists of a finite number of rules), contrary to the answer set programming

---

[5] Note that the tree rules/constraints are trees of one level deep.

introduced in Section 2 where the universe is a superset (possibly infinite) of $\{c, b\}$. However, one can translate $q(X) \leftarrow f(c, b, c)$ into a CLP by grounding it with its Herbrand universe, thus obtaining another finite DLP, and subsequently, a CLP by attaching a variable to it. For the above example, this yields the clauses $q(b)(X) \leftarrow f(c, b, c)(X)$ and $q(c)(X) \leftarrow f(c, b, c)(X)$, with the grounded literals now considered as unary predicates. One obtains the following theorem.

Theorem 3. *M is an answer set of a logic program P iff $(M', \{a\})$, with 'a' a constant, is an answer set of the CLP P' where $M' = \{l(a)|l \in M\}$ and $P' = \{r(X)|r \in P^M_{\mathcal{H}_M}\}$, with $r(X)$ defined such that every literal l in r is replaced by $l(X)$.*

Moreover, several DLs that cannot be simulated by finite answer set programming, because they do not have the finite model property, i.e. some DL knowledge bases have only infinite models, can be simulated by CLPs. Such a DL is for example $\mathcal{SHIQ}$ [16], which is the DL that can provide the formal semantics of the ontology language OIL [17], with transitive closure of roles instead of transitivity of roles, which we called $\mathcal{SHIQ}^*$.

We define the syntax of $\mathcal{SHIQ}^*$ concept expressions as follows.

$$D_1, D_2 \rightarrow A|\neg D_1|D_1 \sqcap D_2|D_1 \sqcup D_2|\exists R.D_1|\forall R.D_1|(\leq n\, Q.D_1)|(\geq n\, Q.D_1)$$

$$Q \rightarrow P|P^-$$

$$R \rightarrow Q|Q^*$$

with A a concept name and P a role name. The semantics of a $\mathcal{SHIQ}^*$ concept expression is given by an interpretation $\mathcal{I} = (\Delta^{\mathcal{I}}, \cdot^{\mathcal{I}})$ which consists of a non-empty (possibly infinite) domain $\Delta^{\mathcal{I}}$, and an interpretation function $\cdot^{\mathcal{I}}$ defined as follows.

$$A^{\mathcal{I}} \subseteq \Delta^{\mathcal{I}} \text{ for concept names } A$$

$$P^{\mathcal{I}} \subseteq \Delta^{\mathcal{I}} \times \Delta^{\mathcal{I}} \text{ for role names } P$$

$$P^{-\mathcal{I}} = \{(y, x)|(x, y) \in P^{\mathcal{I}}\} \text{ for role names } P$$

$$(\neg D_1)^{\mathcal{I}} = \Delta^{\mathcal{I}} \setminus D_1^{\mathcal{I}}$$

$$(D_1 \sqcap D_2)^{\mathcal{I}} = D_1^{\mathcal{I}} \cap D_2^{\mathcal{I}}$$

$$(D_1 \sqcup D_2)^{\mathcal{I}} = D_1^{\mathcal{I}} \cup D_2^{\mathcal{I}}$$

$$(\exists R.D_1)^{\mathcal{I}} = \{x|\exists y : (x, y) \in R^{\mathcal{I}} \wedge y \in D_1^{\mathcal{I}}\}$$

$$(\forall R.D_1)^{\mathcal{I}} = \{x|\forall y : (x, y) \in R^{\mathcal{I}} \Rightarrow y \in D_1^{\mathcal{I}}\}$$

$$(\leq n\, Q.D_1)^{\mathcal{I}} = \{x|\#\{y|(x, y) \in Q^{\mathcal{I}} \wedge y \in D_1^{\mathcal{I}}\} \leq n\}$$

$$(\geq n\, Q.D_1)^{\mathcal{I}} = \{x|\#\{y|(x, y) \in Q^{\mathcal{I}} \wedge y \in D_1^{\mathcal{I}}\} \geq n\}$$

$$(R^*)^{\mathcal{I}} = R^{\mathcal{I}^*} \text{ i.e. the reflexive transitive closure of } R^{\mathcal{I}}$$

A *terminological axiom* is of the form $C_1 \sqsubseteq C_2$, with C_1 and C_2 arbitrary concept expressions. An interpretation $\mathcal{I}$ satisfies a terminological axiom $C_1 \sqsubseteq C_2$ if $C_1^{\mathcal{I}} \subseteq C_2^{\mathcal{I}}$. A *role axiom* is of the form $R_1 \sqsubseteq R_2$, with R_1 and R_2 roles (possibly inverted or transitive closures). An interpretation $\mathcal{I}$ satisfies a role axiom $R_1 \sqsubseteq R_2$ if $R_1^{\mathcal{I}} \subseteq R_2^{\mathcal{I}}$. A knowledge base Σ is a set of terminological and role axioms. An interpretation $\mathcal{I}$ is a *model* of Σ if $\mathcal{I}$ satisfies every axiom in Σ. A $\mathcal{SHIQ}^*$ concept expression

```
<owl:Class rdf:ID="SalesItem">
  <owl:intersectionOf rdf:parseType="Collection">
    <owl:Class rdf:about="#Item"/>
    <owl:Restriction>
      <owl:onProperty rdf:resource="#hasPrice"/>
      <owl:minCardinality
          rdf:datatype="&xsd;nonNegativeInteger">1
      </owl:minCardinality>
    </owl:Restriction>
  </owl:intersectionOf>
</owl:Class>
```

Fig. 1. An OWL DL example ontology

C is *satisfiable* w.r.t. Σ if there exists a model $\mathcal{I}$ of Σ such that C has a non-empty interpretation, i.e. $C^{\mathcal{I}} \neq \emptyset$. It is straightforward to simulate satisfiability checking in $\mathcal{SHIQ}^*$ with CLPs.

Consider for example the small fragment of an OWL DL[6] ontology in Figure 1 which expresses that sales items are the items that have at least one price. The DL knowledge base corresponding to the ontology in Figure 1 consists of the axioms[7]

$$SalesItem \sqsubseteq Item \sqcap \exists hasPrice$$
$$Item \sqcap \exists hasPrice \sqsubseteq SalesItem$$

The corresponding CLP makes $SalesItem$, $Item$, $hasPrice$, and $\neg hasPrice$ free:

$$SalesItem(X) \vee not(SalesItem(X)) \leftarrow$$
$$Item(X) \vee not(Item(X)) \leftarrow$$
$$hasPrice(X,Y) \vee not(hasPrice(X,Y)) \leftarrow$$
$$\neg hasPrice(X,Y) \vee not(\neg hasPrice(X,Y)) \leftarrow$$

and contains rules defining the negation of concept expressions appearing in the knowledge base[8].

$$\neg SalesItem(X) \leftarrow not(SalesItem(X))$$
$$\neg Item(X) \leftarrow not(Item(X))$$
$$\neg \exists hasPrice(X) \leftarrow not(\exists hasPrice(X))$$
$$\neg(Item \sqcap \exists hasPrice)(X) \leftarrow not((Item \sqcap \exists hasPrice)(X))$$

as well as rules defining the intersection and the exists restriction $\exists hasPrice$:

$$(Item \sqcap \exists hasPrice)(X) \leftarrow Item(X), \exists hasPrice(X)$$
$$\exists hasPrice(X) \leftarrow hasPrice(X,Y)$$

---

[6] OWL DL [21] is the most expressive fragment of OWL that corresponds to a DL.

[7] $\exists hasPrice$ corresponds to the concept expression $\exists hasPrice.\top$ where $\top$ is the top concept, i.e. $\top^{\mathcal{I}} = \Delta^{\mathcal{I}}$ for every interpretation $\mathcal{I}$.

[8] Extending CLP to directly support "true negation" ($\neg$) is possible and would simplify the translation.

Finally, we express both DL axioms directly as follows,

$$\leftarrow SalesItem(X), not((Item \sqcap \exists hasPrice)(X))$$
$$\leftarrow not(SalesItem(X)), (Item \sqcap \exists hasPrice)(X)$$

which are the only two rules that are strictly necessary to express the knowledge in the OWL ontology; the other rules simulate the DLs semantics and can be automatically derived.

Formally, we define $\Phi(C, \Sigma)$ to be the CLP, obtained from the $\mathcal{SHIQ}^*$ knowledge base Σ and the concept expression C as follows.

$clos(C, \Sigma)$	$\Phi(C, \Sigma)$	
concepts A	$A(X) \vee not(A(X)) \leftarrow$	(1)
role names P	$P(X,Y) \vee not(P(X,Y)) \leftarrow$	(2)
	$\neg P(X,Y) \vee not(\neg P(X,Y)) \leftarrow$	(3)
expressions D		
$D = \neg E$	$\neg E(X) \leftarrow not(E(X))$	(4)
$D = E \sqcap F$	$E \sqcap F(X) \leftarrow E(X), F(X)$	(5)
$D = E \sqcup F$	$E \sqcup F(X) \leftarrow E(X)$	(6)
	$E \sqcup F(X) \leftarrow F(X)$	(7)
$D = \exists Q.E$	$\exists Q.E(X) \leftarrow Q(X,Y), E(Y)$	(8)
$D = \exists Q^*.E$	$\exists Q^*.E(X) \leftarrow E(X)$	(9)
	$\exists Q^*.E(X) \leftarrow Q(X,Y), \exists Q^*.E(Y)$	(10)
$D = \forall R.E$	$\forall R.E(X) \leftarrow \neg \exists R.\neg E(X)$	(11)
$D = (\leq n\, Q.E)$	$(\leq n\, Q.E)(X) \leftarrow \neg(\geq n+1\, Q.E)(X)$	(12)
$D = (\geq n\, Q.E)$	$(\geq n\, Q.E)(X) \leftarrow Q(X,Y_1), \ldots, Q(X,Y_n),$	
	$\quad E(Y_1), \ldots, E(Y_n), Y_1 \neq Y_2, \ldots$	(13)
$C_1 \sqsubseteq C_2 \in \Sigma$	$\leftarrow C_1(X), not(C_2(X))$	(14)
$R_1 \sqsubseteq R_2 \in \Sigma$	$\leftarrow R_1(X,Y), not(R_2(X,Y))$	(15)

The *closure* $clos(C, \Sigma)$, appearing in the above table, of a concept expression, C and the $\mathcal{SHIQ}^*$ knowledge base Σ, is defined as follows:

- for every concept expression D in $\{C\} \cup \Sigma$ we have $D \in clos(C, \Sigma)$,
- for every D in $clos(C, \Sigma)$, we have one of the following
  $D = \neg D_1, D_1 \in clos(C, \Sigma)$
  $D = D_1 \sqcup D_2, \{D_1, D_2\} \subseteq clos(C, \Sigma)$
  $D = D_1 \sqcap D_2, \{D_1, D_2\} \subseteq clos(C, \Sigma)$
  $D = \exists R.D_1, \{R, D_1\} \subseteq clos(C, \Sigma)$
  $D = \forall R.D_1, \{D_1, \exists R.\neg D_1\} \subseteq clos(C, \Sigma)$
  $D = (\leq n\, Q.D_1)$, then $\{(\geq n+1\, Q.D_1)\} \subseteq clos(C, \Sigma)$
  $D = (\geq n\, Q.D_1)$, then $\{Q, D_1\} \subseteq clos(C, \Sigma)$
- for all $R^* \in clos(C, \Sigma)$, $R \in clos(C, \Sigma)$,
- for all $D \in clos(C, \Sigma)$, $\neg D \in clos(C, \Sigma)$.

Theorem 4. *A $\mathcal{SHIQ}^*$ concept expression C is satisfiable w.r.t. a $\mathcal{SHIQ}^*$ knowledge base Σ iff $C(X)$ is satisfiable w.r.t. $\Phi(C, \Sigma)$.*

Proof Sketch. $\boxed{\Rightarrow}$ C is satisfiable w.r.t. Σ, so there exists a model $\mathcal{I} = (\Delta^{\mathcal{I}}, \cdot^{\mathcal{I}})$ with $C^{\mathcal{I}} \neq \emptyset$. We construct the answer set $A = (M, \mathcal{H}_M)$ out of this interpretation with $\mathcal{H}_M = \Delta^{\mathcal{I}}$ and M as follows

$$M = \{C(a) \mid a \in C^{\mathcal{I}}, C \in \text{cbs}(C, \Sigma)\} \cup \{\neg C(a) \mid a \notin C^{\mathcal{I}}, C \in \text{cbs}(C, \Sigma)\}$$
$$\cup \{Q(a, b), Q^{-}(b, a) \mid (a, b) \in Q^{\mathcal{I}}, Q \in \text{cbs}(C, \Sigma)\}$$
$$\cup \{\neg Q(a, b), \neg Q^{-}(b, a) \mid (a, b) \notin Q^{\mathcal{I}}, Q \in \text{cbs}(C, \Sigma)\}$$

It is then easy to show that $(M, \mathcal{H}_M)$ is an answer set of $\varPhi(C, \Sigma)$.

$\boxed{\Leftarrow}$ Let M be a minimal model of $\varPhi(C, \Sigma)_{\mathcal{H}_M}^M$ with $C(a) \in M$, and define an interpretation $\mathcal{I} = (\Delta^{\mathcal{I}}, \cdot^{\mathcal{I}})$, with $\Delta^{\mathcal{I}} = \mathcal{H}_M$, and $A^{\mathcal{I}} = \{a \mid A(a) \in M\}$, for concept names A, $Q^{\mathcal{I}} = \{(a, b) \mid Q(a, b) \in M\}$, for role names or an inverse Q.

$\mathcal{I}$ is defined on concept expressions as usual, and one can show that $\mathcal{I}$ is a model of Σ such that $C^{\mathcal{I}} \neq \emptyset$. $\square$

Note that while every $\mathcal{SHIQ}^*$ knowledge base can be rewritten, by Theorem 4, as an equivalent CLP, not every CLP can be written as a $\mathcal{SHIQ}^*$ knowledge base expressing the same knowledge. Consider for example the rule

$$g(X, Y) \leftarrow a(X), f(X, Y), b(Y)$$

stating that g is exactly the projection of f on both its first and second coordinate. One direction (the minimality) can be simulated by the three axioms $\top \sqsubseteq \forall g^{-}.a$, $\top \sqsubseteq \forall g.b$ and $g \sqsubseteq f$. The other direction would demand for a more expressive DL including product of concept expressions and intersection of roles [5].

5   Conclusions and Directions for Further Research

We presented conceptual logic programming (CLP) as a language that unifies both answer set programming and expressive description logics, exemplified by $\mathcal{SHIQ}^*$. This was achieved by, on the one hand, allowing inverse predicates and infinite domains and, on the other hand, suitably restricting the form of clauses so as to keep the satisfiability problem decidable.

Because ontology languages such as OIL, DAML+OIL and a large fragment of OWL, obtain their formal semantics through a correspondence with a description logic, CLP is useful to represent and reason about ontologies in a rule-based manner which also supports fine grained modularity, where ontologies can be extended by simply adding intuitive (business) rules. In addition, reasoning using CLP is nonmonotonic (through negation as failure), an important feature in view of the evolving nature of knowledge that is available on the Semantic Web.

Future work includes extending CLP, e.g. by supporting constants and further relaxing the restrictions on tree rules, possibly even dropping the reliance on the tree model property to guarantee satisfiability. In another direction, CLP could be equipped with a preference order on rules, thus introducing another source for nonmonotonic reasoning [12], which would be useful for resolving conflicts resulting from the integration of knowledge from different schema's/ontologies. Finally, we intend to confirm the theoretical results with an implementation of CLP.

References

1. G. Alsaç and C. Baral. Reasoning in Description Logics using Declarative Logic Programming. http://www.public.asu.edu/ guray/dlreasoning.pdf, 2002.
2. F. Baader, D. Calvanese, D. McGuinness, D. Nardi, and P. Patel-Schneider. *The Description Logic Handbook*. Cambridge University Press, 2003.
3. S. Bechhofer, C. Goble, and I. Horrocks. DAML+OIL is not Enough. In *Proceedings of the First Semantic Web Working Symposium (SWWS'01)*, pages 151–159. CEUR, 2001.
4. T. Berners-Lee, J. Hendler, and O. Lassila. The Semantic Web. *Scientific American*, pages 34–43, May 2001.
5. A. Borgida. On the Relative Expressiveness of Description Logics and predicate logics. *Artificial Intelligence*, 82(1-2):353–367, 1996.
6. M. Cadoli, L. Palopoli, and M. Lenzerini. Datalog and Description Logics: Expressive Power. In *Proceedings of the Sixth International Workshop on Database Programming Languages (DBPL'97)*, number 1369 in Lecture Notes in Computer Science, pages 281–298. Springer-Verlag, 1998.
7. F. M. Donini, M. Lenzerini, D. Nardi, and A. Schaerf. AL-log: Integrating Datalog and Description Logics. *J. of Intelligent and Cooperative Information Systems*, 10:227–252, 1998.
8. D. Fensel, I. Horrocks, F. van Harmelen, S. Decker, M. Erdmann, and M. Klein. OIL in a Nutshell. In R. Dieng et al., editor, *Knowledge Acquisition, Modeling, and Management, Proceedings of the European Knowledge Acquisition Conference (EKAW-2000)*, Lecture Notes in Artificial Intelligence. Springer-Verlag, 2000.
9. R. Fikes and D. McGuinness. An Axiomatic Semantics for RDF, RDF-S, and DAML+OIL. http://www.w3.org/TR/daml+oil-axioms, December 2001. W3C Note.
10. M. Gelfond and V. Lifschitz. The Stable Model Semantics for Logic Programming. In Robert A. Kowalski and Kenneth Bowen, editors, *Proceedings of the Fifth International Conference on Logic Programming*, pages 1070–1080, Cambridge, Massachusetts, 1988. The MIT Press.
11. B. N. Grosof, I. Horrocks, R. Volz, and S. Decker. Description Logic Programs: Combining Logic Programs with Description Logic. In *Proceedings of Twelfth International World Wide Web Conference (WWW 2003)*, pages 48–57, 2003.
12. S. Heymans and D. Vermeir. A Defeasible Ontology Language. In Robert Meersman and Zahir Tari et al., editors, *Confederated International Conferences: CoopIS, DOA and ODBASE 2002*, number 2519 in Lecture Notes in Computer Science, pages 1033–1046. Springer, 2002.
13. S. Heymans and D. Vermeir. Integrating Ontology Languages and Answer set Programming. In *Fourteenth International Workshop on Database and Expert Systems Applications*, pages 584–588, Prague, Czech Republic, September 2003. IEEE Computer Society.
14. S. Heymans and D. Vermeir. Ontology Reasoning using an Extension of Answer Set Programming. Technical report, Vrije Universiteit Brussel, Dept. of Computer Science, 2003.
15. I. Horrocks, U. Sattler, and S. Tobies. Practical Reasoning for Expressive Description Logics. In Harald Ganzinger, David McAllester, and Andrei Voronkov, editors, *Proceedings of the 6th International Conference on Logic for Programming and Automated Reasoning (LPAR'99)*, number 1705, pages 161–180. Springer-Verlag, 1999.
16. I. Horrocks and U. Sattler. A Description Logic with Transitive and Converse Roles and Role Hierarchies. LTCS-Report 98-05, LuFg Theoretical Computer Science, RWTH Aachen, Germany, 1998.
17. I. Horrocks. A Denotational Semantics for Standard OIL and Instance OIL. http://www.ontoknowledge.org/oil/downl/semantics.pdf, 2000.

18. J. Kopena. DAMLJessKB. http://plan.mcs.drexel.edu/projects/legorobots/design/software/ DAMLJessKB/, October 2002.
19. V. Lifschitz. Answer Set Programming and Plan Generation. *Artificial Intelligence*, 138(1-2):39–54, 2002.
20. M. Uschold and M. Grüninger. Ontologies: Principles, Methods, and Applications. *Knowledge Engineering Review*, 11(2):93–155, 1996.
21. F. van Harmelen, J. Hendler, I. Horrocks, and L. A. Stein D. L. McGuinness, P. F. Patel-Schneider. Web Ontology Language (OWL) Reference Version 1.0. W3C Working Draft - http://www.w3.org/TR/owl-ref/, February 2003.
22. M. Y. Vardi. Why is Modal Logic so Robustly Decidable? Technical Report TR97-274, Rice University, April 12, 1997.
23. M. Y. Vardi. Reasoning about the Past with Two-Way Automata. In *Proceedings of the 25th Int. Coll. on Automata, Languages and Programming (ICALP '98)*, pages 628–641. Springer, 1998.

Extracting Mathematical Semantics
from LaTeX Documents

Jürgen Stuber[1] and Mark van den Brand[2,3]

[1] LORIA École des Mines de Nancy, 615 Rue du Jardin Botanique,
54600 Villers-lès-Nancy, France
stuber@loria.fr

[2] Centrum voor Wiskunde en Informatica, Department of Software Engineering,
Kruislaan 413, NL-1098 SJ Amsterdam, The Netherlands
Mark.van.den.Brand@cwi.nl

[3] Hogeschool van Amsterdam, Instituut voor Informatica en Electrotechniek,
Weesperzijde 190, NL-1097 DZ Amsterdam, The Netherlands

Abstract. We report on a project to use SGLR parsing and term rewriting with ELAN4 to extract the semantics of mathematical formulas from a LaTeX document and representing them in MathML. The LaTeX document we used is part of the Digital Library of Mathematical Functions (DLMF) project of the US National Institute of Standards and Technology (NIST) and obeys project-specific conventions, which contains macros for mathematical constructions, among them 200 predefined macros for special functions, the subject matter of the project. The SGLR parser can parse general context-free languages, which suffices to extract the structure of mathematical formulas from calculus that are written in the usual mathematical style, with most parentheses and multiplication signs omitted. The parse tree is then rewritten into a more concise and uniform internal syntax that is used as the base for extracting MathML or other semantical information.

1 Introduction

Mathematics is potentially an interesting field of application for the Semantic Web, as the underlying semantics is relatively clear and the main problem is to communicate it in a standard way, so it becomes machine usable, for example by computer algebra systems or theorem provers. However, today the semantics exists solely in the mind of the mathematician, who uses mathematical notation, typically in LaTeX, to communicate it to other mathematicians. The mathematical notation is originally two-dimensional in its graphical representation, take for example the use of subscripts and superscripts, or the notations for fractions and matrices. TeX reduces mathematical notation to a linear form, however as a natural language of humans it leaves out a lot of information that can be easily reconstructed by the human reader, for example the structure of expressions or their types. To enable machines to work with the semantics of mathematical formulas, there needs to be a notation that explicitly denotes expression structure and makes clear exactly which operations and objects are meant in a formula.

F. Bry et al. (Eds.): PPSWR 2003, LNCS 2901, pp. 160–173, 2003.

TEX:

```
\cos(\tfrac{1}{3}t^3+xt)
```

Internal abstract syntax:

```
apply(function("cos"),
  apply("(_)",
    apply("_+_",
      apply("__",
        frac("t",Int("1"),Int("3")),
        superscript(id(Simple,"t"),Int("3"))),
      apply("__",id(Simple,"x"),id(Simple,"t")))))
```

Representation MathML:

```
<mrow>
  <mo>cos</mo>
  <mo>&ApplyFunction;</mo>
  <mrow>
    <mo stretchy="false">(</mo>
    <mrow>
      <mrow>
        <mfrac displaystyle="false" scriptlevel="1">
          <mn>1</mn>
          <mn>3</mn>
        </mfrac>
        <mo>&InvisibleTimes;</mo>
        <msup><mi>t</mi><mn>3</mn></msup>
      </mrow>
      <mo>+</mo>
      <mrow><mi>x</mi><mo>&InvisibleTimes;</mo><mi>t</mi></mrow>
    </mrow>
    <mo stretchy="false">)</mo>
  </mrow>
</mrow>
```

Fig. 1. Blowup in the transformation from TEX to Representation MathML

MathML [6] is an emerging standard for representing mathematical formulae, which however is much too verbose to be directly used by humans. For example, a short half-a-line formula in TEX corresponds to about half a page of MathML (see Figure 1). MathML comes in two varieties, Representation MathML which is targeted towards graphical representation for displaying or printing, and Content MathML designed to represent the mathematical semantics for computation or proving. Content MathML contains only basic high-school mathematics, for a wider variety of mathematical objects there is the OpenMath effort [16]. Both MathML and OpenMath address mathematical formulas in isolation, whereas OMDoc [10] allows to express the structure of mathematical documents, for example the relation between definitions, theorems and proofs.

We use ELAN4, which combines the rewriting of ELAN [3] with the powerful parser and development environment of ASF+SDF [7], to extract the semantics of mathematical formulas from a LATEX document and to generate a representation in MathML. In a first stage we use the SGLR parser [4] to parse the expression structure, which is then rewritten to an internal abstract representation, and finally to some form of MathML, currently Representation MathML.

Our project shows that it is feasible to extract mathematical formulas from a mathematical text written in a project-specific form of LATEX. In the particular project we worked on, the Digital Library of Mathematical Functions (DLMF) project (http://dlmf.nist.gov/) of the US National Institute of Standards and Technology (NIST), the subject matter was special functions, which has the properties that there are only few types (real and complex numbers and functions over these), and that there is a large body of macros for specific special functions. The task would be more difficult in subjects like algebra or logic, where there are more levels of abstraction and thus more ambiguity, and fewer easily identifiable mathematical notions.

Due to the time frame of only three months and lack of suitable tools we were not able to really investigate Content MathML, and we concentrated on Representation MathML instead. However, we want to emphasize that in contrast to other LATEX-to-MathML conversion tools [9,17], which transform a sequence of symbols in LATEX into a corresponding `mrow` element in MathML indiscriminately, we deduce the complete expression structure of the formula, and that it would thus would be much easier for us to derive Content MathML. To do this the main thing that is missing is the disambiguation between multiplication and function application, for example by type inference. We applied our tool separately to the sections of the sample chapter on Airy functions[1]. As this is only a proof of concept there are still parts missing, but, for example, we can treat the section on Scorer functions completely[2]. In particular, the current prototype cannot parse equations between expressions of function type[3], the MathML representation for a large number of macros for special functions is still missing, and we currently do not use type inference for a more general disambiguation between multiplication and function application.

Since we currently do not have permission to publish parts of the DLMF chapter we worked on, we will only show small subformulas and point to the version published on the WWW [15] where appropriate. We also use examples from the predecessor of DLMF, the Handbook of Mathematical Functions [1], in particular Section 10.4 on Airy Functions.

2   Mathematical Notation

Mathematical notation is a language invented by human mathematicians for communicating with other human mathematicians. As such it is a natural language, with a tendency to suppress information that can easily be deduced by

---

[1] http://dlmf.nist.gov/Contents/AI/index.html
[2] http://dlmf.nist.gov/Contents/AI/AI.12.html
[3] http://dlmf.nist.gov/Contents/AI/AI.8_ii.html

the mathematician. For example, in contrast to programming languages which are designed to be parsed by machines, mathematical notation leaves out many parentheses and multiplication signs, and there is no global order of priorities to chose the right reading.

We looked at several mathematical texts to deduce rules for parsing mathematical formulas, first and foremost of course the chapter on Airy functions we were working on, the Handbook of Mathematical Functions [1], but also other books chosen for their variety and availability [2,5,8,12,18] to get a wider understanding of the problem. Wolfram [20] describes his understanding of mathematical notation, however we feel that it is not as standardized as he claims.

The omission of multiplication signs leads to an ambiguity between function application and multiplication, which can only be resolved using knowledge about the types. For example, $w(a+b)$ could mean that the function w is applied to $a + b$, or that w is multiplied by $a + b$.

The omission of parentheses complicates the parsing of expressions. In particular, for elementary transcendental functions, such as sin or log, parentheses around arguments are often omitted. Expressions such as $x \sin ax \cos bx$ are to be understood as $x(\sin(ax))(\cos(bx))$ where following factors are also part of the argument to the function, up to the next elementary transcendental functions. For example, this notation is used throughout the chapter on elementary transcendental functions in [1]. However, a formula like $\sin(p\pi)z^{-n/4}$ might also mean $(\sin(p\pi))z^{-n/4}$, i.e. in this case sin could be understood to have parentheses around its argument[4]. We resolve this by parsing a parenthesis immediately following an elementary transcendental function as its argument, excluding following factors. For the DLMF project, and in particular the chapter on Airy Functions, this seems to lead to correct parses. However, there are examples in other books [5, page 1069 (305)] where this will parse formulas incorrectly.

Similar conventions apply to big operators. For example, a sum operator extends typically to the next additive operation $(+, -, \pm, \mp)$, including nested sums. Often this is made clear by the scope of the index variables of the sum, for example the i in

$$\sum_i i \sum_j a_{ij}$$

shows that the scope of the first sum extends over the second. In any case, by the distributivity laws the equality

$$\sum_i (a_i \sum_j b_j) = (\sum_i a_i)(\sum_j b_j)$$

holds, so this ambiguity is usually not a problem. We do not currently treat other big operators, as their interaction with $\sum$ and other operations is not clear to us, and varies in the mathematical literature we surveyed.

For division it is rather unclear whether in $\sin a/b$ the b is part of the argument of sin, in practice this seems to depend on the particular a and b. In the DLMF this is resolved by always using macros for division, which makes this clear.

---

[4] http://dlmf.nist.gov/Contents/AI/about_AI.13.9.html

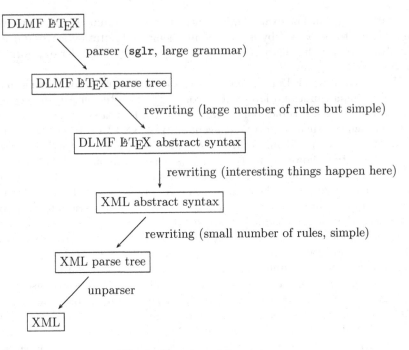

Fig. 2. Overview of the system

All of this can be expressed in an SDF grammar with the help of a hierarchy of sorts for various expressions. We will show such a grammar below for a fragment that contains the elementary transcendental functions.

3   Overall Structure

The technique that we use is to proceed in several stages, using the SGLR parser of ELAN4 to parse expressions and then rewriting them into the desired MathML representation (see Figure 2). Processing of a document begins by parsing it with the SGLR parser, which needs a relatively complex grammar that we describe in Section 4. The rest of the processing is done by several passes of rewriting. We first use a large rewriting system that parallels the grammar to rewrite the parse tree to an internal abstract syntax (Section 5), which is then made more uniform by successive rewriting phases (Section 6). From the final internal representation we produce an abstract version of MathML (Section 7), which is then rewritten to a parse tree for true XML by a small rewrite system (Section 8). From this the resulting XML can be created by the **unparse** tool that is part of ELAN4.

4   Parsing

We use the SGLR parser [4] in ELAN4, which permits to write unrestricted context-free grammars, even ambiguous ones, and has in addition a preference mechanism to choose certain parse trees if there are ambiguities. Grammars for SGLR are written in SDF, the Syntax Definition Formalism. We use preferences in the technique of "island parsing" [13], where a simple and loose subgrammar allows to parse the complete document in a rather flat and meaningless way, the "sea", and wherever possible more detailed subgrammars parse the parts that we are interested in, the "islands". In the case of this work the sea consists of the preamble and textual part, while the islands are the mathematical formulas. The SDF for the standard, non-mathematical part of the grammar is shown in Figure 3. The nonterminal `TeX-Element` is extended in `Math-Env` by environments for mathematical formulas, where all the mathematical parsing takes place. The mathematical part consists in turn of several environments which are specific to the DLMF project, which contain equations or mathematical formulas together with for example labels and comments.

The central component of the grammar for mathematical formulas is the grammar module Equation, which describes the rules according to which mathematical expressions can be formed. This grammar is rather large, it has about 100 productions, so we cannot present it here. Instead we present a fragment of its core that describes basic arithmetic and elementary transcendental functions in Figure 4. As said this is only a small fraction, the real grammar contains many more rules, for example for fractions, differentials, integrals and other, less well-known mathematical operators. Our example grammar relies on the presence of grammars for `AddOp`, `MultOp`, `Function`, `Number` and `Variable`, which are of a very simple structure, either a few lexical definitions or dictionaries of functions. A small example dictionary is shown in Figure 5. In the real grammar the dictionaries are much larger, for example there are about 200 macros for specific functions in the DLMF latex package.

5   Rewriting to Abstract Syntax

The result of parsing is a parse tree that conserves all the syntactical details of a mathematical formula. In particular, each grammar rule becomes a function symbol in the parse term, even though several grammar rules may represent the same mathematical object. For example, in the full grammar the hierarchy of sorts leads to 7 rules for multiplication. This would make it extremely hard to work with, as each of the redundant cases will need to be treated separately. We chose to obtain a more uniform representation as the first step, rewriting the parse tree to an abstract internal representation that is more uniform and closely follows the mathematical structure. The abstract syntax consists of variable-arity terms in prefix notation, with optional annotations. Atoms are either constants or strings. For example, `plus`, `apply(plus,"x","1")` and `mo("(")`{`[xml_attribute(stretchy),"false"]`} are terms in the abstract syntax. The optional annotations consist of a list of pairs of terms in braces; we use it mostly to represent XML attributes. The abstract syntax was chosen so that it is a subset of the textual representation of ATerms [19].

The rewriting system that converts parse tree to abstract syntax parallels the grammar, as grammar rules become function symbols in the parse trees, so

```
module Latex-Document

imports
    Math-Env
    Layout

exports
  sorts
    LaTeX-Document
    Doc-Class
    Tex-Element
    Tex-Token
    Comment
    Text-Token
    Macro
    Special-Macro
    Bracket-Struct

  lexical syntax
    [A-Za-z0-9\-]+                     -> Doc-Class

    [\\] [a-zA-Z]+ [\\]?               -> Macro
    [\\] ~[a-zA-Z]                     -> Special-Macro
    ~[\\\%\ \n\{\}\[\]\#\$]+           -> Text-Token
    [\#][0-9]+                         -> Text-Token
    "%" ~[\n]* [\n]                    -> Comment

  context-free restrictions
    Macro -/- [A-Za-z]
    Text-Token -/- ~[\\\%\ \n\{\}\[\]\#\$]

  context-free syntax
    "\\documentclass{" Doc-Class "}" TeX-Element*
    "\\begin{document}" TeX-Element* "\\end{document}" -> LaTeX-Document

    Comment                 -> TeX-Token
    Text-Token              -> TeX-Token
    Macro                   -> TeX-Token
    Bracket-Struct          -> TeX-Token
    Special-Macro           -> TeX-Token

    TeX-Token               -> TeX-Element

  context-free syntax
    "{" TeX-Element* "}"    -> Bracket-Struct
    "[" TeX-Token+ "]"      -> Bracket-Struct
```

Fig. 3. Top part of island grammar

```
module Expression

imports
    Layout
    Dictionaries

exports
    sorts
        Expression SumProduct ETFProduct SumApplication ETFApplication
        SimpleProduct Power Base SumOp ETFunction

    context-free syntax
                        ETFProduct -> Expression
                  AddOp ETFProduct -> Expression
        Expression AddOp ETFProduct -> Expression

        SimpleProduct                  -> ETFProduct
                     ETFApplication -> ETFProduct
        ETFProduct MultOp ETFApplication -> ETFProduct

        ETFunction SimpleProduct     -> ETFApplication
        ETFunction ETFApplication    -> ETFApplication

                            Power -> SimpleProduct
        SimpleProduct MultOp Power -> SimpleProduct

        Base                       -> Power
        Base "^" "{" Expression "}" -> Power

        Number                   -> Base
        Variable                 -> Base
        "(" Expression ")"       -> Base
        Function "(" Expression ")" -> Base

        "\\sin"                        -> ETFunction
        "\\log" "_" "{" Expression "}" -> ETFunction

        ETFunction -> Function {prefer}
```

Fig. 4. Simplified grammar for mathematical expressions

we essentially need a rule for each of these function symbols. A typical rule is shown in Figure 6. #to_term_expression is the function that converts parse trees of sort (resp. nonterminal) **Expression** to abstract syntax. The general form of the ELAN4 rules that we use (there are other features such as strategies that we do not use currently) is

$$[] \; l => r \quad \text{where} \; t_1 := s_1 \; \ldots \; \text{where} \; t_n := s_n$$

where l, r, s_i and t_i are terms. If l matches a subterm of the current term then the variables in l are bound, and the terms in the right-hand sides s_i of

```
module Dictionaries

sorts
    Integer Number Variable Function LogFunction AddOp MultOp SumOp

exports
    lexical syntax
        [\-]?[1-9][0-9]* -> Integer

    context-free syntax
        Integer -> Number

        "x" -> Variable
        "y" -> Variable
        "i" -> Variable
        "n" -> Variable

        "f" -> Function
        "g" -> Function

        "+" -> AddOp
        "-" -> AddOp

            -> MultOp
        "*" -> MultOp
```

Fig. 5. Dictionary for the example grammar

```
[] #to_term_expression(#$Expression_1# #$PlusOp# #$Expression_2#)
   => apply(#$Term_op#,#$Term_1#,#$Term_2#)
   where #$Term_op# := #to_term_plus_op(#$PlusOp#)
   where #$Term_1# := #to_term_expression(#$Expression_1#)
   where #$Term_2# := #to_term_expression(#$Expression_2#)
```

Fig. 6. Typical rule to rewrite to abstract syntax

the where clauses are successively rewritten to normal form and then matched against the corresponding left-hand side t_i. If this match fails the rule is not applied, otherwise the variables in t_i are bound and the process continues. At the end l is replaced by r in the current term, with the variables in r instantiated by their bound values. In the example variables have the syntax #$Sort_Suffix# where the optional suffix distinguishes several variables of the same sort. The # helps to distinguish them from abstract terms and TEX-text.

This example illustrates that in the internal syntax we represent most mathematical expressions in the form apply(*operation*, *arguments*), except for fractions, large operators, differentials and integrals, which have their special representation.

```
rules

[]  #improve_abstract_syntax(#$Term#)
    => #$Term8#
    where #$Term0# := #collate_tex_text(#$Term#)
    where #$Term1# := #move_macro_argument(#$Term0#)
    where #$Term2# := #transform_text_envs(#$Term1#)
    where #$Term3# := #transform_references(#$Term2#)
    where #$Term4# := #transform_headings(#$Term3#)
    where #$Term5# := #transform_user_macros(#$Term4#)
    where #$Term6# := #transform_equation_envs(#$Term5#)
    where #$Term7# := #transform_text(#$Term6#)
    where #$Term8# := #transform_preamble(#$Term7#)
```

Fig. 7. Phases for rewriting the abstract syntax

6 Improving the Abstract Syntax

The abstract syntax representation obtained in the previous step is still very close to the original grammar, and needs to be refined to exhibit all the information needed in subsequent steps in a convenient format. We use several passes that traverse the complete term and each does a particular operation on the tree (see Figure 7). First, we combine adjacent texts into one to substantially reduce the term size, and we attach arguments to macros, which in the grammar are braces that follow macros. Currently we do not do more sophisticated semantical processing, such as type inference, however this could easily be extended.

The remaining phases **#transform_X** are concerned with generating abstract XML (XHTML and Representation MathML) for output, which we discuss in the following section.

7 Rewriting to Abstract Representation MathML

As the final step within abstract syntax we generate an abstract version of XML for output. XML elements are represented as function applications, text nodes as strings and attributes as annotations. For example, the abstract syntax term

$$\text{mo("(")}\{[\text{xml\_attribute(stretchy)},\text{"false"}]\}$$

represents the XML

$$\text{<mo stretchy="false">(</mo>}.$$

We also have a special notation XML_Reference(*String*) to represent character references, for example XML_Reference("int") becomes ∫.

With this representation of XML in place it is straightforward to write rules that transform our internal representation. Figure 8 contains the fragment of the code that handles the various cases of **apply**, together with a few lines from the dictionary rules to illustrate their format. Here we use the **where** clauses of the

```
[] #to_mrep(apply(#$Term_op#, #$Term_1#, #$Term_2#))
   => mrow(#to_mrep(#$Term_1#),#$Term_mo#,#to_mrep(#$Term_2#))
   where infix(#$Term_mo#) := #to_mrep_op(#$Term_op#)

[] #to_mrep(apply(#$Term_op#, #$Term#))
   => mrow(#$Term_mo#,#to_mrep(#$Term#))
   where prefix(#$Term_mo#) := #to_mrep_op(#$Term_op#)

[] #to_mrep(apply(#$Term_op#, #$Term#))
   => mrow(#to_mrep(#$Term#),#$Term_mo#)
   where postfix(#$Term_mo#) := #to_mrep_op(#$Term_op#)

[] #to_mrep(apply(#$Term_op#, #$Term#))
   => mrow(#$Term_mol#,#to_mrep(#$Term#), #$Term_mor#)
   where fence(#$Term_mol#,#$Term_mor#) := #to_mrep_op(#$Term_op#)

[] #to_mrep(apply(#$Term_op#, #$Term#))
   =>mrow(#$Term_mo#,mo(XML_Reference("ApplyFunction")),#to_mrep(#$Term#))
   where et_function(#$Term_mo#) := #to_mrep_op(#$Term_op#)

[] #to_mrep(apply(#$Term_op#, #$Term#))
   => mrow(#$Term_mo#,
           mo(XML_Reference("ApplyFunction")),
           mo("("),
           #to_mrep(#$Term#),mo(")"))
   where function(#$Term_mo#) := #to_mrep_op(#$Term_op#)

[] #to_mrep(apply("\sqrt", #$Term#))
   => msqrt(#to_mrep(#$Term#))

[] #to_mrep(apply("\sqrt", #$Term_exp#, #$Term#))
   => msqrt(#to_mrep(#$Term#),#to_mrep(#$Term_exp#))

[] #to_mrep_op("_+_") => infix(mo("+"))
...
[] #to_mrep_op("+_") => prefix(mo("+"))
...
[] #to_mrep_op("_!") => postfix(mo("!"))
...
[] #to_mrep_op(function("sin")) => et_function(mo("sin"))
...
[] #to_mrep_op(function("AiryAi")) => function(mo("Ai"))
...
[] #to_mrep_op("(_)") =>fence(mo("("){[xml_attribute(stretchy),"false"]},
                              mo(")"){[xml_attribute(stretchy),"false"]})
[] #to_mrep_op("\left(_\right)") => fence(mo("("),mo(")"))
[] #to_mrep_op("|_|") => fence(mo("|"),mo("|"))
```

Fig. 8. Transformation to MathML of apply

ELAN4 rules to distinguish the different operation types, in order to generate
different output. For example, in

```
where infix(#$Term_mo#) := #to_mrep_op(#$Term_op#)
```

```
[] <#term_to_XML_element(#$Identifier#(#$Term,+#) #$Annotation?#)#>
=> <$QName $Attributes><#terms_to_XML_nodes(#$Term,+#)#></$QName>
where $QName := #term_to_qname(#$Identifier#)
where $Attributes := <#opt_annotation_to_attributes(#$Annotation?#)#>
```

Fig. 9. A core rule in the transformation from abstract syntax to XML

the rewriting of the term on the right-hand side results in a normal form. If this normal form has the function symbol `infix` at the root it matches the left-hand side, its argument gets bound to the variable `#$Term_mo#` and the rule is executed. In this way it is easy to write dictionaries for a large number of operators.

8   Generating XML

We have written an SDF grammar for XML with namespaces that can be used both for parsing and generating XML documents, which has the side effect that generated documents must be syntactically correct. We use a small rewrite system of 27 rules to generate XML from internal abstract syntax, which is not specific to MathML. As an example we show the core rule that creates an XML element from a function symbol in Figure 9. There are more rules for traversing the term and for the other XML nodes. In particular the rules for traversing make heavy use of list matching, since for example nodes below an element are described in the grammar by a * operator. The strange syntax with <, # and $ characters is again used to ensure that operations and variables are not parsed as TeX or XML text.

Using `unparse` on the resulting XML parse tree produces an XML document that can be passed to other tools as input, in our case for example Mozilla for Representation MathML display.

9   Performance

Of the 17 sections in the DLMF sample chapter on Airy functions we can handle the mathematical formulas completely in 6, partially in 5 (without the transformation to MathML), and 6 remain incomplete.

The grammar currently contains approximately 1000 productions, of which ca. 350 are dictionaries. There are about 550 rewrite rules. There are fewer rewrite rules than grammar rules, partly because dictionaries can be treated uniformly by manipulating literals, and partly because it is still incomplete with respect to the grammar.

On a 1.8GHz Pentium 4 compiling the grammar and rules takes about a minute, while parsing is relatively fast, on the order of a few seconds for the complete chapter. The result is a parse tree of several hundred thousand nodes. Rewriting it is comparatively slow, on the order of several minutes, since it is done by an interpreter. We do not currently have a compiler for ELAN4.

We feel that the limit of what can be achieved with ELAN4 is not yet reached.

10   Conclusion

SGLR permits a very flexible syntax, which allows to represent both LaTeX and XML directly. However, having these two markup languages, where almost every input string except for some escape characters is legal, lead to problems in correctly parsing the rewrite rules. These were overcome by designing a special syntax for internal variables and function symbols, as these can also be chosen freely.

Our project shows that parsing mathematics in the form of LaTeX documents written to project-specific rules is feasible, but due to the variations in notation the grammar needs to be engineered specifically for the project, or even for different chapters written by different mathematicians (e.g. the chapter on elementary transcendental functions and on Airy functions).

In this kind of work there will also always be some part that cannot treated automatically. For example, the example chapter contains the formula

$$\int\int \cdots \int f(t) \, (dt)^n,$$

which, even if we could parse it, we would not know how to represent in Content MathML.

The use of ELAN4 is not a prerequisite but was a convenient vehicle due to its combination with SDF. We could also have used ASF, since we currently do not use ELAN's strategies, however these might be useful for type inference. Writing an equivalent grammar with, for instance, LEX+YACC will probably next to impossible. It would also have been possible to keep the SGLR parser and the grammar, but to use other tools for the transformation, in particular JAVA tools like TOM [14] or JJForester [11]. The advantage of using ELAN4 or ASF over these is that use of user-defined syntax for both the input format as well as the output format ensures syntactically correct results. Another possible route would be to translate the parse trees into XML and to express the transformation in XSLT.

Parsing mathematical formulas in LaTeX documents is a real challenge. In this paper we only address the translation to Representation MathML, due to time constraints. The translation to Content MathML is a next step in this project and would create a link with computer algebra systems like Mathematica or Maple. We feel that to generalize and extend these results further some of the implicit mathematical semantic information, in particular type information, needs to be encoded in the document and used by more semantically directed parsing techniques.

Acknowledgments

We thank Gaurav Kwatra from IIT Delhi, who has worked with us on this project as a summer intern, Claude Kirchner and Michael Kohlhase for initiating the project, and Bruce R. Miller from NIST for making available the sample chapter.

References

1. Milton Abramowitz and Irene Stegun, editors. *Handbook of Mathematical Functions*. National Bureau of Standards, USA, 1964.
2. Martin Aigner and Günter M. Ziegler. *Proofs from THE BOOK*. Springer, 1998.
3. Peter Borovanský, Horatiu Cirstea, Hubert Dubois, Claude Kirchner, Hélène Kirchner, Pierre-Etienne Moreau, Christophe Ringeissen, and Marian Vittek. ELAN V 3.3 User Manual. LORIA, Nancy (France), third edition, December 1998.
4. M.G.J. van den Brand, J. Scheerder, J.J. Vinju, and E. Visser. Disambiguation Filters for Scannerless Generalized LR Parsers. In *Compiler Construction (CC'02)*, LNCS 2304, pages 143–158, Grenoble, France, 2002. Springer. See http://www.cwi.nl/projects/MetaEnv/.
5. I. N. Bronstein, K. A. Semendjajew, G. Musiol, and H. Mühlig. *Taschenbuch der Mathematik*. Harri Deutsch, 5th edition, 2000.
6. David Carlisle, Patrick Ion, Robert Miner, and Nico Poppelier, editors. *Mathematical Markup Language (MathML) Version 2.0*. W3C, 21 February 2001. http://www.w3.org/TR/2001/REC-MathML2-20010221/.
7. A. van Deursen, J. Heering, and P. Klint, editors. *Language Prototyping: An Algebraic Specification Approach*, volume 5 of *AMAST Series in Computing*. World Scientific, 1996.
8. Ronald L. Graham, Donald E. Knuth, and Oren Patashnik. *Concrete Mathematics*. Addison-Wesley, 2nd edition, 1994.
9. Eitan M. Gurari. Tex4ht: Latex and tex for hypertext. http://www.cis.ohio-state.edu/~gurari/TeX4ht/mn.html.
10. Michael Kohlhase. OMDoc: An open markup format for mathematical documents, 2003. See http://www.mathweb.org/omdoc/.
11. T. Kuipers and J. Visser. Object-oriented tree traversal with JJForester. *Science of Computer Programming*, 47(1):59–87, November 2002.
12. Serge Lang. *Algebra*. Addison-Wesley, Reading, Mass., 3rd edition, 1993.
13. Leon Moonen. Generating robust parsers using island grammars. In *Proc. 8th Working Conf. on Reverse Engineering*, pages 13–22. IEEE Computer Society Press, 2001.
14. Pierre-Etienne Moreau, Christophe Ringeissen, and Marian Vittek. A Pattern Matching Compiler for Multiple Target Languages. In G. Hedin, editor, *12th Conference on Compiler Construction, Warsaw (Poland)*, volume 2622 of *LNCS*, pages 61–76. Springer-Verlag, May 2003.
15. Frank W. J. Olver. *Digital Library of Mathematical Functions*, chapter Airy and Related Functions. National Institute of Standards and Technology, 2001. http://dlmf.nist.gov/Contents/AI/index.html.
16. OpenMath. http://www.openmath.org/.
17. John Plaice and Yannis Haralambous. Produire du MathML et autres ...ML à partir d'Ω : Ω se généralise. In *Cahiers GUTenberg no 33 — actes du congrès GUT'99*, Lyon, May 1999.
18. Günter Scheja and Uwe Storch. *Lehrbuch der Algebra*. B. G. Teubner, Stuttgart, 2nd edition, 1994.
19. M. G. J. van den Brand, H. A. de Jong, P. Klint, and P. A. Olivier. Efficient annotated terms. *Software, Practice and Experience*, 30(3):259–291, 2000.
20. Stephen Wolfram. Mathematical notation: Past and future. Transcript of a keynote address presented at MathML and Math on the Web: MathML International Conference 2000. Available at http://www.stephenwolfram.com/publications/talks/mathml/.

Reasoning in Attempto Controlled English

Norbert E. Fuchs and Uta Schwertel

Institut für Informatik, Universität Zürich
{fuchs,uschwert}@ifi.unizh.ch
http://www.ifi.unizh.ch/attempto

Abstract. Attempto Controlled English (ACE) – a subset of English that can be unambiguously translated into first-order logic – is a knowledge representation language. To support automatic reasoning in ACE we have developed the Attempto Reasoner RACE (Reasoning in ACE). RACE proves that one ACE text is the logical consequence of another one, and gives a justification for the proof in ACE. Variations of the basic proof procedure permit query answering and consistency checking. Reasoning in RACE is supported by auxiliary first-order axioms and by evaluable functions. The current implementation of RACE is based on the model generator Satchmo.

1 Reasoning in Natural Language

Knowledge representation requires a language suited to the problem domain investigated. Traditional candidates for knowledge representation languages are natural language and formal languages. Discussing the pros and cons of natural language versus formal languages one could easily overlook that natural language is not on a par with these other languages, but plays an important and privileged role. First, it is the prototypical means of human communication, and also offers itself as a user-friendly means to interact with computers. Second, it serves as the meta-language for all other languages, informal or formal ones. Third, natural language effectively serves as its own meta-language, thus supporting representation, explanation, argumentation, and analysis all in one and the same notation. Fourth, natural language needs no extra learning effort, and – provided we exercise some care to avoid vagueness and ambiguity – is easy to use and to understand.

Some researchers go as far as to consider natural language "the ultimate knowledge representation language" [18]. Arguably, natural language also has a great potential for semantic web applications. This potential will be explored by the EU Network of Excellence "Reasoning on the Web with Rules and Semantics (REWERSE)".

Likewise, we use natural language to perform common sense reasoning that involves logical inference operations like deduction, abduction, and induction. Knowing that

> Every company that buys a machine gets a discount.
> Hardware Corporation is a company and buys a machine.

F. Bry et al. (Eds.): PPSWR 2003, LNCS 2901, pp. 174–188, 2003.

we deduce that

`Hardware Corporation gets a discount.`

Natural language and reasoning in natural language have concerned people since ancient times. In more recent years researchers have increasingly employed computers to investigate the potential of natural language for knowledge representation and its suitability for automated reasoning [9,20]. The systems described in these publications usually process unrestricted natural language, typically do not use first-order logic but richer representations, and try to perform "one-step" inferences by introducing a large number of specialised inference rules that should closely mimic informal human reasoning in natural language.

These approaches have two major drawbacks. First, the large number of inference rules – requiring a combination of forward and backward reasoning – makes it hard to find an effective and efficient inference strategy, and can lead to a combinatorial explosion of inferences. Second, each new language construct can introduce additional inference rules threatening to further aggravate the inference process. Arguably, these objections apply to all approaches that perform one-step inferences – inferences that in first-order predicate logic would require several elementary steps.

Here we suggest an alternative approach to using natural language for knowledge representation and reasoning. Our approach differs in three essential aspects from the approaches mentioned above.

First, realising that we cannot hope to process full natural language on a computer, we use a tractable subset of English called Attempto Controlled English (ACE) – where tractable refers to both parsing and reasoning.

Second, ACE texts are translated into first-order logic. Our conviction that first-order logic is the adequate tool for our purposes is precisely expressed by "... besides expressive power, first-order logic has the best-defined, least problematic model theory and proof theory ... " [18] . Further support for the use of first-order logic in the context of natural language processing can be found in [8,2].

Third, to show that a set T of theorems expressed in ACE is the logical consequence of a set A of ACE axioms we automatically translate A and T into their equivalent first-order representations LA and LT, try to deduce LT from LA with the help of a standard first-order theorem prover, and then report the success or failure of the proof – together with a justification – again on the level of ACE.

The advantages of our approach are twofold. First, we can rely on the correctness, completeness and efficiency of first-order theorem provers and model generators available off-the-shelf. Second, adding language constructs to ACE will not affect in any way the inference rules and the inference strategy used on the logical level. However, as will be seen in the sequel some language constructs of ACE require auxiliary first-order axioms that necessarily enlarge the search space for inferences.

In section 2 we briefly describe Attempto Controlled English (ACE) and its translation into first-order logic. In section 3 we list and motivate our requirements for the Attempto Reasoner RACE (Reasoning in ACE), in section 4 we present our candidate Satchmo as the basis of RACE, and in section 5 we sketch how we satisfy the requirements for RACE. Section 6 presents RACE's basic functionality, while section 7 demonstrates RACE's application to the no- toriously difficult processing of plurals using auxiliary first-order axioms and evaluable functions. In section 8 we briefly discuss the performance of RACE. Finally, in section 9 we conclude and point to open issues and further research.

2   Attempto Controlled English

Information on the language Attempto Controlled English (ACE) in particular, and on the project Attempto in general, can be found at the Attempto web-site [www.ifi.unizh.ch/attempto]. Here, we briefly recall ACE's main features.

ACE is a controlled subset of standard English that allows users to express technical texts precisely, and in the terms of the respective application domain. ACE texts are computer-processable and can be unambiguously translated into first-order logic. Concretely, ACE is equivalent to the subset of closed sentences of FOL. ACE appears perfectly natural, but – being a controlled subset of English – is in fact a formal language with the semantics of the underlying first-order logic representation. It is exactly this logic underpinning that allows us to reason in ACE.

The Attempto system and Attempto Controlled English are intended for domain specialists – e.g. engineers, economists, physicians – who want to use formal notations and formal methods, but may not be familiar with them. Thus the Attempto system has been designed in a way that allows users to work solely on the level of ACE without having to take recourse to its internal logic representation.

Here is an ACE text from the example domain used in the sequel.

```
Every company that buys a standard machine gets a discount.
A British company buys a standard machine.
```

The Attempto Parsing Engine APE translates this ACE text unambiguously into the following discourse representation structure [10]:

```
drs([A,B,C,D,E],[drs([F,G,H,I,J],[structure(G,atomic),
quantity(G,cardinality,count_unit,F,eq,1),
object(G,company),structure(I,atomic),
quantity(I,cardinality,count_unit,H,eq,1),
property(I,standard),object(I,machine),
predicate(J,event,buy,G,I)])=>drs([K,L,M],[structure(L,atomic),
quantity(L,cardinality,count_unit,K,eq,1),
object(L,discount),predicate(M,event,get,G,L)]),
structure(B,atomic),quantity(B,cardinality,count_unit,A,eq,1),
property(B,'British'),object(B,company),
structure(D,atomic),quantity(D,cardinality,count_unit,C,eq,1),
property(D,standard),object(D,machine),
predicate(E,event,buy,B,D)])
```

The discourse representation structure drs/2 uses a syntactic variant of the language of first-order predicate logic. The first argument of drs/2 is a list of discourse referents, i.e. quantified variables naming objects of the domain of discourse. In our example the discourse referents A, B, C, D, E, K, L, M are existentially quantified, and F, G, H, I, J being introduced in the precondition of an implication are universally quantified. The second argument of drs/2 is a list of simple and complex conditions for the discourse referents. The list separator ',' stands for logical conjunction. Simple conditions are logical atoms, while complex conditions are built from other discourse representation structures with the help of the logical connectors negation '-', disjunction 'v', and implication '=>'.

Logical atoms are formed from a small set of predefined predicates like object/2, property/2, or predicate/5. For example, instead of the usual company(D), we reify the relation company, and write object(D,company). This 'flat notation' allows us to quantify over the arguments of the predefined predicates and thus to express general aspects of relations in first-order axioms that otherwise would require higher-order logic [8].

The discourse representation structure gets a model-theoretic semantics [10] that assigns an unambiguous meaning to the ACE text from which it was derived. Thus the Attempto system treats every ACE sentence as unambiguous, even if people not familiar with ACE would perceive the same sentence as ambiguous with respect to full English.

3   Requirements for the Attempto Theorem Prover

For the Attempto Reasoner (RACE) we determined a number of requirements most of which take our decision for granted to base RACE on first-order logic. Some requirements reflect the particular needs of the typical users of the Attempto system, that is to say domain specialists who may be unfamiliar with logic and theorem proving. Other requirements concern complementing ACE as RACE's main input language by alternative notations. Still other requirements refer to the efficient and flexible implementation of RACE.

Input and Output of RACE Should Be in Attempto Controlled English. To accommodate the needs of the typical user of the Attempto system the input and output of RACE should be in ACE. Alternative forms of input should be available for users familiar with first-order logic.

RACE Should Generate all Proofs. If an ACE text is unsatisfiable, RACE should generate all minimal unsatisfiable subsets of sentences of the text, i.e. sets of sentences that are unsatisfiable and all of whose strict subsets are satisfiable.

There can be several proofs of ACE theorems from ACE axioms, specifically several answers to ACE queries. Furthermore, an ACE text can have several inconsistent subsets. Users should be given the option to get all results.

RACE Should Give a Justification of a Proof. RACE should provide a justification of a successful proof, either as a trace of the proof or as a report which minimal subset of the axioms was used to prove the theorems. Especially the second alternative is of utmost practical relevance if the ACE text is a software specification and users want to trace requirements.

RACE Should Combine Theorem Proving with Model Generation. If an ACE text is satisfiable, RACE should generate a minimal finite model if there is one.

Theorem provers and model generators complement each other. If a problem is unsatisfiable a theorem prover will find a proof. If, however, the problem is satisfiable and admits finite models then a model generator will find a finite model. Finally, if the problem is satisfiable, but does only have infinite models, we can encounter non-termination for both theorem provers and model generators.

Besides complementing theorem provers, model generators generating (minimal) finite models offer additional advantages [3], foremost the possibility to construct comprehensive answers to queries.

RACE Should Allow for the Definition of Auxiliary Axioms in First-Order Logic. ACE is primarily a language to express domain knowledge. However, deductions in ACE presuppose domain-independent knowledge, for instance general linguistic knowledge like the relations between plural and singular nouns, or mathematical knowledge like comparisons between natural numbers. This domain-independent knowledge is best expressed in auxiliary axioms using the language of first-order logic. Users may even prefer to state some domain knowledge, for instance ontologies, in first-order axioms instead of in ACE. In still other cases users may want to state something in first-order logic that cannot yet be conveniently expressed in ACE.

RACE Should Have an Interface to Evaluable Functions and Predicates. Auxiliary first-order axioms, but also ACE texts can refer to functions or predicates, for instance to arithmetic functions or Boolean predicates. Instead of letting users define these functions and predicates, it is much more convenient and certainly more efficient to use the evaluable functions and predicates that are provided by the execution environment.

Using RACE Should not Presuppose Detailed Knowledge of Its Workings. Many theorem provers allow users to control proofs through options and parameters. Often these options and parameters presuppose detailed knowledge of the structure of the problem, of the internal working of a theorem prover, or of theorem proving in general, that a typical user of the Attempto system may not have. Thus, RACE should preferably run automatically, and at most expect users to set familiar parameters like a runtime limit, or the number of solutions found.

4   A Basis for the Attempto Reasoner

Many first-order theorem provers and model generators are freely available off-the-shelf. Since these tools have already reached a high level of maturity, we decided to base RACE on one of them.

Since RACE's requirements imply extensions and possibly modifications of the selected tool we wanted to have the tool locally available. This decision precludes solutions like MathWeb [www.mathweb.org] that farms out an inference task simultaneously to theorem provers and model generators available on the internet and then uses the first result returned. However, this competitive parallelism that leads to super-linear speed-ups can also be implemented as parallel processes on one single machine [21].

After an extensive and necessarily subjective evaluation of candidates – involving deduction rules for discourse representation structures [15], leanT^AP [1], EP Tableaux [4,22], Otter [13] and Mace [14] – we decided to base the implementation of RACE on the model generator Satchmo [12,5].

Satchmo accepts first-order clauses in implication form, or Horn clauses in Prolog notation. Negation is expressed as implication to false.

If the set of clauses admits a finite model, Satchmo will find it. Satchmo is correct for unsatisfiability if the clauses are range-restricted – which can always be achieved – and complete for unsatisfiability if used in level-saturation manner – technically achieved with the help of Prolog's set predicates [5].

Satchmo is highly efficient since it delegates as much as possible to the underlying Prolog inference engine.

5   Fulfilling the Requirements for the Attempto Reasoner

RACE consists of a set of Prolog programs with an extended version of Satchmo at its core. Some of RACE's requirements are already fulfilled by Satchmo, while others are satisfied by RACE's Prolog code making use of Satchmo's basic functionality and of special features of the logical representation of ACE texts.

Input and Output of RACE Should Be in Attempto Controlled English. RACE proves that ACE theorems T are the logical consequence of ACE axioms A, translating the ACE texts T and A into Satchmo clauses CT and CA, showing that $CA \cup \neg CT$ have no model, and then reporting the result of the proof $A \vdash T$ using the original texts T and A.

RACE should Generate all Proofs. As a model generator Satchmo searches for a model of a set of clauses. However, if the set is unsatisfiable, Satchmo will stop immediately once it detected unsatisfiability. The requirement to generate all proofs amounts to finding not just the first, but all cases of unsatisfiability. We have extended Satchmo so that it will find all minimal unsatisfiable subsets of the clauses, and thus all minimal unsatisfiable subsets of the ACE sentences from which the clauses were derived.

RACE Should Give a Justification of a Proof. RACE generates for each proof a report which minimal subset of the axioms was used to prove the theorems. The implementation of this feature relies on an extended internal representation of an ACE text called a paragraph. The example

```
Every company that buys a standard machine gets a discount.
A British company buys a standard machine.
```

of section 2 is actually translated into

```
paragraph(drs([A,B,C,D,E],[drs([F,G,H,I,J],[structure(G,atomic)-1,
quantity(G,cardinality,count_unit,F,eq,1)-1,object(G,company)-1,
structure(I,atomic)-1,quantity(I,cardinality,H,count_unit,H,eq,1)-1,
property(I,standard)-1,object(I,machine)-1,
predicate(J,event,buy,G,I)-1])=>drs([K,L,M],[structure(L,atomic)-1,
quantity(L,cardinality,count_unit,K,eq,1)-1,object(L,discount)-1,
predicate(M,event,get,G,L)-1]),structure(B,atomic)-2,
quantity(B,cardinality,count_unit,A,eq,1)-2,property(B,'British')-2,
object(B,company)-2,structure(D,atomic)-2,
quantity(D,cardinality,count_unit,C,eq,1)-2,property(D,standard)-2,
object(D,machine)-2,predicate(E,event,buy,B,D)-2]),text(['Every
company that buys a standard machine gets a discount.','A
British company buys a standard machine.']))
```

where drs/2 is a slightly extended version of the discourse representation structure discussed in section 2. The structure text/1 contains a list whose elements are the input sentences represented as character strings. A logical atom Atom occurring in drs/2 is actually written as Atom-I where the index I refers to the I'th element of the list in text/1, i.e. to the sentence from which Atom was derived.

The discourse representation structure is translated into Satchmo clauses of the general form

```
satchmo_clause(Body,Head,Index)
```

where Body, respectively Head, are the body and head of the Satchmo clause, and Index is either axiom(I) or theorem(I) indicating that the clause was derived from the I'th ACE axiom or from the I'th ACE theorem.

During a proof RACE collects the indices of atoms participating in a proof in a sorted list. There is one list for each proof. These lists are then used to generate reports showing which ACE axioms were used to derive which ACE theorems.

RACE Should Combine Theorem Proving with Model Generation. Satchmo, and consequently RACE, can be used both as a theorem prover and a model generator. If a set of Satchmo clauses is satisfiable and admits a finite model then RACE will generate a minimal finite model that is returned as a list of ground instances of atoms.

RACE Should Allow for The Definition of Auxiliary Axioms in First-Order Logic. RACE accepts auxiliary first-order axioms of the form

```
fol_axiom(Number,Formula,Text)
```

where Number labels the axiom, Formula is a closed first-order formula, and Text is a string describing the axiom. All auxiliary axioms are conjoined with the first-order formula derived from the ACE axioms, and the conjunction is translated into Satchmo clauses. While an auxiliary axiom is processed the atoms A of its Formula are changed into A - fol_axiom(Number) so that the Text of the auxiliary axiom becomes accessible to the justification of the proof via the index fol_axiom(Number).

RACE Should Have an Interface to Evaluable Functions and Predicates. Satchmo accepts and executes any Prolog predicate – be it user defined or built-in.

Using RACE Should not Presuppose Detailed Knowledge of Its Workings. Satchmo does not offer any options or parameters, nor can users interact with Satchmo.

6   Using the Attempto Reasoner

In its basic form RACE proves that one ACE text – the theorems – follows logically from another ACE text – the axioms – by showing that the conjunction of the axioms and the negated theorems leads to a contradiction. Variations of this basic proof procedure allow users to check the consistency of an ACE text, or to answer queries expressed in ACE. These two forms of deduction are especially interesting for the analysis of specifications written in ACE, for instance for their validation with respect to requirements.

The following examples are deliberately simple to clearly demonstrate the basic usage of RACE. We will only show the ACE input and output of RACE and omit the internal logical representation into which the ACE input is transformed by the Attempto parser before being fed to RACE.

Given the three ACE axioms

```
Every company that buys a standard machine gets a discount.
A British company buys a standard machine.
A French company buys a special machine.
```

and the ACE theorem

```
A company gets a discount.
```

RACE will prove the theorem and generate the following output

```
RACE proved that the sentence(s)
  A company gets a discount.
can be deduced from the sentence(s)
  Every company that buys a standard machine gets a discount.
  A British company buys a standard machine.
```

Note that since RACE generates minimal unsatisfiable subsets, we only see the two axioms actually used in the proof.

Given the same three axioms and the ACE query

```
Who buys a machine?
```

RACE generates the two answers

```
RACE proved that the query (-ies)
  Who buys a machine?
can be answered on the basis of the sentence(s)
  A British company buys a standard machine.

RACE proved that the query (-ies)
  Who buys a machine?
can be answered on the basis of the sentence(s)
  A French company buys a special machine.
```

All possible answers are generated, and for each answer we see only the ACE axiom(s) used to derive that answer.

Similarly we can check the consistency of an ACE text. If the text is inconsistent, RACE will identify all minimal unsatisfiable subsets. Given the ACE text

```
Every company that buys a standard machine gets a discount.
A British company buys a standard machine.
A French company buys a standard machine.
There is no company that gets a discount.
```

we get the two results

```
RACE proved that the sentence(s)
  Every company that buys a standard machine gets a discount.
  A French company buys a standard machine.
  There is no company that gets a discount.
are inconsistent.

RACE proved that the sentence(s)
  Every company that buys a standard machine gets a discount.
  A British company buys a standard machine.
  There is no company that gets a discount.
are inconsistent.
```

showing that the text contains two inconsistent subsets.

The preceding examples demonstrated the basic usage of RACE. More advanced applications making use of auxiliary first-order axioms and evaluable functions will be shown in the next section.

7 Plural Inferences via Auxiliary First-Order Axioms

Plural constructions in natural language raise hard linguistic and semantic problems [17], and trigger complex inferences. There are for example plural disambiguation processes activated by world-knowledge, inferences induced by linguistic knowledge about the structure and interpretation of plurals, or inferences that are driven by mathematical knowledge. Linguistic and mathematical inferences can be modelled by extending RACE with auxiliary domain-independent first-order axioms for lattice-theory, equality and integer arithmetic. The examples used in this section may give the impression of being simple, and are in fact easily solved by human beings. However, as will become apparent, they are not at all trivial when solved by a computer.

Lattice Theoretic Axioms. The representation and processing of natural language plurals in first-order logic requires additional axioms describing the properties of plural entities. For the practical implementation we had to settle with an axiom system that provides a good trade-off between empirical adequacy and computational tractability. For conciseness we can only show a selection of the axioms that were implemented in RACE.

From the two ACE sentences

```
Every company that buys a machine gets a discount.
Six Swiss companies each buy a machine.
```

where the second sentence contains a plural construction we want to infer the singular sentence

```
A company gets a discount.
```

To perform this inference we need to deduce from the second sentence the existence of a company that buys a machine. The logical representation of the second sentence is

```
paragraph(
drs([A,B],[structure(A,group)-2,drs([C],[structure(C,atomic)-2,
part_of(C,A)-2])=>drs([],[object(C,company)-2,property(C,'Swiss')-2]),
quantity(A,cardinality,count_unit,B,eq,6)-2,
drs([D],[structure(D,atomic)-2,part_of(D,A)-2])=>drs([E,F],
[object(E,machine)-2,structure(E,atomic)-2,
predicate(F,event,buy,D,E)-2])]),
text(['...','Six Swiss companies each buy a machine.']))
```

This representation assumes a lattice-theoretic structure of the domain of discourse partially ordered by the relation part_of/2. Additionally it is assumed that for any subset S of the domain there exists a unique least upper bound (supremum) of the elements of S with respect to part_of/2. Thus, apart from atomic individuals (atoms) there are complex individuals (groups) formed by the supremum operation which serve as the denotation of plural nouns. This lattice-theoretic approach allows for a first-order treatment of plural objects [11]. In the above representation each object variable is typed according to its position in the lattice. Lines 2 and 3 of the structure express that there is a group A the atomic parts of which are Swiss companies, the fourth line that the cardinality of A equals 6, and lines 5 to 7 express the distributive reading triggered by the cue word each.

Since from this representation the existence of a company that buys a machine cannot be directly deduced we add to RACE the following auxiliary first-order lattice-theoretic axiom stating that each group consists of atomic parts:

```
fol_axiom(1,forall([X],(structure(X,group) =>
exists([Y],(part_of(Y,X) & structure(Y,atomic)))))),
'Every group consists of atomic parts.').
```

Note that the axiom is not domain specific since it models the meaning of plurals in natural language. Hence the axiom has to be available for each proof in each domain. Calling RACE with the conjunction of the clauses derived from the ACE text and from the auxiliary axiom we get the desired deduction and RACE outputs

```
RACE proved that the sentence(s)
  A company gets a discount.
can be deduced from the sentence(s)
  Every company that buys a machine gets a discount.
  Six Swiss companies each buy a machine.
using the auxiliary axiom(s)
  Every group consists of atomic parts.
```

RACE includes other lattice-theoretic axioms, e.g. the reflexivity, transitivity and antisymmetry of the part-of relation, the proper-part-of relation, or an axiom that states that atoms do not have proper parts. Commutativity, associativity and idempotence of the lattice-theoretic join operation – needed for the representation of noun phrase coordination – are not directly implemented via first-order axioms but more efficiently simulated by list processing operations like permutation.

Equality. Many inferences require the interaction of several auxiliary axioms whereby equality plays an important role. Asking the query

```
Who buys machines?
```

we expect to retrieve the second sentence

```
Six Swiss companies each buy a machine.
```

of the above example since the bare plural machines in the query is indeterminate as to whether one or more machines are bought. To model this we represent both the query word who and the bare plural machines as underspecified with respect to the position in the lattice (structure(V,dom)). The query representation is

```
paragraph(
drs([A,B,C,D],[structure(A,dom)-1,query(A,who)-1,
structure(C,dom)-1,quantity(C,cardinality,count_unit,B,geq,1)-1,
drs([E],[structure(E,atomic)-1,part_of(E,C)-1])=>
drs([],[object(E,machine)-1]),predicate(D,event,buy,A,C)-1]),
text(['Who buys machines?'])).
```

Using the auxiliary axiom 1 introduced above and additionally the following three auxiliary axioms

```
fol_axiom(2,forall([X],(structure(X,atomic) => structure(X,dom)))),
'Atom is a subtype of the general type dom.')

fol_axiom(3,forall([X,Y],(structure(X,atomic) & part_of(Y,X) =>
is_equal(X,Y))), 'Atoms do not have proper parts.')

fol_axiom(4,forall([X,Y,P],(is_equal(X,Y) & object(X,P) =>
object(Y,P))), 'Identical objects have the same properties.')
```

will licence the deduction of the query from the second sentence. The relation is_equal/2 models equality and is defined as reflexive, symmetric and transitive via other auxiliary axioms. Equality substitution axioms like the fourth axiom can be formalised directly in first-order logic due to our flat notation. Defining equality in this way may seem naïve, but since Satchmo does not provide methods like paramodulation or demodulation there is no alternative.

Mathematical Axioms. Assume the slightly modified ACE text

```
Every company that buys at least three machines gets a discount.
Six Swiss companies each buy one machine.
A German company buys four machines.
```

Answering the query

```
Who gets a discount?
```

needs mathematical knowledge about natural numbers.

In RACE mathematical knowledge about natural numbers can be straightforwardly implemented by triggering the execution of Prolog predicates during the proof. For the current example we need the user-defined predicate

```
quantity(_A,_Dimension,_Unit,Cardinality,geq,NewNumber):-
  number(NewNumber),
  quantity(_A,_Dimension,_Unit,Cardinality,eq,GivenNumber),
  number(GivenNumber),
  NewNumber =< GivenNumber.
```

With this predicate it can be proved that an object has a Cardinality greater or equal to NewNumber (here 3) if that object has a Cardinality that equals GivenNumber (here 4) and if NewNumber is less or equal than GivenNumber. Instantiation problems – that we encountered when working with the theorem prover Otter – can be easily avoided by the Prolog predicate number/1.

Domain-Specific Axioms. Even domain-specific knowledge – for instance on-tologies – could analogously be formalised as auxiliary first-order axioms, al-though the formulation in ACE is preferable.

8   Performance of RACE

Since RACE is an extended and modified version of Satchmo, we will compare its performance with that of the original version of Satchmo. To put the performance figures into the correct perspective, some comments are in order, though.

If a set of clauses is unsatisfiable, Satchmo will stop immediately once it detects the first inconsistency. Since RACE generates all minimal unsatisfiable subsets it has to cope with a much larger search space that must be traversed exhaustively. This affects RACE's performance negatively.

Satchmo owes much of its efficiency to the underlying Prolog inference engine. While implementing RACE we have tried to preserve as much as possible of Satchmo's original code. However, to implement RACE's additional functionality we had to operate on a meta-level that necessarily introduces a performance loss.

Satchmo has one source of inefficiency, though. While trying to find a model, Satchmo again and again checks the same clauses for (un-) satis-fiability. RACE eliminates some of this inefficiency by pruning all clauses `satchmo_clause(true,Head,Index)` from the Prolog data base once they have been used. Furthermore, RACE uses a simple, but effective algorithm [16] to select relevant clauses for the (un-) satisfiability check. Other authors have proposed alternative algorithms to identify relevant clauses. A recent proposal for such an algorithm, and references to older ones, can be found in [7].

Since the original version of Satchmo used Schubert's steamroller [19] as one of its examples, we will report here RACE's performance figures for the steamroller.

We compared the original version of Satchmo with two versions of RACE, one that generates all solutions and a modified version that stops after the first solution. We used these three versions with the standard representation of the steamroller and contrasted it to the flat Attempto representation introduced in section 2. The following times were measured on a Macintosh 500 MHz G4 running under Mac OS X 10.2.6 and using SICStus Prolog 3.10.

Representation	Standard	Attempto
Satchmo (original)	15 ms	2050 ms
RACE (all)	230 ms	2100 ms
RACE (first only)	70 ms	990 ms

The runtimes for the Attempto representation may seem excessive when com-pared to the runtimes of the standard representation of the steamroller. However, we have to realise that this is a consequence of the much richer first-order lan-guage necessary to adequately represent aspects of natural language, for instance verb phrase modification and plural.

Furthermore, the comparison between the original Satchmo and RACE (all) is not completely fair since Satchmo finds the single solution of the steamroller and then stops, while RACE – after finding this solution – searches for alternative solutions. Thus we slightly modified RACE to stop after the first solution, and got the results listed for RACE (first only).

A more thorough investigation of RACE's performance remains to be done.

9   Conclusions

The Attempto Reasoner (RACE) proves that one text in Attempto Controlled English (ACE) can be deduced from another one and gives a justification for the proof in ACE. Variations of the basic proof procedure permit query answering and consistency checking. Extending RACE by auxiliary first-order axioms and evaluable functions and predicates we can perform complex deductions on sentences with plurals and numbers.

Though small, the examples of this paper already exhibit the practicality and potential of our approach. Much more remains to be done, though, besides investigating the scaling up of RACE. To support the analysis of ACE specifications hypothetical reasoning ('What happens if ... ?'), abductive reasoning ('Under which conditions does ... occur?'), and the execution of ACE specifications [6] using ACE scenarios would be helpful. These and other problems will be investigated within the EU Network of Excellence REWERSE.

Acknowledgements

We would like to thank Johan Bos, François Bry, Stefan Höfler, Michael Kohlhase, William McCune, Rolf Schwitter, John Sowa and Sunna Torge for fruitful discussions. We also thank the anonymous reviewers of a first draft of this paper for their constructive comments. Our research was partially funded by grant 2000-061932.00 of the Swiss National Science Foundation.

References

1. B. Beckert and J. Posegga. leanT^AP: Lean, Tableau-Based Deduction. *Journal of Automated Reasoning*, 15(3):339–358, 1995.
2. P. Blackburn and J. Bos. Computational Semantics. *Theoria*, 18(1):27–45, 2003.
3. J. Bos. Model Building for Natural Language Understanding, ms., 2001. Draft at www.iccs.informatics.ed.ac.uk/~jbos.
4. F. Bry and S. Torge. A Deduction Method Complete for Refutation and Finite Satisfiability. In *Proc. 6th European Workshop on Logics in Artificial Intelligence*, volume 1489 of *Lecture Notes in Artificial Intelligence*. Springer, 1998.
5. F. Bry and A. H. Yahya. Positive Unit Hyperresolution Tableaux and Their Application to Minimal Model Generation. *Journal of Automated Reasoning*, 25(1):35–82, 2000.

6. N. E. Fuchs. Specifications Are (Preferably) Executable. *Software Engineering Journal*, 7(5):323–334, 1992. Reprinted in: J. P. Bowen, M. G. Hinchey, *High-Integrity System Specification and Design*, Springer-Verlag London, 1999.

7. L. F. He. UNSATCHMO: Unsatisfiability Checking by Model Rejection. In R. Goré, A. Leitsch, and T. Nipkov, editors, *International Joint Conference on Automated Reasoning IJCAR 2001, Short Papers*, pages 64–75, Siena, Italy, 2001.

8. J. R. Hobbs. Ontological Promiscuity. In *23rd Annual Meeting of the ACL*, pages 61–69, University of Chicago, Illinois, 1985.

9. L. M. Iwanska and S. C. Shapiro, editors. *Natural Language Processing and Knowledge Representation*. AAAI Press/MIT Press, Menlo Park, CA, 2000.

10. H. Kamp and U. Reyle. *From Discourse to Logic. Introduction to Modeltheoretic Semantics of Natural Language, Formal Logic and Discourse Representation Theory*. Kluwer, Dordrecht, 1993.

11. G. Link. The Logical Analysis of Plurals and Mass Terms: A Lattice-Theoretical Approach. In R. Bäuerle, C. Schwarze, and A. von Stechow, editors, *Meaning, Use, and Interpretation of Language*, pages 302–323. de Gruyter, Berlin, 1983.

12. R. Manthey and F. Bry. SATCHMO: A Theorem Prover Implemented in Prolog. In E. L. Lusk and R. A. Overbeek, editors, *Proc. CADE 88, Ninth International Conference on Automated Deduction*, volume 310 of *Lecture Notes in Computer Science*, pages 415–434. Springer, Argonne, Illinois, 1988.

13. W. W. McCune. Otter 3.0 Reference Manual and Guide. Technical Report ANL-94/6, Argonne National Laboratory, 1994.

14. W. W. McCune. Mace 2.0 Reference Manual and Guide. Technical Memorandum ANL/MCS-TM-249, Argonne National Laboratory, 2001.

15. U. Reyle and D. M. Gabbay. Direct Deductive Computation on Discourse Representation Structures. *Linguistics and Philosophy*, 17:343–390, 1994.

16. H. Schütz and T. Geisler. Efficient Model Generation through Compilation. *Information and Computation*, 162(1-2):138–157, 2000.

17. U. Schwertel. Controlling Plural Ambiguities in Attempto Controlled English. In *3rd International Workshop on Controlled Language Applications (CLAW)*, Seattle, Washington, 2000.

18. J. F. Sowa. *Knowledge Representation: Logical, Philosophical, and Computational Foundations*. Brooks Cole Publishing Co., Pacific Grove, CA, 2000.

19. M. E. Stickel. Schubert's Steamroller Problem: Formulation and Solutions. *Journal of Automated Reasoning*, 2(1):89–101, 1986.

20. J. Sukkarieh. Quasi-NL Knowledge Representation for Structurally-Based Inferences. In *3rd Workshop on Inference in Computational (ICoS-3)*, Siena, Italy, 2001a.

21. G. Suttcliffe and C. Suttner. Results of the CADE-13 ATP System Competition. *Journal Automated Reasoning*, 18(2):259–264, 1997.

22. S. Torge. *Überprüfung der Erfüllbarkeit im Endlichen: Ein Verfahren und seine Anwendung*. Ph.D. thesis, University of Munich, 1998.

Systematics and Architecture for a Resource Representing Knowledge about Named Entities

Klaus U. Schulz and Felix Weigel

CIS, University of Munich
schulz@cis.uni-muenchen.de, weigel@informatik.uni-muenchen.de

Abstract. Named entities are ubiquitous in documents in the web and other document repositories. The information that a human user associates with named entities occurring in a document often suffices to derive a simplified picture, or a fingerprint, of its contents. Quite generally, background knowledge on named entities simplifies proper document understanding. In order to use this kind of information in automated document processing, resources are needed that make information implicitly carried by named entities explicit, formalizing it in an appropriate way. We describe the systematics and architecture of an experimental resource that contains a thematic-geographic-temporal hierarchy for classifying named entities, positions named entities of various kinds with respect to the hierarchy, lists synonyms, and gives formal descriptions of these entities and their relations. The resource should offer a general basis for semantic annotation, indexing, retrieval, querying, browsing and hyperlinking of (semi-)textual web documents, structured documents and flat texts.

1 Introduction

Named entities of various categories, such as "Ludwig van Beethoven", "Daimler-Chrysler", "Dresdner Bank", "Kofi Annan", "Second World War", "Coca-Cola", "International Conference on Logic Programming", "February", "Royal Albert Hall", "Niagara Falls" etc. are ubiquitous in (semi-)textual documents, including documents in the web. Typically they carry a large amount of implicit semantic information and associations that help human users to get a simplified picture of the contents of the document. From the occurrence of "Beethoven", "Royal Albert Hall", "February 7, 2004", "Fidelio" we can guess that the document announces or describes a classical concert in London. Documents with occurrences of "Beckenbauer", "FIFA" and "World-Championship 2006" are likely to describe some current political affair in the world of football. Documents with occurrences of "Putin" and "George W. Bush" in general are related to the field of global politics. Hence, named entities occurring in a document yield an interesting fingerprint of its general content. Furthermore, in order to "understand" contents or meta-information of a given document it might be necessary to know, say, that "Regensburg" is a town in "Bavaria/Germany" and "Christmas" is in "December".

F. Bry et al. (Eds.): PPSWR 2003, LNCS 2901, pp. 189–207, 2003.

Currently, techniques for automated analysis of documents only start to make use of this kind of information. In the area of information retrieval (IR), sometimes special dictionaries for important categories of named entities (e.g., persons, geographic entities) are used. However, the adequate role of these entities in the general process of indexing and similarity search is not yet clarified in a satisfactory way. Going beyond classical IR, analysis of named entities could obviously support various ambitious document understanding/processing tasks such as, e.g., extraction of meta-information, deduction, "semantic" document transformation, automated hyperlinking and others. However, not much of this potential role is realized in actual systems.

As a first step towards an automated analysis of named entities, a more precise picture of the semantic information that comes with specific kinds of named entities has to be developed. In this paper we focus on four general types of information. First, any named entity is associated with a collection of *thematic fields*. Second, many named entities (e.g., "Olympic Games", "International Conference on Logic Programming") are associated with a *temporal period*, or a collection of temporal periods. Third, named entities are often related to a *geographic location*, or to a collection of places. Fourth, characteristic *relations* exist between named entities of various categories (e.g., "Leonardo da Vinci" is the creator of the painting "Mona Lisa" which is located in the "Louvre"). As a matter of fact, these relations may be temporarily restricted.

Before we may use semantic information associated with named entities for document understanding/processing and reasoning tasks we have to make it explicit. A special resource is needed where information on named entities of the above type is formalized and encoded in an appropriate way. Both design and construction of such a knowledge base are difficult tasks. From a conceptual point of view a suitable hierarchical structure has to be found where thematic areas, temporal periods, locations and entities are ordered using a well-defined set of meaningful semantic relations. Using this scheme, knowledge on real world entities and topics has to be formalized and imported. From a practical point of view, the number of relevant entities is huge and associated with all kinds of thematic areas. In a way, the intended resource covers an important part of encyclopedic knowledge. On this background it makes sense to distinguish three tasks, design of a suitable architecture, realization (filling) of the resource, and adaption to specific applications.

In this paper we concentrate on the first task. We describe our actual picture of an architecture for a resource that encodes the above-mentioned types of information for named entities. An experimental version of the resource based on this architecture is currently realized in our group, concentrating on entities in non-scientific "common-sense" thematic areas. The resource is structured using three levels. Level 1, the *navigational level*, positions named entities of various categories in a thematic-geospatial-geotemporal hierarchy. Each named entity, as well as every field in the hierarchy, comes with a short formal description including main name, synonyms and others. The ordering structure of the hierarchy is induced by meaningful operations for refining and combining entries. Level 2, the *logical level*, describes relations between entities in the hierarchy. It refines and complements the relationships implicitly encoded in the hierarchy, adding explicit relations in the form of datalog facts. Level 3, the *linguistic level*, is used to associate natural language words and phrases with the entries of the hierarchy. This should support indexing mechanisms that include thematic information as well as geospatial and temporal information. Our ideas for Level 3 are only preliminary and we largely ignore this level here.

The paper is structured as follows. Taking the experimental nature of the resource into account, the following section collects some pictures and ideas that guide the design of the resource. In Section 3 we describe syntax and meaning of the identifiers that are used for the thematic-geographic-temporal hierarchy and show how the ordering relations of the hierarchy are derived from the set of identifiers of entries. Section 4 briefly describes the structure of a single entry of the hierarchy. Section 5 indicates how relations between named entities are described in Level 2 using facts. Section 6 adds some concluding remarks.

2 Motivation: Goals, Pictures, and Intended Applications

In the following description, which explains the motivation behind the development of the resource in more detail, we distinguish between

- general scientific goals that are associated with the design and construction of the resource,
- pictures and ideas that influenced the design, and
- intended applications of the resource.

It should be stressed that the general development is not governed by a fixed set of intended applications. However, some ideas of future applications are needed to guide design principles.

Goal 1. Systematics for thematic areas, periods and locations with a semantic meaning. By *systematics* we mean an abstract ordering scheme for positioning entries of a structured knowledge base, together with a scheme for assigning *identifiers* to the entries that reflect the organization. In the area of documentation languages many distinct systematics can be found for organizing collections of thematic fields in a structured way. Most systematics yield a tree structured classification scheme that is based on a single topic/subtopic ordering relation (e.g. ACM Computing Classification Scheme [ACM01]). Other systematics, such as the universal decimal classification [UDC], are more complex, but not very explicit as to the meaning of syntactic constructs used for composing identifiers. We would like to have a "typed" systematics that reflects the difference between main categories of entries (thematic fields, temporal periods, locations, entities, classes of entities, etc.). It should be possible to combine entries of distinct categories in a flexible way (e.g., ⟨"Germany","Politics"⟩ ↦ "German Politics") and to refine thematic fields and other entries (e.g., "Politics" ↦ "Foreign Politics", "Germany" ↦ "Bavaria"). Refinement and combination operations should have a defined *semantic meaning*. Further desirable properties are the following. *Stability:* local changes (e.g., addition of subentries, deletions) should not affect other parts of the identification scheme. *Arbitrary depth and branching degree:*

the identification scheme should allow an arbitrary number of levels for organizing concepts and topics. Similarly it should be possible to have an arbitrary number of immediate subtopics for a given topic. *Multiple parents:* the scheme should not be restricted to tree structures. It should be possible to consider an entry as a child of distinct parent topics. *Multiple subdivision of entries* should be supported. Many entries can be further subdivided using distinct criteria (e.g., the category of politicians can be subdivided by gender, nationality, administrative role, etc.) It should be possible to encode the criterion that gives rise to a certain division into subentries. *Efficient computational access* to subordinate and superordinate concepts should be supported.

Goal 2. Providing a basis for geospatial and geotemporal reasoning. The data contained in the resource should help to realize simple forms of geospatial and geotemporal reasoning. To this end, the *locational or temporal position* of entities and objects should be described. For example, the resource should make clear that "Munich" is part of "Bavaria", which is part of "Germany". It should encode that "Christmas" is in "December" and "December" is in the "Second Half of a Year". A reasoning component may then conclude that a given event in Munich in December 2004 is an event in Germany in the second half of 2004. In a similar way the resource should provide basic numeric information on distances that can be used to deduce, say, that the town "Holzkirchen" is within a 50 km neighbourhood of "Munich". To this end, temporal periods ("Second World War") and locations ("Munich"), as well as other classes of entities (e.g., conferences, concerts and other events) are described with the help of calendar dates and geo-coordinates[1]. In addition we use symbolic temporal and spatial relations such as inclusion or overlap. From a practical point of view, a large set of entities carrying temporal and/or locational information has to be covered.

Goal 3. Connecting textual expressions and vocabulary with thematic fields. As one vision going beyond analysis of named entities would like to be able to associate with any content word of a given dictionary a set of topical areas or domains of the hierarchy where the word has an important status. For example, the noun "heart" typically points to a small selection of topics such as "Love", "Popsongs", and "Medicine". We plan to realize a partial mapping from words/phrases to typical topics. This is the role of the above-mentioned Level 3.

Picture 1. A logical model of prominent entities of the world. From one point of view, with Levels 1 and 2 we would like to describe a simplified formal model of a part of the "real world" that includes time periods, places, individuals of distinct type, their relations etc. The model does not try to capture "deep knowledge" such as aspects of causality. It "merely" represents a (partial) collection of relational facts. Still, many details of this picture remain to be clarified. For example it is not really clear how the intuitive notion of a "thematic area" should be modelled in logical terms.

Picture 2. Chaining of associations. Any real-world topic or entity can be seen as a "mental container" for a whole class of related topics, places, periods

---

[1] As a starting point we intend to describe locations numerically using a single pair of geo-coordinates, marking a central point within the location. Clearly it is desirable to integrate more precise descriptions.

and entities. Opening this container, or looking at it with a magnifying glass, we find new subordered topics etc. With "chaining of associations" we mean a mental process where we start with a topic or entity, move to a subtopic, find new subtopics and continue up to a certain point. One characteristic feature of chaining is that it is possible to reach a given topic on distinct paths. As an example, consider the event "Olympic Games Munich 1972". One chain, starting from "Munich" could have the form

Munich → History of Munich → Munich in the 1970ies → Events in Munich in the 1970ies → Sport Events in Munich in the 1970ies → Olympic Games Munich 1972

Further chains leading to "Olympic Games Munich 1972"could start, e.g., from "Sports", or from the period "1970ies". When browsing the hierarchy we would like to support chaining of associations. It should be possible to find a specific entity or topic starting from distinct points. As an immediate consequence, our hierarchical structure cannot be tree-formed. Still we definitely want to avoid cycles. When finding an entry of the hierarchy such as "Olympic Games Munich 1972" in a document we would like to be able to derive superordinate entries ("Munich", "Sports", "1970ies"). Once we have cycles, the notion of "superordinate" entries does not make sense.

Intended application 1. Semantic annotation and semantic indexing of web-documents and document repositories. With "annotation" we mean a process where pieces of meta-information are attached to a document, or to specific elements of a document. Based on the planned resource we may, e.g., enumerate named entities of a particular type found in the document/element in a syntactically normalized way, attach thematic areas, temporal periods and locations associated with these entities to documents/elements. Furthermore, Level 3 of the resource helps to map arbitrary words and phrases occurring in the document to thematic areas, and to use this mapping for semantic annotation. With "indexing" we mean the related process where we create a simplified description for each document in a given repository. We may use the resource to create specialized subindexes that (conceptually) map named entities, thematic areas, time periods and locations of the hierarchy to documents in the repository. Semantic annotation and semantic indexing support the following practical applications.

Intended application 2. "Semantic" document querying and transformation. A popular vision is that future generations of query/transformation languages for data on the web are equipped with special mechanisms for dealing with semantic information of distinct types. Using semantic annotations of the above-mentioned form, such languages could be able to access, query and transform documents based on topical, temporal and locational conditions. A possible web-inquiry could be: "Find web pages that mention transport enterprises in a neighbourhood of 100 km around Munich. Order them by distance from Munich."

Intended application 3. Semantic Retrieval. Semantic retrieval is similar, but does not involve transformation steps. Locational, temporal or topical conditions in queries bring IR closer to data base querying. Possible retrieval tasks to be supported are, e.g. "Find documents that mention international jazz musicians and locations in Bavaria.", or "Find documents that mention banks in Bavaria, contain the keyword 'mortgage', and refer to each of the last twelve months."

Intended application 4. Typed hyperlinking. Based on the resource we may introduce links between web-pages that support special navigation/mining tasks. We may, say, link documents that refer to the same entity of category X (person, event, film, composition, organization,...), or to some entity in a given thematic area (jazz in the 1970ies). We may use the relations of Level 2 to link documents that mention at least two compositions of Ludwig van Beethoven. Using the hierarchy, links can be typed, say, with topics like "Music", "Politics" etc.

Intended application 5. Browsing. The hierarchy will include a small collection of web-addresses that are relevant for a given entry. Hence it can be used as a special (limited) kind of web-directory. Based on the above-mentioned indexing mechanisms we may also use the hierarchy to support document retrieval by interactive browsing techniques. For example, during a retrieval session where we use conventional keyword querying we may open a parallel window where we browse through the hierarchy. We may restrict a given large result set to those documents that mention at least one entity of the special category X of the currently visited entry of the hierarchy. From more general point, the knowledge available in the hierarchy is used to reduce complexity of searching and answer navigation.

3   Systematics and Organization

Thematic fields and domains, as well as geographic regions and temporal periods, can be organized in at least two conceptually distinct ways. Following an *analytical organization scheme*, topics and entities are ordered using a logical perspective. Consequently, concepts that have the same analytical status are introduced at the same level, or depth. On the other hand we may use a *relevance-based* perspective. This would mean that we try to have "important" topics close to the root of the hierarchy. As a matter of fact, the notion of "importance" is relative and depends on a given application. For example, assume that the hierarchy is used to classify news in Germany. When following an analytical ordering, the two states "Germany" and "Portugal" should be on the same level: both are European states. When using a relevance-based ordering, "Germany" has to be found on a higher level than Portugal. With our systematics we would like to support a twofold organization with an analytical principal ordering and a relevance-based secondary ordering.

3.1   Syntax of Identifiers

We use the following general philosophy. Each entry of the hierarchy has a unique identifier. Identifiers have a well-defined term structure. The syntactic structure of the identifier of an entry reflects its analytical position in the hierarchy: all analytical parent- and ancestor-relations are derived from the term structure of identifiers, in a way to be explained.

In order to support a secondary relevance-based organization we may specify for a given entry a set of "godfather entries". In the visual representation we do not only enumerate the analytical children of an entry but also its godchildren. In this way an entity like "David Beckham", who might perhaps be introduced as an "Current British Football Player of Real Madrid" at a deep level of the analytical hierarchy, can be made directly visible, say, under "Sportsmen". The use of godfather parents is not only relevant for browsing. For classification tasks it might be important to know that David Beckham belongs to a small group of prominent sportsmen, which implies that documents mentioning David Beckham are related to sports, but not necessarily to the actual equipe of Real Madrid.

Definition 1. *There are seven basic types of identifiers, E (category of entities), e (individual entity), G (category of geographic areas), g (individual geographic areas), T (category of temporal periods), t (individual temporal period), F (thematic field). With $\mathcal{T} = \{E, e, G, g, T, t, F\}$ we denote the set of basic types.*

Example 1. Entity categories (type E) can be considered as unary predicates that refer to a set of entities. Examples are "Persons", "Composers", "Organizations", "Paintings". Examples for individual entities (type e), which can be interpreted as individual constants, are "George W. Bush", "Beethoven", "Picasso", "BMW", "The Rolling Stones". Possible categories of geographic areas (type G) are, e.g., "Continents", "States", "Industrial Regions". Individual geographic areas (type g) are, e.g., "Austria", "Germany", "Pacific Ocean", "Alps". Categories of temporal periods (type T) are, e.g., "Political Epochs", "Epochs in Art", "Centuries". Individual temporal periods (type t) are, e.g., "Middle Ages", "Second World War", "1970ies". Thematic fields (type F) are "Politics", "Arts", "Music", "Mathematics and Music in Ancient Greece".

Definition 2. *The set of possible identifiers, $\mathcal{I}(\mathcal{T}, \mathbb{N})$, is recursively defined as follows:*

1. Root Identifier. *The empty sequence, written ( ), is a possible identifier.*
2. Local Introduction. *If φ is an identifier, n is a positive integer, and if $X \in \mathcal{T}_0$ is a basic type, then $(X\varphi.n)$ is a possible identifier.*
3. Symmetric Intersection. *If φ and ψ are possible identifiers, then $(\varphi \& \psi)$ is a possible identifier. The operator "$\&$" is considered to be associative, commutative and idempotent. Hence expressions $(\varphi_1 \& \varphi_2 \& \ldots \& \varphi_n)$ are well-formed. The root identifier ( ) is treated as a neutral element w.r.t. "$\&$", which means that expressions $(\varphi \& ( ))$ and φ are equivalent.*
4. Focus. *If φ and ψ are identifiers, and if φ has type E, G, T, or F, then $(\varphi : \psi)$ is an identifier. The root identifier ( ) is treated as a right neutral element w.r.t. "$:$", which means that expressions $(\varphi : ( ))$ and φ are equivalent.*

We use the following *notational conventions*: If $\varphi = ( )$ we write $(X.n)$ for $(X\varphi.n)$. Expressions $(X\varphi.n.k)$ are shorthand for $(X(X\varphi.n).k)$. Similarly $(X.n.k)$ is shorthand for $(X(X.n).k)$.

Remark 1. In order to account for the above equivalences, identifiers are *normalized* in the actual system. This means that nested symmetric intersections are flattened in the obvious way. Conjuncts "( )" are suppressed, as well as multiple conjuncts, the remaining conjuncts are ordered lexicographically. For example, the normal form of $(((\;)\&(F.1))\&(((F.3)\&(F.2))\&(F.3))$ is $((F.1)\&(F.2)\&(F.3))$. Furthermore, any focus on $(\;)$ is erased.

In the sequel, we write $\mathcal{I}^n(\mathcal{T}, \mathbb{N})$ for the set of normalized identifiers. If not mentioned otherwise, with an identifier we always mean a normalized identifier.

Remark 2. For points deeply embedded in the hierarchy, identifiers tend to be notationally complex and long. In the implemented version, each entry is mapped to a unique integer that represents a second, numerical identifier. An identifier of the form $(\varphi\&\psi)$ can then be written more compact in the form $(n\&m)$ where n and m respectively denote the numerical identifiers corresponding to φ and ψ.

3.2 Meaning of Identifiers

The following remarks explain the intuition behind the above three operations and describe the meaning. Clearly, since we model parts of the real world we cannot expect to have a fully formalized semantics as, say, in mathematical logic. Still, persons that fill the hierarchy and persons that use the results should have a common picture that is as precise as possible.

Local Introduction. When moving to a specific topic, φ, we may find new entity classes, thematic subtopics, temporal periods, geographic areas etc. that are specific for the given topic in the sense that they do not play a major role "outside" the topic. In such a case, the entity class (or the thematic subfield, the period, the geographic area etc.) is introduced into the hierarchy using a local introduction $(X\varphi.n)$. For example, consider an entry "Music" with identifier φ. The category of entities "Compositions" is only relevant inside the area of music. We might introduce it using an identifier $(E\varphi.1)$. If φ stands for Europe, the European Commission might be introduced as $(e\varphi.1)$, the 20 commissioners as $(E\varphi.1)$. An entry "Politics" with identifier ψ might be refined using a local introduction $(F\psi.5)$ to "Foreign Politics". In contrast, assuming that "Germany" is an entry of the hierarchy, "German Politics" would not be introduced by a local introduction, but as a symmetric intersection (s.b.). The following list illustrates the formal relationship between an entry φ and a local introduction $(X\varphi.n)$. Due to type differences there are 49 possible instances of the local introduction scheme. Hence we cannot describe all cases here. In the sequel we use superscripts to denote types. Outermost superscripts represent the type of the resulting expression.

1. $(t\varphi^t.n)^t$: a subperiod of the temporal period φ.
2. $(T\varphi^T.n)^T$: a subcategory of the category of temporal periods φ.
3. $(T\varphi^t.n)^T$: a category of temporal periods, all overlapping with temporal period φ. We do not demand containment in φ. As an example, assume that we want to introduce as a category the "Years of the Second World War" using $\varphi =$ "Second World War". Then 1945 would be a member of the category, even if the war was finished before the end of 1945.
4. $(t\varphi^T.n)^t$: a member of the category of temporal periods φ.
5. $(G\varphi^g.n)^G$: a category of locations, all overlapping with the location φ.

6. $(e\varphi^e.n)^e$: a subentity of the structured (complex) entity φ.
7. $(E\varphi^e.n)^E$: a category of entities, all subentities of the complex entity φ.
8. $(e\varphi^E.n)^e$: a member of the category of entities φ.

Symmetric Intersection. Given two thematic fields φ^F and ψ^F the symmetric intersection $(\varphi\&\psi)$ denotes the thematic intersection of the two fields. A symmetric intersection is used if any subtopic of $(\varphi\&\psi)$ can be considered as a common subtopic of both φ and ψ, which means that $(\varphi\&\psi)$ is a subarea of both arguments. Given the analytical hierarchy defined below, $(\varphi\&\psi)$ will always be a child both of φ and ψ. For unbalanced combinations where the second argument only selects a specific subarea of the first argument the focus operator is used (s.b.). In the general case the meaning of the operator "&" depends on the types of the arguments. We list some examples.

1. $(\varphi^t\&\psi^t)^t$: a temporal period representing the intersection of temporal periods φ and ψ.
2. $(\varphi^t\&\psi^T)^T$: the category of temporal periods obtained by restricting category ψ to those periods that overlap with period φ (cf. Case 3 above).
3. $(\varphi^g\&\psi^G)^G$: category of locations obtained restricting category ψ to those locations that overlap with location φ. For example, "Danubian states" are states overlapping with the Danube, and not states within the Danube.
4. $(\varphi^F\&\psi^t)^F$: thematic field φ restricted to "temporal window" ψ. For example, if φ denotes "Politics" and ψ denotes "Second World War", then $(\varphi^F\&\psi^t)^F$ means "Politics During the Second World War".
5. $(\varphi^F\&\psi^g)^F$: thematic field φ restricted to location ψ. The interpretation is liberal in the sense that subtopics only must have some strong relationship to location ψ. For example if φ denotes "Politics" and ψ means "Germany", then "German Politics" can be introduced as $(\varphi^F\&\psi^g)^F$. Still, events of the field "German Politics" might happen, say, in Paris, Warsaw, or Washington.
6. $(\varphi^F\&\psi^G)^F$: thematic field φ restricted to locations of the category ψ. If φ denotes "Education" and ψ denotes "European States" then "Education in European States" can be introduced as $(\varphi^F\&\psi^G)^F$.
7. $(\varphi^E\&\psi^F)^E$: a subcategory of the class of entities φ^E. Only entities are considered that are relevant for the thematic field F (entities "in the area" F).
8. $(\varphi^E\&\psi^e)^E$: a subcategory of the class of entities φ^E. Only entities are considered where entity e plays a dedicated role. If φ denotes "Symphonies" and ψ denotes "Haydn" then "Symphonies of Haydn" can be introduced as $(\varphi^E\&\psi^e)^E$.

Focus. The focus operation $(\varphi : \psi)$ is used for a kind of combination where the first argument φ, which has type $X \in \{T, G, E, F\}$, is more privileged than the "focussed" argument ψ. Typically, ψ represents just a kind of "object", an "orientation" of φ, the type of $(\varphi : \psi)$ is always the type of φ. For example, "French Policy concerning Germany" could be modelled as "French Policy" focussing "Germany". As a second example, consider the difference between "Political Sciences" (German word: "Politikwissenschaft") and "Policy of Science" (German word: "Wissenschaftspolitik"). The former can be modelled as "Science" focussing "Policy", the latter as "Policy" focussing "Science". Similarly "Policy of Education" would be modelled as "Policy" focussing "Education", "Political Films" as "Films" focussing "Policy". It should be mentioned that in practice we found a considerable number of cases where it is difficult to decide if a symmetric intersection or a combination using the focus operation is more appropriate. For example, under one possible interpretation, "Religious Arts" can also be considered as "Arts" focussing "Religion". The problem is to decide if icons and other paintings of the field of "Religious Arts" really have some kind of religious status. If this is typically the case, then the use of a symmetric intersection is appropriate.

Remark 3. For some applications it might seem desirable to model the relationship between distinct topics in a more detailed way, introducing further operations. However, we have seen above that even with our coarse scheme it is sometimes difficult to select the "correct" operation. These difficulties tend to grow with an enlarged set of operations.

Remark 4. In order to design special reasoning mechanisms for the information found in the hierarchy it would be interesting to have a formal notion of a "model" of the hierarchy, purely based on algebraic notions. The development of such a notion is one point of future work. Parts of Definition 2 can be considered as a partial axiomatization. Subclasses of models could be characterized using additional axioms such as, e.g., the equivalence between $(\varphi : (\psi_1 \& \psi_2))$ and $((\varphi : \psi_1) \& (\varphi : \psi_2))$.

3.3 Derived Hierarchical Structure

When describing a concrete thematic-geographic-temporal hierarchy we use a finite subset H of the set of all normalized identifiers, $\mathcal{I}^n(\mathcal{T}, \mathbb{N})$. We now want to define an ordering relation on H, based on a suitable parent/child relation. It might seem natural to treat for any symmetric intersection of the form $\varphi := (\delta_1 \& \delta_2)$ the two identifiers δ_1 and δ_2 as analytical parents of φ. However, this leads to counterintuitive results. For example, with this choice, all identifiers of H in the sequence $(\delta \& (F.1)), (\delta \& (F.1.1)), (\delta \& (F.1.1.1)), \dots$ would be treated as unrelated children of $\delta \in H$. Thus the number of children becomes unacceptable and the intuitive internal order among these children is ignored.

Definition 3. *The set* min-gen(φ) *of minimal generalizations of* $\varphi \in \mathcal{I}^n(\mathcal{T}, \mathbb{N})$, *and the set of X-refinements (where $X \in \mathcal{T}$) of a normalized identifier is recursively defined in the following way (exponents n denote normalization):*

1. min-gen$((\ )) := \emptyset$.
2. min-gen$((X\psi.n)) := \{\psi\}$; *the identifier* $(X\psi.n)$ *is an X-refinement of* ψ.
3. min-gen$((\varphi \& \psi)) := \{(\varphi' \& \psi)^n \mid \varphi' \in \text{min-gen}(\varphi)\} \cup \{(\varphi \& \psi')^n \mid \psi' \in \text{min-gen}(\psi)\}$. *Here* $(\varphi \& \psi)$ *is an X-refinement of* $(\varphi' \& \psi)$ *iff* φ *is an X-child of* φ', *and similarly for* $(\varphi \& \psi)$ *and* $(\varphi \& \psi')$.
4. min-gen$((\varphi : \psi)) := \{(\varphi' : \psi)^n \mid \varphi' \in \text{min-gen}(\varphi)\} \cup \{(\varphi : \psi')^n \mid \psi' \in \text{min-gen}(\psi)\}$. *Here* $(\varphi : \psi)$ *is an X-refinement of* $(\varphi' : \psi)$ *iff* φ *is an X-refinement of* φ', *and similarly for* $(\varphi : \psi)$ *and* $(\varphi : \psi')$.

With gen(φ) *we denote the set of all* generalizations *of* φ, *which is obtained using the transitive closure of the min-gen-relation.*

We define $\psi <_{gen} \varphi$ iff $\psi \in$ gen(φ) and call "$<_{gen}$" the *refinement/ generalization order* on normalized identifiers in $\mathcal{I}^n(\mathcal{T}, \mathbb{N})$. It is simple to see that $\psi <_{gen} \varphi$ implies that the notational length of ψ is smaller than the length of φ. As a trivial consequence we obtain:

Lemma 1. *The refinement ordering* "$<_{gen}$" *is a strict partial ordering on* $\mathcal{I}^n$ $(\mathcal{T}, \mathbb{N})$. *It imposes the structure of a rooted directed acyclic graph on* $\mathcal{I}^n(\mathcal{T}, \mathbb{N})$.

Definition 4. *Let* H *be a finite subset of* $\mathcal{I}^n(\mathcal{T}, \mathbb{N})$, *let* $\varphi \in H$. *The set* $R \subseteq$ gen(φ)$\cap H$ *is called a* minimal coverage *of* φ *w.r.t.* H *iff the following conditions hold:*

1. Coverage. *For all* $\psi \in$ gen(φ) $\cap H$ *there exists an element* $\varphi' \in R$ *such that* $\psi \leq_{gen} \varphi'$.
2. Minimality. *If* φ_1 *and* φ_2 *are elements of* R, *then neither* $\varphi_1 <_{gen} \varphi_2$ *nor* $\varphi_2 <_{gen} \varphi_1$.

It is not difficult to see that a minimal coverage always exists and is unique.

Definition 5. *Let* H *be a finite subset of* $\mathcal{I}^n(\mathcal{T}, \mathbb{N})$. *Then the* analytical parents *of* $\varphi \in H$ *w.r.t.* H *are the elements of the minimal coverage of* φ *w.r.t.* H.

Example 2. We illustrate the definition of the analytical parent-child relation with an example from sports where we show how the Spanish football club "Real Madrid" could be positioned in a suitable (fragment of the) hierarchy. Let us assume we have the following entries in H: $(F.9)$ "Sports", $(E.3)$ "Organizations", σ "Spain" (we leave the form of σ open), $((F.9)\&\sigma)$ "Spanish Sports", $((F.9)\&(E.3))$ "Sports Organizations", $(F.9.1)$ "Ball Games", $(F.9.1.1)$ "Football", $((F.9.1.1)\&(E.3))$ "Football Organizations", $((F.9.1.1)\&\sigma)$ "Spanish Football", $(E((F.9.1.1)\&(E.3)).1)$ "Football Clubs", $((E((F.9.1.1)\&(E.3)).1)\&\sigma)$ "Spanish Football Clubs". Then $(e((E((F.9.1.1)\&(E.3)).1)\&\sigma).1)$ might denote "Real Madrid". The analytical parent-child relationship induced by this set-up can be seen in Figure 1. Now assume that we delete entry $((F.9.1.1)\&\sigma)$ "Spanish Football" in H. Then link (1) disappears, and links (2), (3) are merged into a link from "Spanish Sports" to "Spanish Football Clubs".

Note that the semantics of the analytical parent-child relation can be derived from the meaning of the operations. From Section 3.2 it follows that in Figure 1 $((F.9.1.1)\&\sigma)$ "Spanish Football" is a thematic subarea of $(F.9.1.1)$ "Football" obtained by looking only at those aspects/subtopics with a close relationship to the location σ "Spain". Similarly it follows that $((F.9.1.1)\&(E.3))$ "Football Organisations" is obtained from $((F.9)\&(E.3))$ "Sports Organisations" by restricting organisations in the area of sports to organisations in the more specific area of football. Still, the ordering relations of the hierarchy only capture a part the information that is encoded in the identifiers, due to "missing points" in the hierarchy (such as "Spanish Football Organisations" above).

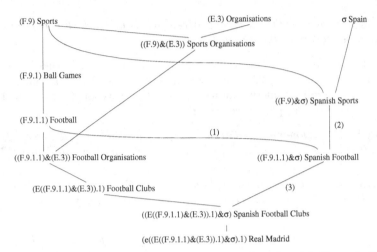

Fig. 1. Parent-child relationship derived from identifiers (cf. Example 2).

Remark 5. The actual computation of analytical parents of an identifier φ w.r.t. a given set $H \subset \mathcal{I}^n(\mathcal{T}, \mathbb{N})$ proceeds in two steps. (1) We first compute a coverage for φ. To this end we "treat" every minimal refinement φ' of φ. To treat φ' means: check if $\varphi' \in H$. In the positive case, add φ' to the coverage for φ. In the negative case, treat the minimal refinements of φ'. (2) Given a coverage C we erase all members that refine other members of C. Details are omitted.

The transitive closure of the analytical parent relation on H is called the *ancestor-relation* on H and denoted "$<^H_{gen}$".

Definition 6. *A subset H of $\mathcal{I}^n(\mathcal{T}, \mathbb{N})$ is called* constructive *iff the following conditions hold: (1) $(\ ) \in H$, (2) $(X\varphi.n) \in H$ implies that $\varphi \in H$ ($X \in \{t, T, g, G, e, E, F\}$ and $n \in \mathbb{N}$), (3) $(\varphi \& \psi) \in H$ implies $\varphi \in H$ and $\psi \in H$, (4) $(\varphi : \psi) \in H$ implies $\varphi \in H$ and $\psi \in H$.*

Lemma 2. *Let H be a constructive subset of $\mathcal{I}^n(\mathcal{T}, \mathbb{N})$. Then the ancestor relationship "$<^H_{gen}$" is a strict partial order on H that imposes the structure of a rooted directed acyclic graph on H.*

Remark 6. In the graphical visualization we not only depict analytical children of a given entry, but also visualize the godchildren. As long as we do not control the introduction of godfathers there is no guarantee that we run into a loop when we follow arbitrary chains of children. For this reason, the visualization of analytical children and godchildren is distinct.

3.4   Examples from the Experimental Version

In order to illustrate the systematics we add two further examples from the experimental version.

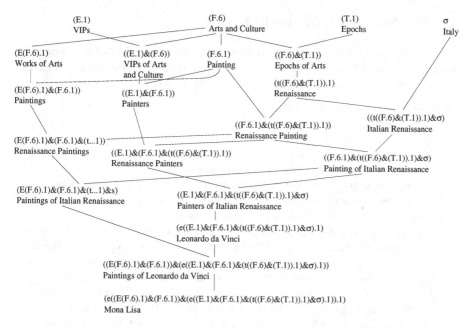

Fig. 2. Part of the experimental hierarchy.

Example 3. The first level (analytical children of the root node) of the current hierarchy has the following entries[2]. (E.1) "Persönlichkeiten" (VIPs), (E.2) "Events", (E.3) "Organisationen und Einrichtungen" (Organisations and Institutions), (F.1) "Politik" (Politics), (F.2) "Wirtschaft" (Economy), (F.3) "Finanzen" (Financial Sector), (F.4) "Recht und Justiz" (Law), (F.5) "Wissenschaft und Technik" (Science and Technology), (F.6) "Kunst und Kultur" (Arts and Culture), (F.7) "Medien und Kommunikation" (Media and Communication), (F.8) "Bildung, Erziehung, Ausbildung und Beruf" (Education and Profession), (F.9) "Sport" (Sports), (F.10) "Religion", (F.11) "Lifestyle", (F.12) "Gesundheit und Ernährung" (Health and Food), (F.13) "Natur und Umwelt" (Nature and Environment), (G.1) "Geophysische Lokationen" (Geophysical Locations), (G.2) "Politische geographische Lokationen" (Political Geographic Locations), (G.3) "Kulturelle und religiöse Lokationen" (Cultural and Religious Locations), (t.1) "Geschichte" (History), (T.1) "Epochen" (Epochs), (T.2) "Jahrhunderte" (Centuries).

Example 4. Figure 2 gives a partial picture of the hierarchy, including temporal and geographic axes, and illustrates how entities such as "Leonardo da Vinci" and "Mona Lisa" are positioned in the hierarchy.

---

[2] The current version of the resource uses German notions. English translations are given in parentheses for convenience.

4   The Structure of the Entries

We have seen how entries are positioned in the hierarchy. In order to complete the description of Level 1 of the resource, some words on the structure of entries are in order. Any entry of the hierarchy has the following components:

1. *Identifier* (element of $\mathcal{I}^n(\mathcal{T}, \mathbb{N})$).
2. *Secondary identifier* (integer).
3. *Main name* (non-empty string).
4. *Explanation* (string, possibly empty). Explains the meaning/use of the main name in the present context. For human readers.
5. *Identifiers of godfather entries* (list, possibly empty). Determines entries of the hierarchy where the given entry is treated as an non-analytical immediate child since it is considered as a relevant subentry.
6. *Synonyms* (list of strings, possibly empty). Collects distinct natural language expressions that can be interpreted (in one reading) as synonyms of the main name. Synonyms are important for recognizing entities and topics in texts. Clearly, a remaining difficult problem is the resolution of ambiguities.
7. *Relationship to entries of other classification schemes.* Explains synonymy, hyperonymy, hyponymy or similarity relations with subject categories from other classification schemes such as the universal decimal classification UDC [UDC] and the IPTC subject classification [IPT].

In addition, all entries of type $X \in \{g, t, e\}$ come with a *formal description* that depends on the category of the entry. In the experimental version, the format of the formal description has only been fixed for a small number if entity classes. As an illustration we describe which kind of data should be included in the formal description of events. Some of these data belong to Level 2 (logical level).

1. *Main URL* (optional). If there is any URL especially for the event.
2. *Useful URLs.* URLs where useful information associated with the event can be found.
3. *Temporal description:*
   (a) Singular or periodical (sin/per).
   (b) First/last occurrence (only for periodical events). Last occurrence: use the last occurrence that is confirmed. This may be a point in future.
   (c) Turnus (for periodical events only). (n days, n weeks, n months, or n years ($n \in \mathbb{N}$).
   (d) Duration. (n days, n weeks, n months, or n years $n \in \mathbb{N}$). May be qualified with "approx.".
   (e) Temporal "home" position. For periodical events list a period that describes the usual temporal position of the event within a year as precisely as possible (upper and lower boundary). Similar for singular events. There are the following alternatives: For specifying a rough period of the year, the categories (first half, second half, spring, summer, autumn, winter) may be used. It is also possible to list an interval of months (from April to August). It is also possible to give a more precise interval such as "from April 15 to August 15".

4. *Location*. A state plus a subcountry (such as Bavaria, optional) plus a city (optional) plus an address (optional). States and cities should be introduced in the hierarchy. We use their identifiers. Exceptions are possible (small unknown towns). For periodical events with distinct places we only give a common location of all instances. (E.g., "Europe" for European championships).
5. *Location URL* (optional). This might be the URL of a concert hall, of a theatre, of a city, of a country,...
6. *Organizer* (optional). This might be another entity of the hierarchy (give identifier and main name), or a freely specified entity.
7. *Organizer URL* (optional).
8. *Importance*. International (i), national (n), or local (l).

5 Level 2: Facts

Level 2 of the planned resource represents a collection of facts that yield a more precise description of the relations between distinct entries of a hierarchy. Facts are classified into several categories.

1. Compositional Facts describe the composition of an entry in terms of other entries.

Definition 7. *A symmetric union has the form* $(\psi_1 \sqcup \ldots \sqcup \psi_n)$ *(n $\geq$ 2) where the components ψ_i are distinct normalized identifers of the same type $X \in F, E, G, T, g, t$ ($1 \leq i \leq n$). $(\psi_1 \sqcup \ldots \sqcup \psi_n)$ has type X.*

The operator "$\sqcup$" is considered to be associative, commutative and idempotent. Read, e.g., $((F.1) \sqcup (F.3))$ as "Union of universal thematic fields 1 and 3", $((G.1) \sqcup (G.3))$ as "Union of the categories of geo-entities 1 and 3", and $((g.1) \sqcup (g.3))$ as "Spatial union of the geo-entities 1 and 3", and $((t.1) \sqcup (t.3))$ as "Temporal union of the temporal periods 1 and 3".

Definition 8. *Let φ denote an identifier, let $\alpha \in D$ be a possible division criterion. A compositional fact for φ has the form $\varphi \equiv (\psi_1 \sqcup \ldots \sqcup \psi_n)$, $\varphi \equiv [\alpha](\psi_1 \sqcup \ldots \sqcup \psi_n)$, $\varphi \sqsubseteq (\psi_1 \sqcup \ldots \sqcup \psi_n)$, or $\varphi \sqsubseteq [\alpha](\psi_1 \sqcup \ldots \sqcup \psi_n)$ where the ψ_i have the same type $X \in \{F, E, G, T, g, t\}$ as φ.*

Example 5. Let fmm $\in D$ stand for the male-female distinction. Let $(E(...).n)$ denote any category of persons, say, politicians. Assume that we have two further entries with identifiers $(E(...).n.k)$ and $(E(...).n.l)$ denoting female and male politicians. Then the axiom $(E(...).n) \equiv [fmm]((E(...).n.k) \sqcup (E(...).n.l))$ expresses that the class of all politicians is the union of the classes of female politicians and male politicians, and that the division follows the male-female distinction.

Example 6. Let adm $\in D$ stand "immediate political-administrative subunit". Then an symmetric union of the German "Bundesländer" (Baden-Wurttemberg, Bavaria, ..., Thuringia) and a compositional fact can be used to express that Germany can be partitioned into 16 immediate political-administrative subunits.

2. Pure Geographic Facts express relations between entities of type g. *Symbolic pure geographic facts* are based on a collection of unary and binary relations between geo-entities.

1. *extended* (unary). Used for geographic areas like states.
2. *linear* (unary). Used for geo-entities like rivers and roads with a linear form on maps.
3. *point* (unary). Used for geo-entities like waterfalls, churches, ... which are represented as points on maps. Cities/towns are not treated as points.
4. *part_of* (binary). Describes spatial inclusion.
5. *common_border_line* (binary). For extended geo-entities with a common borderline such as France and Belgium.
6. *overlaps* (binary). Describes two extended geo-entities where the intersection is extended and a proper subarea of both entities. For example, Austria and the alps overlap.
7. *is-capital-of* (binary).

Numeric pure geographic facts assign a pair of coordinates to a geographic entity. The point described by the coordinates is meant to denote one central point of the geographic entity. Later we perhaps look at more complex spatial descriptions of extended geographic entities.

3. Pure Temporal Facts express relations between entities of type t. As for geographic facts, there are two kinds of pure temporal facts. *Symbolic temporal relations.* We use Allen's 13 relations for temporal intervals [All83]. *Numeric temporal relations* assign a starting date and an end point to a temporal entity.

4. Roles. Recall from the discussion of the local introduction operation that the hierarchy in Level 1 is rich enough to encode elementship in sets represented as entries of type $X \in \{E, G, T\}$. However, the hierarchy does not systematically encode relations of arity $n \geq 2$ between entities. To this end we introduce a set R of *roles* in Level 2. The following is a non-exhaustive and preliminary list. For relations with one temporal argument, this argument may either be an entry of the hierarchy or an explicit date (a century, decade, year, month, or a day).

1. *Is-location-of.* Ternary relation; first argument type e, second argument type G, third argument type g. Used to express locations that are stable. E.g., the location of "Hannover Messe" w.r.t. the category of locations "Towns" is "Hannover". The location of "Carnegy Hall" w.r.t. the category of locations "state" is "USA".
2. *Is-time-of.* Ternary relation; first argument type e, second argument type T, third argument type t. Used for entities that are naturally associated with a temporal period. E.g., the time of the "French Revolution" w.r.t. the category of "Years" is "1789".
3. *Is-the-of-in.* Arity 4. First argument type e, second argument type E, third argument type e or g, fourth argument type t. With this predicate we express that a twofold restriction of an entity category determines a unique person, and that at some moment in time the person satisfied the predicate. E.g., "George W. Bush" is the "President" of the "USA" in "2003". Again we assume that "George W. Bush", "President" and "USA" are entries of the

hierarchy. Similarly person X might be the chief manager of an enterprise in a given year.

4. *Is-the-of-from-until.* These axioms are similar, but they specify two points in time that mark the beginning and the end of the role. Example pattern: X was president of Y from U until V.

5. *Is-a-of-in.* Similar as "Is-the-of-in"-facts, but we do not assume that the role determines a unique person. A person can be a member of a political party in a fixed year. A person can be a member of a football equipe at a moment of time.

6. *Is-a-from-until.* Similar as an "Is-the-of-from-until"-relation, but we do not assume that the role determines a unique entity.

7. *Is-the-location-of-in.* For example, "Edinburgh" is the location of the "ICDAR"-conference in "2003".

8. *Is-the-in.* "Woytila" is the "Roman Pope" in "2002".

9. *Is-the-from-until.*

6   Concluding Remarks

In this paper we introduced a systematics and a three-level architecture for a resource that encodes knowledge about named entities using a thematic-geographic-temporal hierarchy. Though the systematics described in Section 3 is stable, the complete picture of the resource is still preliminary in many respects. We are not aware of another resource or knowledge base with a similar functionality and structure. In our approach the thematic hierarchy - or the corresponding set of identifiers - is considered as a kind of quotient term algebra with a derivable ordering structure that represents a simplified model of real-world thematic areas, entities, and their relations. We think this perspective deserves further attention. We intend to discuss how formal models based on conventional set-theoretic notions can be used to derive a better semantics. This problem is not simple. For example, thematic areas are always described using natural language expressions. The inherent vagueness and context-adaptivity represents one major obstacle.

We only started with second big task, the explicit construction ("filling") and maintenance of the resource. Here we face a considerable number of questions and difficulties. Some of these might give rise to interesting research problems. *(1) Hierarchy construction.* Due to the interleaved nature of the hierarchy and the analytical ordering structure, which is fully derived from identifiers, persons that "fill" a subpart of the thematic hierarchy have to be aware of neighboured areas and their structure/identifiers. Hence hierarchy construction is much more difficult than for any tree-based classification scheme. *(3) Editing the hierarchy.* Intelligent techniques for editing a given hierarchy have to be developed. *(4) Collecting data.* The collection of the data that are necessary to realize the resource represents a huge amount of work. The process should be partially automated.

As a matter of fact, many particular aspects of the resource can be found in other work. A lexical treatment of domains, e.g, is discussed in [GG98]. Thesauri

[DIN] or meta-thesauri [NLM] are obviously close to our resource. In particular, the geographic part of the hierarchy (once fully elaborated) is similar to geographic thesauri such as Getty's thesaurus [GRI]. The graph structure of the hierarchy in Level 1 and some of the motivations in Section 2 indicate a neighbourhood to knowledge bases such as WordNet [Fel98,Eur], perhaps also to conceptual lattices [SW00,GW99]. From the temporal information encoded in the resource we obtain a direct line to interval-based temporal reasoning [All83] and calendar systems [Ohl00]. The idea of reasoning based on taxonomies and classification schemes, which plays an important role for the given hierarchy, has been discussed in [Fal96]. One important application area of the resource is the semantic web [W3C]. Here suitable deduction mechanisms built upon the resource could yield a valuable addition to approaches based on ontologies and description logics [MFHS02,BCM⁺03,ECA98,Sch00]. Eventually, our resource shares some ideas with Topic Maps [Top]. Topic Maps describe distinct entities and thematic fields using typed relations called "associations", and add typed links to "occurrences" (CVs, home pages, etc.) that yield further information on the topics. Associations are similar to the relations in our Level 2, occurrences are close to the URLs that we use in the formal description of events and other entities. Topics Maps do not use identifiers that "describe" the nature of topics and entities. Hence there is no internal ordering between topics derived from identifiers, as in our approach. Furthermore, no special emphasis is given to temporal and geographic data.

Acknowledgements

We thank the anonymous referees for comments that helped to improve the paper.

References

ACM01.   The ACM Computing Classification System, 2001.
           http://www.acm.org/class/1998/homepage.html.
All83.   James F. Allen. Maintaining knowledge about temporal intervals. *Communications of the ACM*, 26(11):832–843, 1983.
BCM⁺03.   Franz Baader, Diego Calvanese, Deborah McGuinness, Daniele Nardi, and Peter Patel Schneider, editors. *The Description Logic Handbook: Theory, Implementation and Applications.* Cambridge University Press, 2003.
DIN.   DIN 1463: Erstellung und Weiterentwicklung von Thesauri. Deutsches Institut für Normung, 1987.
ECA98.   ECAI'98 Workshop on Applications of Ontologies and Problem Solving Methods, 1998.
           http://delicias.dia.fi.upm.es/WORKSHOP/ECAI98/papers.html.
Eur.   EuroWordNet Consortium. http://www.hum.uva.nl/ ewn/index.html♯2.
Fal96.   Andrew Fall. *Reasoning with Taxonomies.* PhD thesis, School of Computing Science, Simon Fraser University, 1996.
Fel98.   Christiane Fellbaum, editor. *WordNet - An Electronic Lexical Database.* The MIT Press, May 1998.

GG98.   G. Gross and F. Guenthner. Traitement automatique des domaines. *Révue francaise de linguistique appliquée*, 1998.

GRI.   Getty Research Institute GRI. Getty Thesaurus of Geographic Names On Line. http://www.getty.edu/research/tools/vocabulary/tgn/.

GW99.   Bernhard Ganter and Rudolf Wille. *Formal Concept Analysis - Mathematical Foundations*. Springer Verlag, Berlin Heidelberg, 1999.

IPT.   International Press Telecommunications Council IPTC. IPTC Subject Reference System. http://www.iptc.org/site/subject-codes/.

MFHS02.   Deborah L. McGuiness, Richard Fikes, James Hendler, and Lynn Andrea Stein. DAML+OIL: An Ontology Language for the Semantic Web. *IEEE Intelligent Systems*, 17(5):72–80, 2002.

NLM.   National Library of Medicine NLM. Unified Medical Language System UMLS. http://www.nlm.nih.gov/research/umls/.

Ohl00.   Hans Jürgen Ohlbach. About real time, calendar systems and temporal notions. In H. Barringer and D. Gabbay, editors, *Advances in Temporal Logic*, pages 319–338. Kluwer Academic Publishers, 2000.

Sch00.   Stefan Schlobach. Description logics and knowledge discovery of data. In H. J. Ohlbach, U. Endriss, O. Rodrigues, and S. Schlobach, editors, *Proceedings of the Seventh Workshop on Automated Reasoning, Bridging the Gap between Theory and Practice*, volume 32 of *CEUR Workshop Proceedings*, July 2000. On-line proceedings are available at http://SunSITE.Informatik.RWTH-Aachen.DE/Publications/CEUR-WS/Vol-32/.

SW00.   Gerd Stumme and Rudolf Wille. *Begriffliche Wissensverarbeitung*. Springer Verlag, Berlin Heidelberg, 2000.

Top.   TopicMaps.Org. XML Topic Maps XTM. http://www.topicmaps.org/xtm/1.0/.

UDC.   Universal Decimal Classification Consortium UDC. Universal Decimal Classification. http://www.udcc.org/outline/outline.htm/.

W3C.   W3C. Semantic Web. http://www.w3.org/2001/sw/.

Author Index

Lecture Notes in Computer Science

For information about Vols. 1–2814
please contact your bookseller or Springer-Verlag

Vol. 2853: M. Jeckle, L.-J. Zhang (Eds.), Web Services – ICWS-Europe 2003. Proceedings, 2003. VIII, 227 pages. 2003.

Vol. 2854: J. Hoffmann, Utilizing Problem Structure in Planning. XIII, 251 pages. 2003. (Subseries LNAI)

Vol. 2855: R. Alur, I. Lee (Eds.), Embedded Software. Proceedings, 2003. X, 373 pages. 2003.

Vol. 2856: M. Smirnov, E. Biersack, C. Blondia, O. Bonaventure, O. Casals, G. Karlsson, George Pavlou, B. Quoitin, J. Roberts, I. Stavrakakis, B. Stiller, P. Trimintzios, P. Van Mieghem (Eds.), Quality of Future Internet Services. IX, 293 pages. 2003.

Vol. 2857: M.A. Nascimento, E.S. de Moura, A.L. Oliveira (Eds.), String Processing and Information Retrieval. Proceedings, 2003. XI, 379 pages. 2003.

Vol. 2858: A. Veidenbaum, K. Joe, H. Amano, H. Aiso (Eds.), High Performance Computing. Proceedings, 2003. XV, 566 pages. 2003.

Vol. 2859: B. Apolloni, M. Marinaro, R. Tagliaferri (Eds.), Neural Nets. Proceedings, 2003. X, 376 pages. 2003.

Vol. 2860: D. Geist, E. Tronci (Eds.), Correct Hardware Design and Verification Methods. Proceedings, 2003. XII, 426 pages. 2003.

Vol. 2861: C. Bliek, C. Jermann, A. Neumaier (Eds.), Global Optimization and Constraint Satisfaction. Proceedings, 2002. XII, 239 pages. 2003.

Vol. 2862: D. Feitelson, L. Rudolph, U. Schwiegelshohn (Eds.), Job Scheduling Strategies for Parallel Processing. Proceedings, 2003. VII, 269 pages. 2003.

Vol. 2863: P. Stevens, J. Whittle, G. Booch (Eds.), «UML» 2003 – The Unified Modeling Language. Proceedings, 2003. XIV, 415 pages. 2003.

Vol. 2864: A.K. Dey, A. Schmidt, J.F. McCarthy (Eds.), UbiComp 2003: Ubiquitous Computing. Proceedings, 2003. XVII, 368 pages. 2003.

Vol. 2865: S. Pierre, M. Barbeau, E. Kranakis (Eds.), Ad-Hoc, Mobile, and Wireless Networks. Proceedings, 2003. X, 293 pages. 2003.

Vol. 2867: M. Brunner, A. Keller (Eds.), Self-Managing Distributed Systems. Proceedings, 2003. XIII, 274 pages. 2003.

Vol. 2868: P. Perner, R. Brause, H.-G. Holzhütter (Eds.), Medical Data Analysis. Proceedings, 2003. VIII, 127 pages. 2003.

Vol. 2869: A. Yazici, C. Şener (Eds.), Computer and Information Sciences – ISCIS 2003. Proceedings, 2003. XIX, 1110 pages. 2003.

Vol. 2870: D. Fensel, K. Sycara, J. Mylopoulos (Eds.), The Semantic Web - ISWC 2003. Proceedings, 2003. XV, 931 pages. 2003.

Vol. 2871: N. Zhong, Z.W. Raś, S. Tsumoto, E. Suzuki (Eds.), Foundations of Intelligent Systems. Proceedings, 2003. XV, 697 pages. 2003. (Subseries LNAI)

Vol. 2873: J. Lawry, J. Shanahan, A. Ralescu (Eds.), Modelling with Words. XIII, 229 pages. 2003. (Subseries LNAI)

Vol. 2875: E. Aarts, R. Collier, E. van Loenen, B. de Ruyter (Eds.), Ambient Intelligence. Proceedings, 2003. XI, 432 pages. 2003.

Vol. 2876: M. Schroeder, G. Wagner (Eds.), Rules and Rule Markup Languages for the Semantic Web. Proceedings, 2003. VII, 173 pages. 2003.

Vol. 2877: T. Böhme, G. Heyer, H. Unger (Eds.), Innovative Internet Community Systems. Proceedings, 2003. VIII, 263 pages. 2003.

Vol. 2878: R.E. Ellis, T.M. Peters (Eds.), Medical Image Computing and Computer-Assisted Intervention - MICCAI 2003. Part I. Proceedings, 2003. XXXIII, 819 pages. 2003.

Vol. 2879: R.E. Ellis, T.M. Peters (Eds.), Medical Image Computing and Computer-Assisted Intervention - MICCAI 2003. Part II. Proceedings, 2003. XXXIV, 1003 pages. 2003.

Vol. 2880: H.L. Bodlaender (Ed.), Graph-Theoretic Concepts in Computer Science. Proceedings, 2003. XI, 386 pages. 2003.

Vol. 2881: E. Horlait, T. Magedanz, R.H. Glitho (Eds.), Mobile Agents for Telecommunication Applications. Proceedings, 2003. IX, 297 pages. 2003.

Vol. 2883: J. Schaeffer, M. Müller, Y. Björnsson (Eds.), Computers and Games. Proceedings, 2002. XI, 431 pages. 2003.

Vol. 2884: E. Najm, U. Nestmann, P. Stevens (Eds.), Formal Methods for Open Object-Based Distributed Systems. Proceedings, 2003. X, 293 pages. 2003.

Vol. 2885: J.S. Dong, J. Woodcock (Eds.), Formal Methods and Software Engineering. Proceedings, 2003. XI, 683 pages. 2003.

Vol. 2886: I. Nyström, G. Sanniti di Baja, S. Svensson (Eds.), Discrete Geometry for Computer Imagery. Proceedings, 2003. XII, 556 pages. 2003.

Vol. 2887: T. Johansson (Ed.), Fast Software Encryption. Proceedings, 2003. IX, 397 pages. 2003.

Vol. 2888: R. Meersman, Zahir Tari, D.C. Schmidt et al. (Eds.), On The Move to Meaningful Internet Systems 2003: CoopIS, DOA, and ODBASE. Proceedings, 2003. XXI, 1546 pages. 2003.

Vol. 2889: Robert Meersman, Zahir Tari et al. (Eds.), On The Move to Meaningful Internet Systems 2003: OTM 2003 Workshops. Proceedings, 2003. XXI, 1096 pages. 2003.

Vol. 2891: J. Lee, M. Barley (Eds.), Intelligent Agents and Multi-Agent Systems. Proceedings, 2003. X, 215 pages. 2003. (Subseries LNAI)

Vol. 2893: J.-B. Stefani, I. Demeure, D. Hagimont (Eds.), Distributed Applications and Interoperable Systems. Proceedings, 2003. XIII, 311 pages. 2003.

Vol. 2895: A. Ohori (Ed.), Programming Languages and Systems. Proceedings, 2003. XIII, 427 pages. 2003.

Vol. 2897: O. Balet, G. Subsol, P. Torguet (Eds.), Virtual Storytelling. Proceedings, 2003. XI, 240 pages. 2003.

Vol. 2899: G. Ventre, R. Canonico (Eds.), Interactive Multimedia on Next Generation Networks. Proceedings, 2003. XIV, 420 pages. 2003.

Vol. 2901: F. Bry, N. Henze, J. Maluszyński (Eds.), Principles and Practice of Semantic Web Reasoning. Proceedings, 2003. X, 209 pages. 2003.

Vol. 2902: F. Moura Pires, S. Abreu (Eds.), Progress in Artificial Intelligence. Proceedings, 2003. XV, 504 pages. 2003. (Subseries LNAI).

Vol. 2905: A. Sanfeliu, J. Ruiz-Shulcloper (Eds.), Progress in Pattern Recognition, Speech and Image Analysis. Proceedings, 2003. XVII, 693 pages. 2003.